D0909105

FORECASTING FINANCIAL MARKETS

TECHNICAL ANALYSIS AND THE DYNAMICS OF PRICE

TONY PLUMMER

JOHN WILEY & SONS

New York • Chichester • Brisbane • Toronto • Singapore

Copyright © Tony Plummer, 1989, 1990, 1991
First published in 1989 by
Kogan Page Ltd.
120 Pentonville Road
London N1 9JN

Revised edition, 1990

Library of Congress Cataloging-in-Publication Data

Plummer, Tony.
    Forecasting financial markets : technical analysis and the
dynamics of price / Tony Plummer. — Rev. ed.
        p.   cm. — (Wiley finance editions)
    Includes index.
    ISBN 0-471-53408-0
    1. Stock price forecasting.   2. Investment analysis.   I. Title.
II. Series.
HG4637.P57   1990   90-24550
332.63′222′0112—dc20

Printed in the United States of America
91 92 10 9 8 7 6 5 4 3 2 1

To Glenys

Contents

Foreword by William F. Eng   vii
Acknowledgements   viii

Introduction   ix

Part I: The Logic of Non-Rational Behaviour in Crowds   1

1. Wholly Individual or Indivisibly Whole   3
2. Two's a Crowd   8
3. The Individual in the Crowd   14
4. The Systems Approach to Crowd Behaviour   19
5. Cycles in the Crowd   26
6. Techniques for Forecasting Crowd Behaviour   38

Part II: The Dynamics of the Bull/Bear Cycle   43

7. The Stock Market Crowd   45
8. The Shape of the Bull/Bear Cycle   56
9. The Spiral and Fibonacci   73
10. The Mathematical Basis of Price Movements   85
11. The Shape of Price Movements   98

Part III: Forecasting Turning Points   105

12. Price Patterns at Turning Points   107
13. Price Patterns in Traditional Technical Analysis   113
14. Price Patterns during Trends   130
15. The Elliott Wave Principle   136
16. The Confirmation of Buy and Sell Signals   152
17. Natural Reversal Points   169
18. The Use of Time Cycle Analysis   185
19. The Evidence for Time Cycles   195

Part IV: The Theory in Practice   203

20.   The Equity Market Crash of 1987   205
21.   Summary and Conclusion   227

Appendices   231

1.   The Theories of W. D. Gann   233
2.   Cycles in the UK Gilt-Edged Market   243

Index   255

Foreword

To the average investor or speculator, analysis of market price is secondary to fundamental analysis. But for the professional who makes a living by investing or speculating, fundamental analysis is only the beginning. The market professional is keenly sensitive to time and volume, and their effects on securities prices. Tony Plummer's *Forecasting Financial Markets* thoroughly explains the impact of time on securities markets and will benefit any investor.

Each concept explored in this book can be found in the many volumes written by other experts in technical analysis. However, Plummer is the first to put all these ideas into one very readable book. Readers who are well versed in the practice of using technical analysis to trade markets will find this easy and enjoyable reading. Yet even readers who are not technically oriented will find the volume understandable because the ideas presented are so intuitively clear and appealing.

If one were to remove the jargon of the technical analyst from this book, its concepts would be readily embraced by even the most skeptical reader. In effect, Plummer asks: If the laws of nature are at work everywhere else, why not in the marketplace? Our readiness to dismiss this notion reflects a weakness in the human condition: What we don't understand, we disparage.

Many say that price movements are fundamentally random. But "randomness" arises from a lack of a cohesive framework to guide our observations. Nature has no framework, no benchmarks, no guidelines; it consists solely of an oscillation between extremes, which themselves are unbounded. The framework and the benchmarks must always be manmade. Once intelligent benchmarks are in place, market action becomes less random and more understandable. This book provides that cohesive framework.

Our willingness to believe that markets are incomprehensible reflects another human weakness—our tendency to idolize what we cannot see. By making market action more comprehensible, Plummer helps us move beyond idolatry toward understanding.

I hope that readers will take the concepts presented here and develop them further, and so advance our finite comprehension closer to an understanding of the infinite laws of nature and their reflection in the marketplace.

William F. Eng
President, Financial Options Consultants
Chicago, Illinois

Acknowledgements

Very few authors can have had their work published without the assistance and encouragement of other people. This one is certainly no exception. My sincere thanks to Michael Hughes who patiently read the manuscript in its penultimate life and provided sound advice on how to recreate it in a more acceptable form. Needless to say any errors remain my own. My thanks also to my colleagues at Hambros Bank, especially David Tapper and John Heywood, whose support and advice over the years has been a major influence on my interest in the workings of financial markets. Some of their wisdom has found expression in the following pages albeit in ways they might not immediately recognise! My thanks also to my wife and family. They accepted my commitment and provided complete support for the task, even when I persistently spent long evenings and weekends hunched over a wordprocessor. Finally, my thanks must also go to my travelling companions on the (now defunct) 7.30 am from Audley End. It was their dedication to sleep and crossword puzzles which enabled the earliest version of the manuscript to be written in the first place!

Introduction

This book is about the forces which operate in financial markets. It is about the influence of *crowds* and the way this influence makes it possible to forecast turning points in financial markets. It is about the theory underlying the discipline known as 'technical analysis', which concentrates on forecasting price trends using price-time charts. Ultimately, however, the book is also about some of the natural forces at work in the world, which are easier to deal with once they are understood.

There are therefore two objectives of this book. The first is to provide a straightforward analytical framework which can be used to trade financial markets. The second is to provide a unifying rationale for technical analysis, and thereby help to upgrade it from a 'black box' art to a more acceptable science.

The starting point of the analysis is that it takes only a small adjustment in our assumptions concerning the nature of human motivation to generate a huge leap in our understanding of observed human behaviour. Specifically, if we accept the assumption that individual behaviour is influenced to some degree by the need to associate with – and obtain the approval of – other people, then all economic and financial behaviour can be seen as being ordered rather than chaotic: it becomes more explicable and predictable.

It will be shown that group, or crowd, behaviour is an unavoidable feature of the human condition. Crowds introduce a very large *non-rational*, and *emotional*, element to decisions by making an individual equate his or her own needs with those of the crowd. This influence permeates all economic and financial behaviour, and is particularly noticeable in financial markets. At peaks and troughs of the stock market, for example, very few people will be concentrating on the fundamental economic influences; the vast majority will be concerned only with the recent short-term movements in prices themselves. Consequently, this majority will inevitably be on the wrong foot when a price reversal occurs. It is this fact, more than anything else, which

explains the stock market 'crash' of October 1987. Successful investment therefore depends on an individual's ability to stand aside from
the crowd's influence.

We shall demonstrate that one of the best ways of achieving
independence from the crowd is to focus attention on what the
majority of other investors are thinking and doing. Importantly, *all the
necessary information relating to investor behaviour is contained in the actual
movement of market prices, and in the movement of certain mechanical
indicators of investor activity*. This is so because the influence of the
crowd ensures that price movements and investor activity in all
financial markets follow specific rules. Many of these rules are already
known to market professionals in one form or another, and over the
years a wide range of trading techniques has been developed to take
advantage of them. The problem, however, has been to explain *why*
the rules exist in the first place. This book will help to fill this gap.

Because of the issues involved it has been necessary to conduct the
analysis from 'first principles', and explore some of the existing theory
relating to crowds and 'natural' systems. Had this book been written
in ten years' time, such a procedure might not have been necessary.
As it is, most of the relevant concepts have not yet been fully
integrated into mainstream economic theory: they need to be
explicitly stated in order to place the phenomenon of financial markets
into a broader analytical framework. It is 'chaos theory' in another
guise.

The theory of 'natural' systems will be used to explore the dynamic
processes of financial markets. It will be demonstrated that these
processes create a specific (and continuously recurring) price pattern.
For ease of exposition, we have called this pattern the *price pulse*. It will
also be shown that the price pulse is subject both to simple
mathematical relationships between the price movements which
constitute the pattern, and to regular rhythmic oscillations. Hence, it
is possible to forecast the *profile* of price movements, the likely *extent* of
those price movements and the likely *timing* of price reversals. Finally,
it will be shown that price reversals which are expected as a result of
these forecasts can be *confirmed* in 'real' time by direct reference to
certain simple measures of investor behaviour.

Despite the apparent novelty of the price pulse, it must be
emphasised that it does not in any way supplant other techniques.
Indeed, it will be shown that not only does the price pulse completely
validate *traditional* technical analysis (which incorporates such phenomena as 'trend lines' and 'head-and-shoulders' reversal patterns)
but that it is also the basis of the important 'Elliott Wave Principle'.
Those investors who are prepared to accept the logic of this book (and
then put it into practice) should be able to trade in financial markets
with the minimum of risk and with a great deal of success.

Part I:

The Logic of Non-Rational Behaviour in Crowds

1.

Wholly Individual or Indivisibly Whole

Introduction

Western culture places a great deal of emphasis on the rights of the individual. The concept of freedom of expression and the right of self-determination are enshrined in the democratic political systems of North America and Western Europe, and are so familiar to us that most of us do not give them a second thought. Nevertheless, single-minded concentration on the needs and desires of the individual has encouraged an arrogance which is at once both an asset and a liability. It is an asset because it has catapulted humankind on a voyage of discovery through the universe that is within each of us, but it is also a liability because it has encouraged us to place ourselves above the cosmos of which we are a part.

Many scientists and philosophers now believe that future progress will depend on our ability to recognise and accept that the independence of each individual is a relative condition rather than an absolute one. Humankind takes great pride in its control and direction of certain aspects of the environment, but it still remains true that ultimately we are all dependent on that environment in the crucial sense of being a part of it. In fact one of the most exciting features of scientific research during the last 50 years is the recognition that everything in nature depends on everything else.

The relationships in nature

This finding has significant implications for the development of human knowledge, because it suggests that the most important aspect of the world is not so much the individual *parts* of nature as the *relationships* in nature: the relationships define the parts, and no single part can exist independently of other parts.[1] Hence, it becomes possible to visualise the world in terms of multi-level structures which start at the sub-atomic level and then extend upwards in ever-increasing layers of complexity. As an example, electrons combine to form atoms, atoms combine to form molecules, molecules combine to form organs, organs combine to form organ systems, organ systems combine to form animals and humankind.

The break with tradition

These concepts have been explored in some detail in recent years, [2] and have even given a strong impetus to a *new* discipline, which is known as 'systems theory'.[3]

However, the ideas are not yet widely understood. Part of the difficulty derives from the fact that systems theory marks a distinct break from the traditional analytical procedures which have been favoured ever since the pioneering work of Isaac Newton and René Descartes. These procedures presume that it is possible to understand all aspects of any complex phenomenon by 'reducing' that phenomenon to its constituent parts.

The process of dividing nature into progressively smaller units (a process which is known as 'reductionism') works very well in the context of everyday life. Indeed, the fund of knowledge is actually enhanced as differentiation increases, and so the process is self-justifying. However, in the 1920s physicists found that the process was totally inapplicable at the *sub*-atomic level.[4] Specifically, it was found that electrons do not exist with certainty at definite places and do not behave predictably at definite times.[5] In other words, there was a critical level where 'certainties' disappeared, and where the concept of basic 'building blocks' seemed to become invalid.

The practical solution to the problem was to step back, and to assign characteristics to electrons which accounted both for the uncertainty of the unobserved state of existence, and for the certainty of the observed state. It was hypothesised that electrons had a *dual* nature: on the one hand, the behaviour of an *individual* electron could not be forecast with any degree of certainty; on the other hand, the behaviour of *groups* of electrons could be forecast with a high degree of certainty. In other words, the solution (which is now known as Heisenberg's 'Uncertainty Principle'[6]) lay within the mathematics of probability theory where a large number of *uncertainties* produce a *certainty*.[7] Probability theory can (for example) determine with 100 per cent accuracy the half-life of any radioactive substance, [8] despite the fact that the point in time when one particular radioactive atom will disintegrate is totally unpredictable.

The conceptual revolution

The search for basic building blocks in nature will undoubtedly persist.[9] In the meantime, the revelations of the New Physics (as it is now called despite the fact that it is more than 50 years old) are generating major structural changes in the natural and social sciences.[10] Each discipline is basically having to absorb two related ideas: first, 'wholes' are something greater than the simple arithmetic sum of their 'parts'; second, each 'part' has a tendency both to have a separate identity and to belong to a greater whole.

The problem of motivation

In the social sciences, the changes are leading towards a revolution in our understanding of human behaviour. In economics, for example, the traditional approach had, as a matter of logic, yielded conclusions about the nature of humankind which were decidedly unattractive. Statistical research had indicated that groups of people tend to respond in a predictable way to given stimuli. However, since it was presumed that people were separate entities from their environment and from one another, it was concluded that individuals also tend to respond in a predictable way to given stimuli. Accordingly, human behaviour was essentially seen as being a mechanistic response to external influences

It is certainly true that a great deal of our behaviour *is* mechanistic. Desmond Morris, for example, in his book *'The Naked Ape'*, [11] has been able to identify a substantial number of parallels between animal and human behaviour. However, this comparison cannot be extended indefinitely because it represents a very limited view of the nature of humankind. As E.F. Schumacher[12] observed, the structure of living organisms is a progression of increasing complexity and power: plants have life; animals have life and consciousness; people have life, consciousness, and *self-awareness*. Self-awareness is specifically the ability to be conscious of one's own thinking, [13] and (at the very least) it enables each individual to *choose* between alternative responses to a given situation. The resulting decision will therefore depend partly on the individual's own understanding (or set of beliefs) about the nature of the world.

The dualistic nature of motivation

The important point here is that decisions based on self-aware thought processes are not necessarily predictable by other people. This is an entirely different concept from the traditional view which essentially defines rational behaviour as being 'reasonable' (or 'under-standable') behaviour, and therefore predictable. The problem, however, is to reconcile the implications of self-aware rational thought with the fact that group behaviour appears to be mechanistic.

The answer lies in the concept of a *duality* of characteristics, comparable to that used for sub-atomic phenomena. People have both the ability to be individuals and the tendency to belong to groups. The actual mix of the two characteristics varies over time depending on circumstances: sometimes a person will be relatively individualistic, while at other times the same person will be relatively willing to conform to behavioural patterns pursued or imposed by others. Hence in Figure 1.1, the mix between individuality and conformity varies along the 45° line: the mix is different at I_1/C_1 compared with I_2/C_2. The important difference between the two sets of circumstances is the degree to which a person accepts *other people's* belief systems, thereby limiting his or her personal room for manoeuvre.

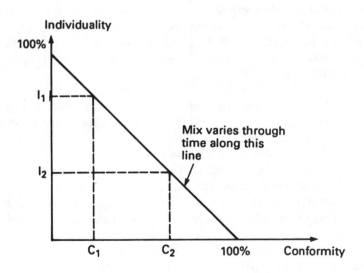

Figure 1.1. *The mix between individuality and conformity*

Conclusion

The idea that motivation has a dual nature represents a major breakthrough in our understanding of human behaviour. Each person simultaneously has a tendency to be an individual with a unique and 'personal' view of the world, and a tendency to belong to groups. Individual behaviour is not easily predictable, but group behaviour is. This duality of character is of the utmost importance to our analysis of investor behaviour in stock markets.

Notes

1. The interconnectedness of nature is actually such that it can sometimes be very difficult to see where each 'part' of a structure starts, or where each 'whole' ends. See David Bohm, *Wholeness and the Implicate Order*. Routledge and Kegan Paul, London, 1980.
2. See, for example, Erich Jantsch, *The Self-Organising Universe*. Pergamon, Oxford, 1980.
3. See Chapter 4.
4. The findings of the New Physics are truly remarkable. It is suggested that interested readers refer, for example, to Gary Zukov, *The Dancing Wu Li Masters*. William Morrow, New York, 1979.
5. Electrons can be viewed as being very abstract packets of energy which have a dual aspect: sometimes they adopt the characteristics of a single entity or *particle*, but sometimes they adopt the characteristics of continuous *waves*. Hence, *prior* to observation, it is impossible to determine whether an electron is particle-like or wave-like. Furthermore, *during* observation, it is impossible to determine *both* the position *and* the velocity of an electron.
6. Werner Heisenberg, *Physics and Beyond*. Allen and Unwin, London, 1971.
7. This point is well made by Arthur Koestler in *Janus: a Summing Up*. Hutchinson, London, 1978.
8. The half-life of a substance is the time required for half the atoms in the substance to disintegrate.
9. The search for basic building blocks of matter has recently focused on smaller phenomena called 'quarks'. However, even ignoring the difficulties regarding the status of electrons, it is not certain that the concept will be validated. See, for example, Stephen W. Hawking, *A Brief History of Time*. Transworld Publishers, London, 1988.
10. See Fritjof Capra, *The Turning Point*. Wildwood House, London, 1982,
11. Desmond Morris, *The Naked Ape*. Jonathan Cape, London, 1967.
12. E.F.Schumacher, *A Guide for the Perplexed*. Jonathan Cape, London, 1977.
13. It is arguable that the specific ability to be aware of one's own thinking is hardly ever used. See J. G. Bennett, *Creative Thinking*, Coombe Springs Press, Masham (Yorks), 1964. However, the term 'self-awareness' can be used as a generic term, which incorporates *all* the factors which enable the human mind to create an inner world which mirrors the outer 'reality'.

2.

Two's a Crowd

Introduction

Investors who have been involved with financial markets for any length of time will readily identify with the concept of a conflicting *two-way pull* on their decisions. On the one hand, their own 'personal' approach to making an investment decision may suggest one course of action; on the other hand, the lure of the 'herd instinct' may be pulling entirely in the opposite direction. Even seasoned professionals, who make a living by anticipating and out-witting the rest of the participants in financial markets, will sometimes find themselves caught up in a common hysteria at just that time when contrary thinking is truly appropriate. It is a rare trader who can honestly say that he or she has not bought stock at the top of a price movement, or sold stock at the bottom of a price movement.

The reason for this two-way pull on each individual lies in the nature of *crowd* membership. On the one hand, each person has a *self-assertive* tendency, or ability to behave in a self-determined, individualistic way. On the other hand, however, each individual also has an *integrative tendency*,[1] which ensures that he or she has a willingness to belong to crowds. Membership of a crowd causes people to behave differently from the way that they would in isolation.

The influence of crowds

Modern crowd theory effectively asserts that crowds emerge as a result of the same basic laws which apply to the rest of nature. As Erich Jantsch[2] has shown, building on the implications of quantum physics, all of nature consists of multi-levelled structures. Each level in this hierarchy has the power to organise its lower levels and use them for its own purposes.[3] Consequently, each level is able to perpetuate itself, or maintain its identity, despite changes in its individual components.[4] This hierarchical structure applies to human society:[5] individuals become members of groups, groups merge to form societies, and societies merge to form civilisations (see Figure 2.1).

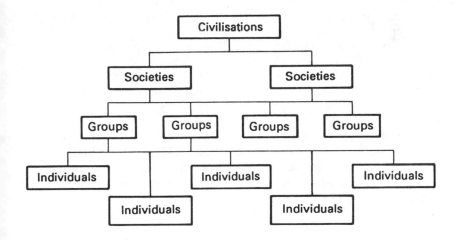

Figure 2.1. *The hierarchical structure of human groupings*

The insights of Gustave Le Bon

One of the first people to analyse the phenomenon of crowds in any detail was Gustave Le Bon.[6] Although his book *The Crowd* was written in 1895, it still stands out as a classic of social psychology. His main conclusions have been validated by subsequent analysts such as Sigmund Freud and Carl Jung, as well as by theorists such as Arthur Koestler. At the time, Le Bon was interested specifically in the causes of the French Revolution, but his analysis is just as applicable to such diverse events as the Nuremberg Rallies in Nazi Germany and the Cultural Revolution in China.

Le Bon saw a crowd as being primarily a *psychological* phenomenon rather than a physical one (although the two concepts are not necessarily mutually exclusive). He considered that any number of otherwise independent and spatially separate individuals could form a crowd, provided that the members had a *common cause*. This implies that 'crowd'-type pressures can be found in a large range of groupings. They can, for example, be found in companies, football teams, armies, riotous mobs, religious sects and patriotic nation states. As we shall see, they can also be found in financial markets. Le Bon himself argued that:[7]

> The most striking peculiarity presented by a psychological crowd is the following: whoever be the individuals that compose it, however like or unlike their mode of life, their occupations, their character, or their intelligence, the fact that they have been transformed into a crowd puts them in possession of a sort of collective mind which makes them feel, think, and act in a manner quite different from that in which each

individual of them would feel, think, and act were he in a state of isolation...

What really takes place (in the formation of a crowd) is a combination followed by the creation of new characteristics, just as in chemistry certain elements, when brought into contact...combine to form a new body possessing properties quite different from those of the bodies that have served to form it.

This profound insight into the nature of crowds used two important concepts which have now become the central tenets of crowd theory: first, a crowd is something other than the sum of its parts – in particular, a crowd has an effective 'mind' of its own; second, each individual's behaviour is altered by membership of a crowd.

The crowd's ability to organise itself

From the crowd's point of view, it is crucial to its own autonomy that it can 'organise' its own membership. This is the only way that energy can be directed towards the overall objectives of the crowd itself. Such 'self'-organisation operates through the crowd's *belief system*. Members of a crowd accept the same beliefs as other members of that crowd, and thereby suppress their own individuality. This situation obviously means that the crowd has a certain cohesion, because the like-mindedness of individuals implies a sense of unity. However, one of the important lessons of the 'Uncertainty Principle' is that each whole is something more than the sum of its parts. In the context of a crowd, this translates into saying that the members develop a sense of altruism towards one another, and therefore (whether they overtly recognise it or not) act with the interests of the crowd at heart. This is where the concept of a crowd 'mind' is truly applicable.

Mind as a dynamic principle

The idea that a crowd has a collective mind (or mind of its own) is not an easy one either to grasp or to convey. The main difficulty is that (despite the propaganda of reductionism) most people think of a mind as being that part of the physical structure of the brain which has the capability of self-aware, rational thought. On this view, *people* have minds, but *animals* do not. The point is, however, that mind is actually a *logical* process involving all the different aspects of self-organisation and learning. It does not need to be encased in any particular physical structure. This was the great insight of the biologist and philosopher Gregory Bateson,[8] who deduced that mind had a metabolic as well as a self-awareness dimension. He found that mind existed within any existed within any process which contained certain characteristics. Broadly, these characteristics involved the control of internal functions, the processing of information, interaction with the environment (in the exchange of energy and information), and the presence of oscillations. In short, 'mind' is the essence of life itself.

The crowd mind

Bateson's criteria for a mind opened up the concept to include all aspects of the living universe, and added an important new feature both to the conclusions of the New Physics and to the framework of the scientific process. Hence it can be used, not only to describe the phenomenon of life but also to describe and explain any particular 'unit' of life. It can be found in both the most simple and the most complex of processes. In terms of human society, it can be found in the dynamics of people's relationships with one another: it can be found in a small group of people, in a physical crowd, in a nation state, or in a whole culture. An individual's mind may (in its non self-aware state) be regarded as a subsystem of a greater whole. Each whole, in turn, has a 'collective mind', which organises its own parts. On this analysis, each crowd (or any other human grouping) may be said to have a collective consciousness.[9]

The human brain

It is intuitively obvious, however, that the collective consciousness of a crowd, or of a whole civilisation, is something different from the self-awareness of an individual human being. The former is essentially simplistic, and is not usually recognised; while the latter is not fully understood, even though it is accepted. Furthermore, why is it that a crowd 'reduces', rather than enhances, an individual?

Part of the answer seems to lie in the structure of the brain itself. The American neurophysiologist Paul D. Maclean[10] calls the brain of humankind a 'triune' brain, consisting of three interrelated parts, each of which stems from different evolutionary periods in the past. Each part is structurally and chemically different from the other parts, and appears to have its own intelligence, its own memory and its own separate functions. The brain stem (the innermost part of the brain) is concerned primarily with instinctive behaviour patterns, biological drives and compulsive behaviour. Surrounding this part is the limbic system, which is mainly involved with the recreation of external experiences in the 'inner' world, and with emotional activity. Finally, the neo-cortex (the outermost part of the brain) deals with the ability both to be aware of the thought process itself, and to anticipate the future and recreate the past.[11]

The neo-cortex

The neo-cortex has developed in humankind only during the last 50 million years or so, compared with more than 150 million years for the limbic system, and more than 250 million years for the brain stem. It is probable, too, that the specific abilities associated with the neo-cortex have developed within a recent period which can be measured in terms of only thousands of years.[12] It has been suggested[13] that the neo-cortex is *such* a recent addition to the brain that it has not yet been properly integrated with the other two parts. Consequently, the operation of the neo-cortex is all too easily suppressed by the emergence of a crowd mentality. As the crowd comes into being, the brain stem and the limbic system hold sway. Crowds accordingly become involved primarily with instincts, biological drives, compulsive behaviour and emotions. Hence, their behaviour is essentially *non-rational* (and is, in fact, often *ir*rational). To paraphrase Arthur Koestler:[14]

> emotion and intellect, faith and reason, [are] at loggerheads. On the one side, [is] the pale cast of rational thought, of logic suspended on a thin thread all too easily broken; on the other, [is] the raging fury of passionately held irrational beliefs, reflected in the holocausts of past and present history.

The 'intelligence' of crowds

This certainly helps to explain the popularly-held delusion that all members of a crowd are unintelligent: it is not that they are unintelligent as such – it is that their ability to remain self-aware, and think logically, becomes suppressed. The overriding dominance of the crowd's belief system then imposes severe limitations on the quality of data which the crowd will recognise as information. Gregory Bateson defined information as 'differences which make a difference'.[15] A crowd mind can usually only perceive differences which are relatively large and which occur over very short periods of time. In other words, a crowd will only recognise 'obvious' changes. Slow changes can be observed only by the lengthy process of continually, and rationally, scanning all the potentially relevant data. Crowds are incapable of such analysis: they think in terms of simple images, and communicate with slogans. Unfortunately, they emerge in times of crisis and change, and are therefore the main vehicle for historical 'progress'.

Notes

1. The terms 'self-assertive tendency' and 'integrative tendency' were popularised by Arthur Koestler.
2. Erich Jantsch, *The Self-Organising Universe*. Pergamon, Oxford 1980.
3. For a very straightforward commentary on this process, see E.F. Schumacher, *A Guide for the Perplexed*. Jonathan Cape, London, 1977.
4. This is called 'homeostasis', and is the source of the phrase *plus ça change, plus c'est la même chose*.
5. The hierarchical structuring, and therefore the crowd phenomenon, obviously exists in the non-human world. It exists, for example, among birds, fish, ants, bees and lemmings. One of the more unusual examples concerns the ability of single-cell amoebae to form themselves into a so-called 'slime mould' in order to search for food as a group. See John Tyler Bonner, Differentiation in social amoebae, *Scientific American*, December 1959.
6. Gustave Le Bon, *Psychologie des Foules*. Reprinted as *The Crowd*. Macmillan, New York, 1922.
7. Ibid.
8. Gregory Bateson, *Mind and Nature – An Essential Unity*. Wildwood House, London, 1979.
9. See Fritjof Capra, *The Turning Point*. Wildwood House, London, 1982.
10. Paul D. Maclean, *A triune concept of the brain and behaviour*, in T. Boag and D. Campbell (eds.), *The Hincks Memorial Lectures*. University of Toronto Press, Toronto, 1973.
11. Erich Jantsch distinguishes between three different types of mental activity, each of which corresponds to one of the different areas of the brain. *Organismic* mental activity is the function of the brain stem, *reflexive* activity is the province of the limbic system, and *self-reflexive* activity is conducted by the neocortex. See Erich Jantsch, op. cit.
12. Dr Julian Jaynes, *The Origin of Consciousness in the Breakdown of the Bicameral Mind*. Houghton Mifflin, Boston, 1976.
13. Arthur Koestler, *Janus: a Summing Up*. Hutchinson, London, 1978.
14. Ibid.
15. Gregory Bateson, op cit.

3.

The Individual in the Crowd

The integrative tendency

We can now look at the crowd phenomenon from the individual's point of view, because it follows that crowd members must have a predilection to belong to groups and that there must be some mechanism whereby they tend to conform to behavioural standards imposed by other group members. In other words, there must be a basis for the *integrative tendency*.

The integrative tendency – the tendency to devote oneself to the crowd – ensures that each crowd member has his or her behaviour altered in a crucial way by the will of the majority. Theoretically, we can observe three aspects of this phenomenon:[1] the first is identification with the crowd, the second is acceptance of the crowd's belief system, and the third is submission to the authority of a leader.

Academic research

There is, indeed, a well-researched predisposition for individuals to reject individuals in other groups, to accept the judgement of the majority in the group to which they belong, and to accept the instructions of a person (or persons) representing authority. In a series of experiments by Henri Tajfel[2] at Bristol University, it was shown that groups of schoolboys aged 14 to 15 could have their behaviour altered merely by telling them that they belonged to a particular group – even an unknown group. Specifically, the schoolboys would automatically associate themselves with other members of the same group, would provide active support for that group, and would take every opportunity to disadvantage members of other groups. These phenomena occurred despite the fact that no indication was given to the schoolboys about the purpose or qualities of the groups.

Furthermore, experiments conducted at Harvard in America[3] showed that, when matching the length of a line with one of three other lines, subjects could have their performance measurably altered by group pressures. When asked to match the lines in isolation from others, participants made a mistake less than 1 per cent of the time. However, when placed in a group which had been schooled beforehand to accept the wrong line, participants agreed with the majority's incorrect judgement more than one-third of the time. This was true even when the actual difference between the lines was *very* significant.

These general conclusions have been confirmed by research conducted at the University of Illinois by Ed Diener. He found that the most important factor in group behaviour was the suppression of self-awareness and therefore of self-regulation. In one particular piece of research,[4] Diener compared behaviour under three different laboratory test conditions: (a) a situation where individuals were self-aware and were isolated from group influences, (b) a situation where individuals were non self-aware but were still isolated from group influences, and (c) a situation where individuals were both non self-aware and involved in a group environment. It was found that individuals in category (c) generally acted spontaneously, had little sense of personal identity, and related closely to other group members. Indeed, the experience was found to be very enjoyable.

The crowd leader

Identification with other members of the crowd and an acceptance of the crowd's belief system is stimulated by each member's willingness to obey a crowd leader. The importance of a leader was Freud's major contribution to the debate, and is based on the concept of a *parent-substitute*.[5] The crowd leader acts as the main interpreter of new information from the environment, determines the appropriate tactical response and directs strategy. Leaders may be dictatorial or democratic, they may be constructive or destructive, but they will always command the attention of each of the crowd members. However, leadership may take on a number of different guises. On the one hand it may be obvious, in the sense that it is vested in a particular individual or in a sub-group of people (such as a committee or board of directors). On the other hand it may be covert: it may, for example, be vested in the democratic decision of a group itself, or in the shared system of beliefs held by members of the crowd, and the code of conduct that it engenders. Covert leadership, however, almost certainly requires some form of 'totem' on which the crowd can focus its attention. Throughout history, crowds have been responsive to national flags, figureheads, icons and statues.

The findings of Stanley Milgram

The classic experiment to discover the limit to which people would be obedient to authority was conducted by Dr Stanley Milgram of Yale University.[6] In the experiment, the subjects were ordered to inflict pain on an innocent victim in the interests of an important cause. Authority (or leader and representative of a crowd belief system) was represented by a scientist in a white coat who would continually urge the experimental subject to proceed with administering electric shocks to a third person. In fact, there was no electric shock involved at all: the experimental subject did not know it, but the third person (the victim) merely behaved as if there had been. At all stages in the experiment the subject was made aware of the effect of his or her actions, both by a dial on the electric shock machine (which indicated the voltage being administered and the degree of danger involved therewith), and by the screams and protests of the victim strapped into a chair. Milgram found that over 60 per cent of the subjects were prepared to obey instructions to administer the highest and most lethal dose of electricity, even after the victim had given up screaming and was to all intents and purposes comatose.

Altruism and conflict

The results of researchers like Diener and Milgram verify that a crowd which is led by a strong leader can be a frightening force. First, people within a crowd develop a sense of altruism towards other crowd members which is very strong. (Sometimes, indeed, it is so strong that, as Emile Durkheim found, it can result in suicide.[7]) Second, the crowd can achieve objectives using methods which independent individuals would regard as being totally unacceptable. It is not surprising, therefore, that men and women are more likely to be involved in states of conflict as *group members* than as *individuals*. Third, and as a corollary, it follows that conflict (or stress) is a perfect catalyst for the formation of a crowd. If, for some reason, an imbalance develops between two groups, each group member will have common cause with other members of the same group in protecting the autonomy of his or her own group. The paramount need of each group may then release the aggressiveness in, or relax constraints on, each individual.

Conclusion

The conclusions of this chapter are simple, although profound. Membership of a crowd involves the abrogation of personal responsibility to some degree: people act differently as crowd participants than they do as independent individuals. A crowd as a whole tends to behave in a non-rational, emotional way in pursuit of its objectives and forces its members to do likewise. The ability of a crowd to organise its members in this way is particularly pronounced under conditions of conflict, when the autonomy of the crowd is in some way threatened.

These observations go some way towards explaining some of the less attractive features of the human condition. They explain, for example, why armies of otherwise rational and humane men are prepared to go to war; they offer an explanation of why avowedly religious groups have tortured and murdered in pursuit of doctrinal purity; they explain why trade union members have been willing to destroy the firms they work for rather than surrender any union 'rights'. The list is endless, and is the more depressing for it.

However, the purpose of this book is other than to bemoan the fate of humanity. The last three chapters have presented a body of theory which explains essentially. *why* group behaviour is an ubiquitous feature of the human condition. For the vast majority of people, some form of crowd pressure provides a major motivating force in all their social, economic, and political activities. Such pressure exists in such diverse structures as friendly societies, corporations, religions, sports teams, and rioting mobs. As we shall demonstrate shortly, it also exists in financial markets. However, so far we have only explained *why* crowds exist. We have not yet shown *how* crowds behave. Let us, therefore, take one further step towards the primary revelations of this book, by analysing the *dynamics* of a crowd system.

Notes

1. Arthur Koestler, *Janus: a Summing Up*. Hutchinson, London, 1978.
2. Quoted in Arthur Koestler, op. cit.
3. Quoted in Michael Talbot, *Mysticism and the New Physics*. Routledge and Kegan Paul, London, 1981.
4. Ed Diener, *Deindividuation: the absence of self-awareness and self-regulation in group members*, in P.B. Paulus (ed.) *The Psychology of Group Influence*. Erlbaum, Hillsdale, New Jersey, 1980.
5. Freud, and others, have argued that the willingness of individuals to respond to a leader is based on the experiences of early childhood. Under normal circumstances, each baby not only learns about its own individuality, but also gains security, from transactions with its parents. Hence a need for both a parent-substitute and the company of others is learnt and carried through into adult life. See, for example, Thomas A. Harris, *The Book of Choice*. Jonathan Cape, London, 1970.
6. Reported in Ralph Crawshaw, 'But everybody cheats', *Medical Opinion and Review*, January 1967.
7. Emile Durkheim, *Suicide: a Study in Sociology*. Routledge and Kegan Paul, London, 1970. Durkheim differentiated between altruistic suicide where

individuals die for the group, and anomic suicide where they die because of separation from the group.

4.

The Systems Approach to Crowd Behaviour

Introduction

The insights of analysts such as Le Bon, Freud and Koestler take us a long way towards understanding the basic crowd phenomenon. However, this does not complete the process. There is one last step to take because it is necessary to understand how *fluctuations* arise. This, as we shall see, is of vital importance to forecasting financial markets.

The analysis of a crowd as a dynamic, fluctuating system can be conducted within the framework of the philosophical approach to living organisms which is known as 'systems theory'. Such an approach – which derives from the pioneering work conducted by analysts such as Ludwig von Bertolanffy,[1] Ervin Laszlo,[2] and Erich Jantsch[3] – proceeds to a new understanding of nature by focusing on *processes* rather than on structures as such. Hence, each living organism is seen as being a *self-organising* system, with a hierarchical structure. Each such structure is *responsive* to disequilibrium, is *open* to the environment for the exchange of information and energy, and is able to *process* information and energy. These characteristics broadly mirror Gregory Bateson's criteria for the existence of 'mind' which we mentioned in Chapter 2. A brief discussion of these characteristics within the context of crowds now follows.

Non-equilibrium conditions

The basic catalyst for the formation of a crowd is a condition of 'non-equilibrium'. Such a condition creates stress, conflict, or competition, and provides the *purpose* for the creation of a crowd. The purpose, quite obviously, is to alter the disequilibrium in order to benefit the crowd's membership. The targeted change may merely be the attraction of additional resources away from the environment (as in the case of a profit-making corporation), or it may be a more fundamental attempt to impose creative evolution on the environment (as in the case of social revolution). A crowd will continue to respond to the implicit non-equilibrium either until the crowd's purpose is achieved or (in extreme cases) until the environment itself damps down the crowd. Obviously, when a crowd's purpose is fulfilled, equilibrium exists and the crowd will disintegrate.

Openness to the environment: the exchange of energy

In order to achieve its objectives, however, a crowd must be 'open' to the environment for the exchange of both energy and information. Energy is continually being used up by crowd members. Consequently the loss of useful energy (known as the build-up of entropy), as individuals leave for whatever reason, has to be surmounted by continuously attracting new members to 'the cause'. The rate of addition may be greater than, equal to, or less than the rate of exhaustion or departure. Obviously, the crowd's ability to survive cannot continue if the rate of arrival of new members is less than the rate of departure. This is one reason why 'spontaneous' street riots rarely persist for any extended length of time, even in the absence of large-scale law enforcement.

Openness to the environment: the exchange of information

This exchange of energy is complemented by an exchange of information.[4] The crowd's need to change, or to manipulate, its environment for its own ends involves a continuous process of information transfer and analysis. The crowd needs to know how its achievements relate to its objectives, and it needs to know how the environment is responding so that countervailing adjustments can be made if necessary. This process therefore involves two levels of analysis: the first is the nature of the mechanism for transmitting information, and the second is the interrelationship between a crowd and its environment.

The mechanism for transmitting information

The nature of the information transmission mechanism is very important. Often the receipt of information from the environment, and transmission of this information, is the prerogative of whoever (or whatever) constitutes the crowd 'leader'. Basically, however, any individual within a crowd can receive information on behalf of the whole crowd and can transmit it to the other members of the crowd. As Gustave Le Bon originally argued,[5] crowd members are in a constant state of expectant attention and are therefore vulnerable to suggestion. Moods, feelings and ideas in such an environment are, of course, very contagious and they spread rapidly. Modern communications, based on high technology, now ensure that the same effects can be quickly achieved even if the crowd is not assembled in one place.

However, the processes of contagion are not necessarily simplistic. Each person not only receives information and transmits it to others; but he or she can also alter it before transmission. The alteration need not only apply to the *quality* of the information, it may also apply to the *emotions* which accompany the transmission of the information. Hence, even where the information is 'hard' data which cannot be directly altered, it will be *interpreted* by individuals, and will almost certainly be retransmitted in the context of an emotion (anger, greed, sadness, indifference, optimism, pessimism etc). The end result is that crowd members all experience the same beliefs and emotions about the information which is being transmitted.

Feedback loops and the transformation of information

The idea that a crowd can process, and respond to, information in this way can usefully be described in terms of what are called *'feedback loops'*. Feedback loops transform information. The process of transforming information means that there is a difference between the *input* of information at any stage in the loop, and the *output* of information from the same stage (see Figure 4.1).

The resultant output then becomes an input of information to the next stage. Thus part A may affect part B, part B may affect part C, and C may feed back the (transformed) information to A. Each input of information therefore triggers a process which generates new information.[6] Interestingly, there are two possibilities here (see Figure 4.2): in the first, information is given a positive gain at each stage, thereby leading to a *runaway* system;[7] in the second, information is given a negative influence (usually by some form of 'governor') at some stage in the chain, thereby leading to an *oscillating* system.

Oscillating systems

Although the presence of negative feedback always creates oscillations, it does not necessarily generate *stable* oscillations. In fact, it may generate one of three types of oscillation – namely, damped, stable or unstable. These three possibilities are shown in Figure 4.3.

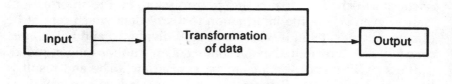

Figure 4.1. *Information transformation*

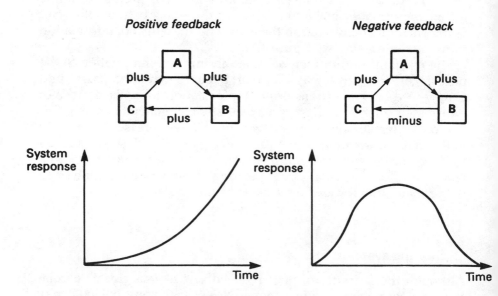

Figure 4.2. *Feedback loops and adjustment paths*

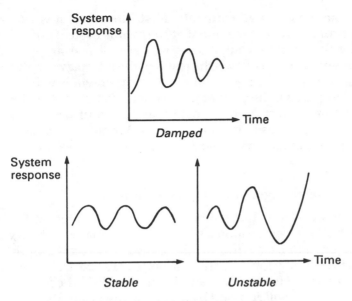

Figure 4.3. *Negative feedback loops*

The role of the crowd leader

Within a crowd, the role of the 'governor' is essentially performed by the crowd leader. The leader ensures that crowd behaviour is either magnified through positive feedback, or damped down by negative feedback. Where the leadership acts to damp down the oscillations of a crowd, that crowd operates harmoniously with its environment. Such behaviour is typical of bureaucratic organisations. Obviously, however, there are occasions when the leadership attempts to magnify the oscillations of the crowd. Indeed, since many crowds form with the specific intention of changing the environment in a fundamental way, the leadership may have a vested interest in magnifying the friction created by the crowd. Under these circumstances, society itself will attempt to protect its own autonomy by suppressing the 'runaway' behaviour of the crowd. This is the basis of police riot control. However, at an extreme, a mob may enforce evolution through revolution.

The source of change: internal fluctuations

In this sense, change and 'progress' come about as a result of a dynamic interplay, both between individuals and the crowd to which they belong, and between a crowd and its environment. Any conflict creates compensating adjustments. First, therefore, it is true to say that the progressive development of *any* overall system is determined partly by the creative components within it. For example, cultural development in any society is the result of the interplay of creative free thinking and conservative traditions. The larger whole will invariably seek to damp down the smaller parts, but ultimately the smaller parts *must* have an impact on the whole if any form of progress is to be achieved. Recent cases in point are the Women's Movement and ecologically-oriented groups such as Greenpeace.

The source of change: external fluctuations

Second, independent fluctuations in the environment itself can lead to a number of different responses by a crowd. Initially, a change in the environment imposes *stress* on the crowd. The crowd is therefore unable to respond properly, and it seeks to stabilise itself by changing its metabolism.[8] Hence, for example, an established company faced with falling sales will respond by accepting lower profits, an increase in bank overdrafts and a rise in stock levels.

Subsequently, of course, the crowd will 'acclimatise' itself to enduring changes in the environment by adjusting its operating ability without actually changing its structure.[9] Hence, a company faced with falling sales would eventually need to take positive action in terms of a cutback in its operations if it was to survive.

Ultimately the crowd may adapt to permanent changes in the environment as a result of 'revolutionary' changes. The crowd moves to a new, but stable, operating structure; in particular, the objectives of the crowd become altered.[10] Inevitably, therefore, a company faced with a permanent decline in demand for its products would have to diversify its operations if it were not to go out of business. It is interesting to note the relationship between chance and necessity in this view of evolution. In the old Darwinian view, chance mutation is *followed* by the survival of the fittest. However, in the newer systems view, chance and necessity are *complementary* principles. The initial perturbation which creates the instability in the system may appear to be random from the system's point of view, [11] but the need to survive forces the system to adapt. The system itself makes its own decisions about the nature of its new structure. Evolution is thus the unfolding of order and complexity in the process of learning.

Conclusion

To summarise the analysis of this chapter, we may argue as follows: a crowd is essentially part of the hierarchical structure of nature, and each crowd can be defined in terms of its processes rather than its physical characteristics. Theoretically, these processes are triggered by differences (or non-equilibrium conditions), utilise feedback loops, and therefore involve oscillations. The processes are continually energised by the crowd's access to the environment and are sufficiently complex to facilitate some degree of 'self-knowledge'. Energy and self-knowledge, in turn, contribute to the crowd's ability to be self-organising. Self-organisation involves the control of the crowd's members, and this enables the crowd to maintain its autonomy as well as to learn, adapt and evolve. In somewhat technical language, we have described the behavioural characteristics of Le Bon's "crowd"!

Notes

1. Ludwig von Bertalanffy, *General Systems Theory. Foundation, Development, Applications*. Braziller, New York, 1968.
2. Ervin Laszlo, *Introduction to Systems Philosophy: Towards a New Paradigm of Contemporary Thought*. Gordon and Breach, New York, 1972.
3. Erich Jantsch, *The Self-Organising Universe*. Pergamon, Oxford, 1980.
4. The environment 'recognises' a crowd by responding both to the difference made by that crowd's initial presence and to the difference made by its subsequent activities; while the crowd itself 'recognises' its own existence by responding to the resulting differences in the environment.
5. Gustave Le Bon, *Psychologie des Foules*. Reprinted as *The Crowd*. Macmillan, New York, 1922.
6. Such systems are called 'autocatalytic'.
7. The growth may be either exponential or hyperbolic. Exponential growth results in increases which are proportional to the amount present and in which the doubling time remains constant. Hyperbolic growth results in increases which are the square of the amount present, and in which the doubling time is halved with every doubling.
8. Metabolism means those chemical changes, occurring in living organisms, which are essential to sustain life.
9. Such 'somatic' changes, however, are not necessarily permanent because they are reversible. Consequently, the changes generally amount to an internalisation of stress.
10. Fluctuations in the components, caused by environmental changes, are reinforced by feedback loops. The system is then driven into a new structure by 'order through fluctuation'. Erich Jantsch, op. cit.
11. The perturbation is usually part of a larger *cyclical* fluctuation. However, it appears to the lower-level structures as a shock (see Chapter 5).

5.

Cycles in the Crowd

Introduction

The important feature of any self-organising system, whether it be a crowd or a living organism, is that it *oscillates* during the transfer of energy and information. Indeed, the presence of continuous fluctuations can be taken as *prima facie* evidence of the presence of 'mental' activity (as defined by Gregory Bateson). There are, however, a number of different 'types' of oscillation which can usefully be distinguished. We shall now look at each of these in turn.

The life cycle

The first point to make is that every crowd has both a beginning and an end. There will be a time *before* the crowd existed and there will be a time *after* it has disappeared. In other words, each crowd has a *life cycle*. Life cycles essentially consist of the three phases – namely, growth, maturity, and decline (see Figure 5.1).

Birth and growth

Crowds initially come into being as a result of both a change which creates a change (ie an item of information) and an ability to respond purposefully to that change.[1] Once a crowd with common values and a common objective has been established, it will then respond positively to the input of new items of information from the environment. In particular, it will draw a dynamic response from the most creative elements of the crowd, especially from the crowd leadership.[2] During the growth stage of its life cycle a crowd is completely able to maintain its integrity, even in the face of a hostile environment.

Maturity

At maturity, however, the crowd becomes self-orientated and therefore

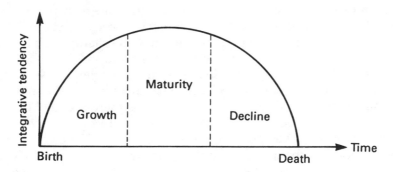

Figure 5.1. *The crowd life cycle*

inflexible. It is able to feel comfortable, basking in the glow of its achievements, and will therefore seek to control the creativity of its smaller parts rather than the other way round. Consequently, low-level fluctuations are quickly suppressed.

Decline and death

Eventually, however, this rigidity will mean that the crowd is unable to adjust any further to changes in the environment. The expectations of the crowd are unchanging, and increasingly become divergent from actual events. There then begins a decline which is marked by internal discord, uncertain leadership and hostility towards that leadership. Ultimately comes the shock which causes the crowd to disintegrate entirely. The life cycle is thus complete, and individuals are released to participate in other crowds. Hence generation and degeneration are succeeded by regeneration in a continuous process.

It is apparent that the receipt of an item of information by a crowd will have a different effect depending on the stage of its life cycle. Bad weather, for example, may stimulate the resolve of pickets in the early stages of a dispute, or it may encourage them to pack up and go home if the cause already appears to be lost; invasion of one country by another may stimulate heroic resistance, or passive acceptance; innovations may be enthusiastically embraced (as in the case of micro-chips), or vehemently opposed (as in the case of the Luddite riots).

Co-evolution

We have seen that natural dynamic systems process information by using feedback loops. The essential feature of life as we know it, is that it uses *negative* feedback loops and therefore generates continuous fluctuations. Negative feedback loops are designed basically to allow any self-organising system (including a crowd) to cope with change in its environment so that it can survive. Indeed, there are two options open to it: either it can seek directly to correct the original change in the environment, or it can change itself to meet the change. In either case, there is a *mutual* development between the system and the environment.

This mutual development involves an interesting and important concept – namely, that of *co-evolution*. The early work on the subject was conducted by Vito Volterra in 1926, and was then extended by Alfred Lotka[3] in 1956. Their basic theory was centred on the existence of a complementary development between predators and their prey: predators respond to changes in both the quantity and quality of their prey, but the prey species constantly introduces countervailing measures to predator developments. Hence neither side wins, and both survive.

The theory was subsequently developed into a more complete theory of co-evolution by the American biologists Paul Ehrlich and Peter Raven[4] in 1965. They argued that there is a mutual complementarity between different levels of any hierarchical structure: lower-level changes could not occur without higher-level changes, and higher-level changes could not develop without lower-level changes.

More recently, James Lovelock[5] has sought to extend the basic analysis to the idea that the whole of the earth's biosphere has developed into its current form through co-evolution between living organisms and their environment. For example, life could not have been created by the so-called 'Big Bang' if the necessary fundamental elements had not already been in existence, nor could it have been created out of the basic elements if the 'Big Bang' had not occurred. Now, of course, oxygen-breathing/carbon dioxide-creating animals could not live without oxygen-creating/carbon dioxide-using plants. The eternal 'chicken and egg' paradox is resolved by the concept of complementary and simultaneous development.

Limit cycles

The theory of co-evolution relies on the fact that the relevant feedback loops generate stable fluctuations between a particular system and a higher-order system. Actually, and more precisely, this relationship exists between a particular system, and a *niche* in the higher-order system. Mathematicians have a name for these stable fluctuations: they call them *limit cycles*.[6] The term 'limit' relates to the fact that the system oscillates within specific parameters, and the term 'cycle' refers to the fact that the oscillations continually return to the same point of departure.[7] If the limit cycle is stable, the oscillations will spiral on to the solution path from a wide range of initial states. If, on the other hand, the cycle is unstable, a disturbance will cause the oscillations to spiral away from that solution path. It follows that co-evolving systems utilise stable limit cycles (see Figure 5.2).

Each limit cycle expresses the relationship between two specific variables: as one variable moves, so does the other. In the diagrams, the variables are represented as x and y. However, within the context of our current analysis, we could assume that the x-axis represents an index of crowd behaviour and that the y-axis represents an index of environmental change. As presented, the limit cycle does not actually take a circular shape on the two-dimensional x-y surface (known as the 'phase plane'); nor does it need to do so. It may be oval or elliptical, as well as circular. The important point is that the oscillations occur between predetermined upper and lower limits, and these limits determine the *amplitude* of the cycle.

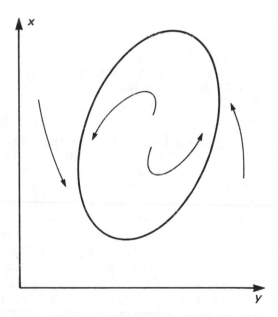

Figure 5.2. *Idealised stable limit cycle*

Limit cycles through time

A moment's reflection will reveal that the two-dimensional limit cycle relating x and y (or the crowd and the environment) actually unfolds through *time*. In other words, the cycle effectively operates in three dimensions. Let us assume that the limit cycle unfolds at a constant rate through time, and include 'time' as the third dimension in a diagram. Then the solution path takes the form of a cylinder (see Figure 5.3).

Furthermore, if we now change the perspective of the diagram, and collapse one of the x-y dimensions (say y, which corresponds to the environmental change) then the resulting solution path yields a regular cyclical pattern in the other variable (x, which corresponds to crowd behaviour). Successive peaks will occur at regular intervals, as will successive troughs (see Figure 5.4). The regularity of the intervals between peaks and troughs defines the periodicity of the cycle. However, because a limit cycle can take any number of forms, there is no reason why the shape of the cycle should be balanced around the peaks and troughs: the up phase of the cycle may be longer or shorter than the down phase. If we collapse the time dimension, of course, we are returned to the basic limit cycle.

Limit cycles in nature

There is, in fact, substantial evidence that limit cycles occur throughout nature. The human body, for example, literally pulsates with the rhythms of limit cycle fluctuations: the heart beats regularly; the neural activity of the brain proceeds in bursts of pulses;[8] the activity of breathing is basically rhythmic. Furthermore, Professor Rex Hersey of the University of Pennsylvania found that each individual has a personalised *emotional* cycle lasting for an average of 35 days.[9] In each case, lower-level systems are oscillating regularly in harmony with each other and with the higher-level system (which is the body itself); in turn, the metabolism of the body is integrated with the wider environment. There is, for example, a natural metabolic rate of activity and rest which harmonises with the day/night cycle. Hence, the rate of urine production peaks each day at around the same time, [10] and the ability of the blood to coagulate on a wound is lowest in the morning. Furthermore, the rate of body metabolism is generally higher during the spring and summer than it is during the autumn and winter. It appears, in fact, that subtle electro-magnetic changes in the geophysical environment induce electro-chemical changes in the human body.[11]

Multiple limit cycles

There are three important features of all natural cycles. First, cycles at all

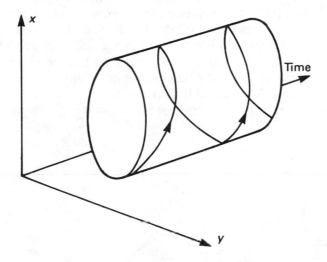

Figure 5.3. *Three-dimensional limit cycle*

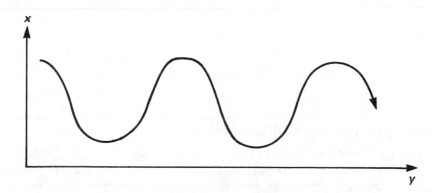

Figure 5.4. *Two-dimensional limit cycle*

levels of the hierarchy of nature will *harmonise* with one another, since the processes of nature do not allow discord. Second, each different hierarchical level has a different time dimension attached to it, so that higher-level cycles take longer to develop than do their lower-level counterparts. Third, the *trend* of each lower-degree cycle is formed by a higher-degree cycle. The situation can be presented as in Figure 5.5. For simplicity, it is assumed that only two levels of limit cycle exist, although in theory any number of levels could be included. Figure 5.5 shows a small, short-term cycle integrated with a larger, longer-term cycle in three-dimensional space. As before, the three dimensions could be an index of crowd behaviour, an index of environmental change, and time. The short-run fluctuations continue throughout each complete long-run cycle.

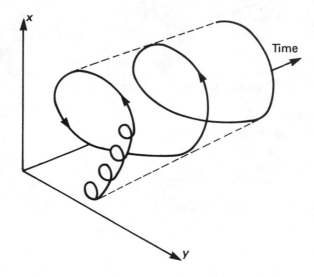

Figure 5.5. *Two-limit cycles in three dimensions*

Multiple cycles in two dimensions

In order to obtain a clearer picture of this theoretical construct, we can visualise it in two dimensions: first, by collapsing the 'time' dimension while keeping the other two dimensions unchanged; second, by collapsing the y (or 'environment') dimension while keeping the other two dimensions unchanged (see Figure 5.6). The effect of higher-level fluctuations on the lower-level fluctuations should be perfectly clear.

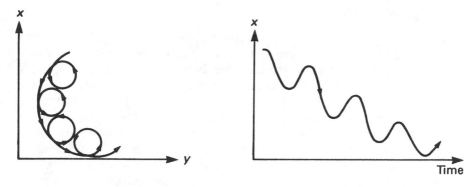

Figure 5.6. *Two-limit cycles in two dimensions*

The impact of shocks

Although limit cycles are the main mechanism whereby a self-organising system copes with fluctuations in its environment, they do not fully represent the adjustment processes which are involved. By definition, items of information become available only in discontinuous or discrete time intervals. The adjustment process depends on whether or not the recipient system is prepared for the information. If the information is 'expected', then the system can adjust very quickly to suit the changed circumstances. If, however, the information is 'unfamiliar' to the system when it is received, [12] then that information impacts as a *shock*, and the system may have to change its dynamic structure in order to cope.

The concept of shocks as applied to group behaviour is not a new one. As early as 1933, Ragnar Frisch[13] sought to show that business cycles could be simulated by subjecting a linear model to random shocks. However, the theme being developed in this book presents a substantially different view of the world from that visualised by Frisch and many subsequent economic theorists. In particular, cyclical behaviour is here seen as an intrinsic part of nature, whereas the classical view of economics assumes *linear* behaviour which would converge on a 'steady state' if it were not upset by exogenous changes such as strikes, crop shortages, changes in government policy, changes in tastes and so forth.

In practice, then, shocks are delivered to systems which are already oscillating in a limit cycle pattern with their niche in the environment. The situation can be viewed as a *family* of limit cycles operating in three-dimensional space. Each sub-system bears a limit cycle relationship with a higher system; each higher system has a limit cycle relationship with its local environment; the local environment has a limit cycle relationship with the global environment. Divergences between lower-level cycles and higher level cycles are rectified by shocks, and the lower-level cycle will then move to meet the upper-level cycle.

The profile of shocks

The important feature of the analysis of shocks is the *form* taken by the subsequent adjustment process. First, a shock delivered to a lower subsystem destabilises the relationship between that subsystem and a higher-level system. Second, every attempt by the subsystem to re-establish its original relationship will now be met by a countervailing response from the higher system. Third (and as a consequence) every adjustment by the higher system will result in an additional response from the subsystem. Fourth, these fluctuations will continue *at least* until the limit cycle of the next higher degree is able to reassert control.[14] This process of adjustment in three-dimensional space reveals itself as a *spiral* as shown in Figure 5.7. Such a spiral could, for example, materialise after a crowd had initially been 'born', and was moving towards a stable relationship with its environment. Alternatively, it could represent the adjustment processes *within* the crowd as it responded to an externally imposed shock.

Shocks in two dimensions

If we now review the solution path in *two* dimensions, two familiar patterns emerge (see Figure 5.8). First, we have a *spiral* formation between x (eg an index of crowd activity) and y (eg an index of environmental change). Second, we have an *unstable* cycle, involving either x or y, through time. As we shall see in Part II of this book, these two patterns are of profound importance to our analysis.

Some insights into social change

The dynamics of hierarchical crowd systems therefore involve three types of oscillation: first, there are the life cycles of the crowd systems involved; second, there are the limit cycles; third there are the unstable fluctuations. During the life cycle of any particular crowd, its own internal cycles are bound by the requirements of higher-level oscillations, and divergences are rectified by shocks. This conclusion leads us to a number of important insights into social and economic developments. The first is that because higher-level cycles are often so slow to develop, the social and geophysical environments usually appear static and immutable to the majority of participants. Individuals do not therefore recognise that changes have taken place until some form of catastrophe occurs. Revolutions, large-scale population migrations, and wars are invariably the results of complex changes which have been developing over long periods of time. However, they are often triggered

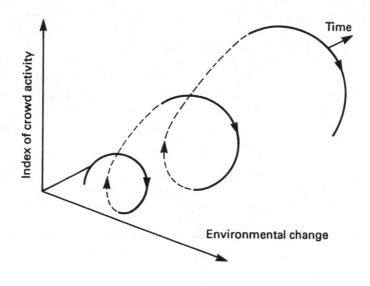

Figure 5.7. *The spiral adjustment process*

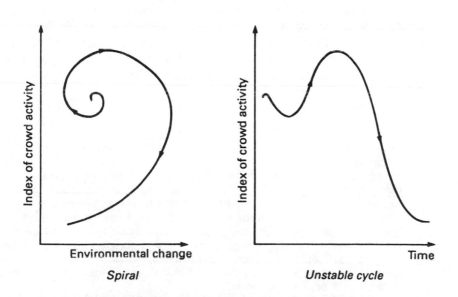

Figure 5.8. *The adjustment process in two dimensions*

by apparent 'local' causes or even by relatively insignificant events. The resulting gap between personal expectations and the reality of the situation invariably adds to the chaos by imposing stress and uncertainty on individuals in unfamiliar circumstances.

The second implication is that some of the events which are usually assumed to be random (such as the 'acts of God' invoked by insurance companies) may in fact be predictable. It will always be difficult to forecast the exact timing and location of some events, but this does not mean it is impossible to forecast that they will occur within specific time frames. There is now substantial evidence to suggest that such diverse occurrences as wars, [15] earthquakes and climatic changes exhibit cyclical behaviour. Most individuals do not recognise the rhythmic nature of the phenomena because they are exposed to their consequences irregularly, if at all, in the course of a single lifetime. However, the concept of cyclical fluctuations in the hierarchy of nature implicitly confirms that irregular events are more regular than we care to suppose.

Third, the analysis highlights the fact that short-term and long-term developments are intricately related to one another. Evolution occurs at all levels, and in all degrees, in a largely complementary fashion. Consequently, the difference between short-term cycles and long-term trends is not one that only involves quantity, but one that also involves *quality*. In other words, dynamic structures are continually changing in a largely irreversible fashion between one situation and another. As each short-run cycle swings down, the quantitative retracement of the previous rise is not entirely matched by a reversal in qualitative changes. Even in the case of a simple heartbeat, for example, there is a subtle ageing process between one beat and another. In the the case of economic activity, each quantitative cycle in inventories (or stock levels) is accompanied by important changes in the quality of the investment. 'All change', it is said, 'is growth; and growth is life!'

Notes

1. This raises an interesting point. A crowd can only form in response to the receipt of information which gives the crowd a purpose; but the concept of purpose presupposes that individuals are in some way pre-programmed to recognise the validity of a specific objective. Each individual has to be able to place the information in a context which triggers his or her integrative tendency: the one is impotent without the other. Contexts are essentially learnt either directly or through genetic transmission. This confirms the need for learnt common values to ensure that societies survive. It also confirms the 'biological' nature of crowd behaviour.
2. If necessary, new common values and traditions will emerge which will ensure the stability of the crowd.
3. Alfred J. Lotka, *Elements of Mathematical Biology*. Dover Publications, New York, 1956.

4. See Erich Jantsch, *The Self-Organising Universe*. Pergamon, Oxford, 1980.
5. James E. Lovelock, *Gaia*. Oxford University Press, Oxford, 1979.
6. A limit cycle is defined as the (isolated) periodic oscillation between two variables, and is represented graphically by an (isolated) closed non-linear path. See, for example, D.W. Jordon and P. Smith, *Nonlinear Ordinary Differential Equations*. Oxford University Press, Oxford, 1977.
7. The time between successive troughs or successive peaks is known as the periodicity of the cycle.
8. Walter J. Freeman, *Mass Action in the Nervous System*. Academic Press, New York, 1975.
9. R.B. Hersey, 'Emotional cycles of man', in *Journal of Mental Science*, 1931. Hersey found that the cycle of each individual, taken separately, varied quite markedly from the average: some had cycles of 16 days, others had cycles of as long as 63 days. The important point, however, is that each individual had a personalised cycle which persisted over the sampling period.
10. See Lyall Watson, *Supernature*. Hodder and Stoughton, London, 1973
11. There is an expanding body of literature which records the striking correlation between electro-magnetic fluctuations in the solar system, electro-magnetic fluctuations in the earth's biosphere, and electro-chemical changes in the human body. The implication is that we are more influenced by events such as sunspot cycles and lunar cycles than we sometimes care to believe. See, for example, Michael Gaugelin, *The Cosmic Clocks*. Granada, London, 1973.
12. That is, there is no previous context within which to place the information.
13. Ragnar Frisch, 'Propagation problems and impulse problems in dynamic economics', in *Essays in Honour of Gustav Cassel*. George Allen and Unwin, London, 1933.
14. During the adjustment process, the upper-level cycle does not therefore accurately reflect the *trend* of the lower cycle.
15. Some of the evidence for the striking phenomenon of cycles in warfare is discussed in Edward R. Dewey with Og Mandino, *Cycles – the Mysterious Forces that Trigger Events*. Hawthorn, New York, 1971.

6.

Techniques for Forecasting
Crowd Behaviour

Introduction

The idea that behaviour in financial markets is essentially a crowd phenomenon is the basis of a comprehensive approach to accurate forecasting in equity, bond, and foreign exchange markets. At one extreme, a self-aware individual is potentially unpredictable except within the very broadest of guidelines. However, at the other extreme, people as a group *are* predictable. This is the essence of the crowd phenomenon, and it implies that price movements in financial markets are also intrinsically predictable.

Methods of predicting price movements

Deciding that financial markets are predictable is, however, not quite the same thing as deciding *how* such prediction may be arrived at. In essence, there are two main lines of thought. The first is that financial market prices ultimately reflect fundamental values in the economy. On this view, financial prices are determined by actual and expected developments concerning these values, and forecasting financial prices is therefore a matter of forecasting fundamentals.[1] The second approach argues that most of the actual and expected information concerning fundamental values is already discounted by the market at any given point in time. Hence, market price movements tend to forecast developments in fundamental values, and forecasting financial market prices therefore becomes a matter of deciding what the market is already 'saying' about itself.

Economic forecasting

Despite the fact that political and social trends often have to be taken into account, forecasting financial markets on the basis of fundamentals is essentially the province of *economics*. Economic theory argues that the price of any asset is determined by the interaction of demand and supply: the price will rise if demand rises or supply falls; and the price will fall if demand falls or supply rises. Hence, the main task of an economist is to isolate the forces which will influence the demand for, and supply of, financial assets over time. The main tools are economic theory itself and statistics – the former to provide the logical framework and the latter to provide some form of quantification to the analysis and conclusions.[2]

Problems with economic forecasting

The different theories concerning the specific relationships involved will not be discussed here, since they are beyond the scope of this book. However, it is worth while commenting briefly on the methodology involved. Economic forecasting can be very accurate in providing *trend* forecasts for markets, particularly over relatively short time periods. However, the fact remains that they have some difficulty in coping with the *level* and *timing* of turning points. This is because most economic forecasting models are still steeped in the traditions of 'reductionism' (which was discussed in Chapter 1). Economic models tend to be 'closed' systems which are divorced from the wider environment in which they operate; indeed, the environment is normally represented by 'assumptions' which are made by the forecasters. In addition, the models tend to assume that individuals behave mechanistically, [3] and therefore in a linear fashion, [4] to given stimuli.

These characteristics of economic models create three sources of potential forecasting errors. First, there is no automatic feedback loop between the model and its environment[5] and consequently the internal relationships in the model gradually break down over time. Second, assumptions made by the forecaster about the environment are subject to human error. Third, the techniques do not recognise the importance of crowd emotions, and hence of significant swings in sentiment.[6]

In fairness, it has to be said that economists are acutely aware of these difficulties, and seek to compensate for them. But the difficulties undoubtedly compromise the potential accuracy of the forecasts. Nowhere was this more true than in the case of equities during the 1986-87 bull run and the subsequent collapse. It is not that economic analysis is necessarily incorrect; it is just that the available techniques are inadequate for the task of providing exact forecasts for the levels and timings of market turning points. The practical value of economics is therefore limited to providing excellent background forecasts against which to judge the current trends of particular markets.

Technical analysis

The alternative (or at least complementary) method of forecasting financial market behaviour is known as *technical analysis*. When using technical analysis, no account is taken of fundamental values, because it is assumed that investors' expectations concerning those values (and a lot more information besides) are already reflected in prices. To paraphrase Oscar Wilde's view of the cynic, a technical analyst therefore knows the price of everything and the value of nothing. This implies that financial markets will, in fact, always be trying to *anticipate* the future, and that therefore changes in financial market prices *precede* changes in fundamental conditions. In many cases, it should be possible to use price behaviour to forecast fundamentals, rather than the other way around!

The past and present as a guide to the future

This, in itself, would be a sufficient reason for focusing attention on the behaviour of financial asset prices. However, the claim of technical analysis is that it is actually possible to forecast the future performance of a particular market *entirely* by reference to the actual and historical performance of that market. In other words, no external factors need to be included in the analysis.[7] For many years, analysts have recognised that certain price patterns have a predictive value, that the extent of some price movements can be calculated in advance, and that there are regular price cycles operating in some markets. More recently, the use of technical analysis has become an increasingly large part of the investment decision-making process because it is both simple and profitable. The big problem, however, is that very few people understand *why* the forecasting techniques actually work. This has created tremendous difficulties of communication within the investment industry. On the one hand there are those who know that technical analysis works, but cannot explain why; on the other hand there are those who know that fundamental analysis does not work to the required degree of accuracy, but continue to use it because it is at least explicable.

The rationale behind technical analysis

The preceding chapters should have given a strong indication of the *raison d'être* of technical analysis. Natural forces encourage people to indulge in group behaviour. Groups behave as single organisms: they therefore respond in a predictable way to information shocks, they have metabolic (emotional) cycles, and they follow a definable path of growth and decay. Unlike any other crowd, however, the behaviour of financial market crowds is clearly reflected in simple, and specific, indicators. These are the price movements themselves, and certain mechanical indices of the underlying activity and energy of the crowd, such as trading volumes.[8] Logically, these indicators should reflect the operation of the appropriate 'natural' laws.

We shall therefore now demonstrate that price movements, and indices of investor activity, actually do behave in accordance with the analytical framework presented in the previous chapters. We shall show that all price movements are part of a very simple pattern which is the response to information shocks, and that prices oscillate rhythmically in response to the metabolic fluctuations of the crowd. We shall show how the cohesiveness of the crowd ensures that each price movement is *mathematically* related to preceding price movements. We shall therefore show that it is very easy to differentiate between *trends* and *turning points*.

Notes

1. Because, on the face of it, new information tends to become available *randomly*, current economic analysis tends to accept the hypothesis that stock prices are randomly determined (the so-called 'Random-Walk Hypothesis'). It is, in fact, true that stock price movements usually appear to be uncorrelated with one another over particular time periods. However, the hypothesis is essentially no more than a truism. It fails to recognise the ordered nature of the underlying process, and fails to take account of actual investor behaviour. Furthermore, it has recently been shown that an unusually long run of correlated price changes occurred during the October 1987 'crash' in the US (see G. J. Santoni, 'The October Crash', *The Federal Reserve Bank of St. Louis Review*, May/June 1988). The Random Walk Hypothesis cannot therefore explain the 'crash'. For a particularly relevant, and amusing, critique of the Random Walk Hypothesis see Adam Smith, *The Money Game*. Vintage Books, New York, 1976.
2. See, for example, Carl F. Christ, *Econometric Models and Methods*. John Wiley and Sons, New York, 1966.
3. It has been argued that the assumptions used in a theory are not as important as the conclusions, or predictions, of that theory. (See, for example, Milton Friedman, *Essays in Positive Economics*. University of Chicago Press, Chicago, 1953.) This argument has some validity under two circumstances. It is acceptable when the assumptions are designed to neutralise external interferences. In this way, it becomes possible to analyse the response of specific variables to changes in a limited number of other variables, with outside influences being held unchanged. The argument is also acceptable when the assumptions simply affirm the 'truth' of previous research. Serious philosophical problems arise,

however, when the assumptions are used to neutralise complications *within* a particular system because, by definition, these complications are part of the system.

4. Linear relationships are usually used even in those mathematical models which are able to create cyclical fluctuations. A great variety of linear relationships allow for oscillations. These include derivatives, integrals, fixed delays, and lags of various distributed forms. See R.G.D. Allen, *Macro-Economic Theory*. Macmillan, London, 1967.

5. This exacerbates the problems of trying to forecast the effects of shocks. Shocks are continually occurring, and indeed they are the main catalyst for change. They can be caused by events such as wars, bad weather, interruptions to supplies of raw materials, labour disputes and strikes, and bankruptcies. However, 'closed' linear economic models cannot be used to forecast the effects of such shocks with any degree of accuracy. Not only is each shock associated with a change in the environment within which economic and financial activities have to take place, but people's *attitudes* to such activities are likely to alter. Therefore, it is usually possible to calculate only the *direction* of economic changes caused by a particular shock.

6. Economic theory essentially regards such swings as being abnormal. Excesses of optimism and pessimism occur relatively infrequently. Therefore it is certainly consistent with the evidence that emotional upheavals are unusual. Manias and panics are accordingly treated as idiosyncracies rather than as special examples of a general phenomenon.

7. In practice it is, however, wise to take account of fundamental factors.

8. Financial markets are therefore an ideal source of information about *all* crowd behaviour.

Part II:

The Dynamics of the Bull/Bear Cycle

7.

The Stock Market Crowd

Introduction

The physical structures of any financial market, and the institutional arrangements for settling transactions in that market, vary throughout the world. Many markets are centred on physical arenas known as 'exchanges'; others are established purely by telephone conversations between willing buyers and sellers. All, however, have common characteristics. The first of these, strangely enough, is that it is actually very difficult to identify a physical body of people that constitutes the market 'crowd'. The investment community is a far larger, far more amorphous and far less tangible construct than the group of people who are physically on the floor of an exchange, or who are actually transacting bargains over the telephone at any given time.

The individual investor

The basic unit in the investment hierarchy is the individual investor. Essentially an investor is anyone who has a *trading position*. In this context, the term 'trading position' has two meanings because it may reflect a view either that market prices are going to rise, or that market prices are going to fall. In the former instance an investor will be a 'bull' (or will be 'long') of a market, while in the latter instance an investor will be a 'bear' (or will be 'short') of a market. Hence a bullish investor will either own an equity, bond or commodity, or have a 'right' to own an underlying security at some future date.[1] On the other hand, a bearish investor either will have a direct holding of cash (or its equivalent, such as a bank deposit or a building society account) while awaiting an opportune moment to purchase a security (or securities), or will hold an investment which confers the 'right' to sell stock at some future date.[2]

The individual investor may be dealing on his or her own behalf (a *private* investor) or be dealing on behalf of an organisation (an *institutional* investor). The investor's objective is to maximise total returns, subject to a preferred split between capital and income. The reasons for the separation of capital and income need not concern us unduly here. Suffice to say that each investor faces a fixed tax regime and a future set of liabilities (dependent on his or her age[3]), and has a natural attitude towards the acceptance of risk. The tax regime will help to determine whether or not capital is preferred to income over short periods, and the future liabilities will help to determine whether capital is preferred to income over longer periods. However, the most important consideration will be the extent to which an individual is prepared to accept the possibility of uncertain capital gains as opposed to the probability of a certain income[4] whatever the time period concerned.

The dealing strategy

The strategy used by the individual investor to achieve a maximum total return is to buy securities before the market price rises and to sell them after the price has done so. There are slight variations on this theme, depending on whether performance is judged against the rate of return on short-term money deposits, or against a 'fully invested' position. Private individuals fall into the former category and will simply aim to buy at low prices and sell at high ones. Some institutional investors employed by pension funds and insurance companies, on the other hand, fall into the latter category. These individuals may simply hold up purchases within limited time frames to ensure that they are at least buying cheaply. Alternatively, they may switch investments from underperforming securities to better performing securities. For all groups, however, the basic philosophy remains exactly the same: 'buy cheap and sell dear'.

The bulls and the bears

The next higher level in the investment hierarchy consists of two groups of investor: the 'bullish' crowd and the 'bearish' crowd. The former crowd anticipates a rise in security prices, while the latter anticipates a fall. We have seen that crowds are not necessarily physical assemblies, but that they are psychological phenomena. This is especially true of financial market crowds, of whatever persuasion. Members of the bullish crowd or of the bearish crowd all have a specific belief as to the future direction of security prices. Further-more, they are linked to each other via the communications network. Newspapers, television, telephones and market reports all supple-ment the sort of direct contact which habitually occurs in daily professional and personal life. This network of contacts ensures that price-sensitive information is speedily disseminated and assimilated, and that like-minded individuals are brought into contact with each other.

The mechanism of price fluctuations

The presence of *two* crowds in a financial market, with diametrically opposite views, ensures that a state of conflict exists within the rules of the investment game. The presence of stress is the main catalyst for the formation of a crowd-mind, and its associated behaviour, and conditions of conflict certainly ensure that stress exists. If everybody always thought the same thing at the same time, there would be no 'market' as such, and consequently no graduated price movements: prices would jump up and down randomly, if they changed at all, and no-one would trade. However, the influence of differing views as to the future course of prices, and the fact that the conflict between the bulls and the bears takes time to resolve, ensures that prices move up and down *through time*.

The influence of emotions

When an individual buys or sells securities, an *emotional* commitment is being made. Initially, of course, this commitment is being made to a trading position. The decision to deal may have been arrived at rationally, but the *act* of dealing creates a financial involvement, and an associated need to 'get it right'. The investor will have a trading position whose market value is outside his or her control. There will be a feeling of pleasure as the price goes in his or her favour, but there will be a feeling of displeasure (dismay, anger, depression, fear) if the price does the opposite. These feelings of pleasure or displeasure will be associated with biochemical changes in the body. The heartbeat changes, the rate of respiration alters, and the palms sweat.

The herd instinct

These feelings of pleasure or displeasure are intensified when an individual associates with other people. If the trading position is 'right', the personal advantages in terms of wealth and self-esteem are supplemented by communicating with other investors who have similar trading positions. Conversations with others will confirm both the validity of the trading position and the decision-making process which preceded it; satisfaction will be felt when newspaper articles or brokers' reports provide supportive evidence; members of the same group will engage in a continuous process of congratulating each other; attention will be focused on the immediate future, where critical analysis is less necessary, rather than on the longer term.

More than this, however, investors who are members of the 'right' crowd will tend to emphasise the weakness of the arguments of the 'wrong' crowd. There will be a continuous propaganda stream aimed at the latter who, in any case, will already feel at a disadvantage. Initially, members of the 'wrong' crowd will feel the need to associate together for protection. They will try to confirm each others' views as being correct, and will emphasise the ultimate errors of the 'right' crowd's case. Indeed, there will be a tendency to ignore the 'right' crowd's arguments altogether. Members of the 'wrong' crowd will commiserate with one another and emphasise the longer term rather than the immediate future.

It is apparent from these comments, therefore, that a commitment to a trading *position* is only the beginning of the story. No matter how rational was the original decision to enter into a trading position, the very *act* of dealing moves an individual into a less rational, crowd-type environment. Specifically, the investor accepts one of the two crowds' beliefs about the future trend in prices, and identifies strongly with other members of that same crowd. He or she becomes a committed crowd member.

The bull/bear life cycle in emotions

The intensity of this emotional commitment to a particular crowd seems to vary depending on the phases and duration of a particular bull/bear cycle. We shall be analysing these different phases in more detail in later chapters. However, the following comments can be made now.

At the early stages of a *new* price trend, the majority of investors still remain committed to the *old* price trend. The previous trend has already finished, but its termination has not yet been generally recognised. A minority of investors will have begun to suspect that a price reversal is at hand, and will be altering the balance of their portfolios. However, even for this group, there will be some degree of uncertainty about the future course of prices: portfolio balances will be altered to only a relatively small degree and there will be a tendency to reverse profitable trades very quickly rather than take the longer term view. At the beginning of a bull trend the fear of making losses still predominates, while at the start of a bear trend greed (or a fear of missing further profits) tends to stop people from selling a significant proportion of their investments. Consequently at the early stages of a price trend the emotional commitment of the (ultimately) successful crowd to that trend is quite weak.

Subsequently, however, there comes a stage during a price movement when the emotional commitment becomes more intense. This is the stage when most of the investment community recognise that the movement in prices has become a *trend* either upwards or downwards and emotional conviction replaces any rational doubts that still persist. Investors therefore 'chase' the trend and open new trading positions.

This feature of investor behaviour then leads on to the next phase of the cycle. Once there has been a general recognition that a bullish or bearish price trend is in full swing, the foundation is laid for a *price reversal*. The trend will obviously persist for some time, but the fact remains that the more people who commit themselves to believing in a particular trend, and to investing in that trend, the fewer people there are in fact left to perpetuate it. A price reversal therefore inevitably occurs when the vast majority of investors believe that it will not (yet) happen.

The objectives of technical analysis

It should be apparent from this (admittedly brief) analysis that the obvious rule for successful investment is to keep a close watch on what other investors are saying and doing, and then, when a vast majority are saying and doing the same thing, do the reverse. This is one of the most valuable aspects of using technical analysis: it is a rational approach to a non-rational phenomenon, and encourages the user to stand aside from the crowd pressures.

The influence of price movements on crowd psychology

There are two important points to remember here. The first is that crowds have objectives of their own, even if the individual members do not specifically recognise them as such. The second is that crowds respond very quickly and simply to leadership. It is an important feature of financial markets that prices play a crucial part in *both* of these aspects of crowd behaviour. First, it is the prime objective of each of the bullish and bearish crowds to move security prices in their own favour; second, the leadership role is partly provided by movements in prices themselves. Let us now analyse each of these forces in turn.

The contest between the two crowds

The ability of a bullish or bearish crowd to move security prices in its own favour depends primarily on the financial resources which can be marshalled and committed one way or the other. Eventually, the conflict between the bulls and the bears is resolved when one of the groups disintegrates and transfers its resources to the other side. The strategy used to win this conflict is: first, to ensure that every member of the crowd is fully committed to membership, and second, to bombard the opposition (which includes all those who are not yet participating in the market *at all*) with a continuous stream of propaganda. Hence, as a persistent move by prices in a particular direction develops, the integrative tendency of the successful crowd will ensure that each member's trading position is as large as possible. Rational behaviour by the individual becomes more difficult, and non-rational (emotional) behaviour becomes increasingly easy. Trading positions are opened on the basis that the successful crowd's belief system (be it rising or falling prices) will continue to be correct, and critical judgement accordingly wanes. Personal interest ultimately becomes subordinated to the group interest, and over-trading begins to occur.

The influence of prices on behaviour

As more and more resources are committed to the successful crowd's point of view, prices will continue to respond favourably. This, in turn, justifies the successful crowd's existence and excites members of that crowd further. Simultaneously, of course, the vested interests involved in keeping prices moving in one direction will be increased. Consequently, brokers, market-makers and investors alike will provide a continuous stream of favourable comment to the media, and the latter will promote the cause to the widest possible audience.

Meanwhile, individuals in the unsuccessful crowd will already be vulnerable to coercion and will tend to desert to the successful crowd. As this process develops, market prices will continue to move in the direction required by the successful crowd. These changes in prices are a clear signal[5] to members of the unsuccessful crowd that their arguments are ineffectual. No matter how powerful these arguments might appear on a longer term view, the short term message cannot be ignored. The beliefs of the unsuccessful crowd are shown to be incorrect. Eventually, the stress created by the combined forces of adverse price movements, shrinking numbers and unfavourable propaganda becomes too much, and the trickle of deserters from the unsuccessful crowd becomes a flood. Prices will suddenly rise or fall very sharply as this change occurs: it is an emotional period, usually accompanied by high volume turnover in the market place.[6] Further-more, those investors who join the successful crowd at this stage are 'converts' and, as such, tend to be the more committed. They are therefore the least likely to change their minds quickly, and will provide sufficient finance to keep the trend intact.

The limit cycle between prices and behaviour

On this analysis, it is apparent that price movements are not just a passive response to market forces: there is a feedback effect which ensures that market forces are themselves responsive to price move-ments. In other words, there is a limit cycle relationship between prices and investor behaviour. This observation is important, and is in direct contrast to the assumptions of classical economics. (Indeed, within the classical framework, prices cannot be determined if the demand/supply functions are allowed to shift in response to a change in prices.) Crowd behaviour ensures that a price movement triggers an emotional response among members of opposing crowds, and thereby helps to ensure that the most recent movement in prices is continued into the future.

Beliefs and leadership

The reason for behaviour being dependent on prices is that a price movement in a particular direction represents the beliefs of one of the two crowds, and helps to fulfil the *leadership* function for that crowd. Because our experience of life through time is (apparently) linear and sequential, and because (for most of us) our thought processes are of the same nature, there is a natural tendency to believe that what has *just* happened will also *continue* to happen in the immediate future. If, for example, security prices have just risen, not only will the bulls feel satisfied but there will also be a tendency to assume that the rise will continue. There is therefore a clear 'instruction' to investors to buy more stock if possible. In a bullish environment, therefore, a rise in prices is the flag to which investors flock and pledge allegiance; in a bearish market a fall in prices represents the harsh and terrible god to which cowed investors ultimately bend their knees!

Individuals as crowd leaders

The role of price movements in the leadership function does not actually rule out the influence on crowd psychology of particular individuals. Indeed, the emergence of a spokesman to publicise the belief of the successful crowd greatly enhances the effect of recent price movements. From time to time, certain market traders or advisers *do* gain a reputation for 'getting the market right'. Usually this reputation comes either from making an accurate forecast (or 'call') of a market when no-one believed it, or from sticking to a particular view of the market trend longer than anyone else. At certain moments in a market price trend, sentiment may actually be influenced by such individuals.

However, there are, two important points to be made about the people who provide this type of 'leadership'. First, attention is given only to individuals who have already earned a reputation: very few people will actually believe a new 'guru' the first time he or she makes a forecast, no matter how accurate those forecasts subsequently turn out to be. Second, it becomes increasingly difficult for a particular individual to influence price movements on a regular basis. This apparent paradox occurs because, as was pointed out earlier, the more people who believe in a trend, the fewer people there are left to perpetuate it. Sooner or later, a successful 'call' will be self-defeating because too many people will believe in it. The price move generated by the call will be quickly reversed, and a large number of people who followed the leader will actually lose money. Hard-won reputations, based on a high-profile exposure, are easily lost and can rarely be fully regained.

The conditions for effective leadership

The identity of those individuals who are able to influence markets therefore changes with time. Furthermore, this type of 'leadership' is certainly not exercised as an ongoing influence: it is essentially a transitory phenomenon which can only occur when market conditions are right. Specifically, there needs to be a state of tension between the opposing bullish and bearish crowds. Conditions of stress ensure that the reported comments, or behaviour, of a particular 'leader' can act as the trigger for the large scale desertion of investors from the unsuccessful crowd to the successful one. 'Leadership' exercised by individuals can only be utilised within the context of the successful crowd.

Investment advisers

Leadership of this nature needs to be differentiated from the regular day-to-day leadership provided by investment advisers to small groups of investors. Investment advisers basically distil the plethora of available economic, political and financial information, and form an investment view which they dispense to their clients. They therefore provide positive leadership which, generally speaking, is acted upon. However, in relation to the phenomenon which we are analysing, investment advisers essentially lead sub-groups within a bullish or bearish crowd. Crowd theory certainly applies to each sub-group. Nevertheless, each sub-group will remain dominated by the main crowd to which it belongs. The strategy to which each sub-group responds emotionally is the strategy of the 'parent' crowd. Successful advisers will not in fact usually make recommendations which are completely independent of market conditions: indeed, they will themselves be part of the crowd to a greater or lesser degree. However, even those rare individuals who are capable both of recognising market sentiment, and of remaining aloof from it, and who are consequently capable of providing contrary opinion advice, cannot fulfil the role of leader for the *whole* crowd. More precisely, it is *because* they remain aloof that they cannot be market crowd leaders. Only the happy minority will follow their advice, while the majority react either too slowly or not at all.

Conclusion

We have thus arrived at the following conclusions in this chapter. The pursuit of trading profits as a common objective for investors ensures that stock market behaviour is a crowd phenomenon. The emotional commitment of individual investors to a particular set of trading positions translates into an emotional commitment to either a bullish or bearish crowd: each investor accepts the bull or bear argument of the crowd to which he or she belongs, each investor identifies strongly with that crowd, and each investor submits to the leadership provided both by the direction of price movements and by spokesmen (insofar as they emerge) for that crowd.

The existence of two crowds in the stock market provides the mechanism through which cyclical behaviour transmits itself. Because of the bull/bear split, conditions of uncertainty and conflict exist. The associated stress encourages a crowd to protect its autonomy as well as pursue its strategic objectives with respect to prices. Consequently, an individual's integrative tendency is stimulated to ensure that trading positions are marshalled for maximum effect. Trading decisions therefore tend to become increasingly non-rational as a price trend develops. As crowd members' resources are thereby committed, the internal strength of the crowd transmutes itself into external strength. Propaganda against the losing crowd intensifies.

The latter eventually respond to stress by joining the successful crowd. New trading positions assist in fulfilling the successful crowd's primary objective of ensuring that security prices move favourably. Ultimately extremes of euphoria or pessimism occur, and the conditions for a price reversal are created.

This analysis provides only the most basic framework for understanding the behaviour of financial markets, but even as far as it goes it has a number of far-reaching implications. First, it provides a theoretical framework which helps to explain both normal *and* abnormal behaviour in financial markets. The same concepts can be used to explain last week's movements in share prices, as well as the South Sea Bubble of 1720 or the Wall Street Crash of 1929. Second, it provides the theoretical basis for the dynamics of behaviour in financial markets which result in excesses of over-trading and which create the conditions for price reversals. In other words, it explains the internal mechanism through which the bull/bear cycle operates. Third, it treats behaviour in financial markets as being a natural phenomenon which is subject to natural forces. (This raises some interesting possibilities as to the role of external influences, such as the weather, on crowd psychology.) The analysis has therefore moved a long way from the simplistic view that price movements in financial markets are the wholly unpredictable outcome of wholly rational decisions taken by completely independent people.

Notes

1. This involves the purchase of a call option or a futures contract. There is an important difference between the two. If held to expiry, an option is a 'right' to buy or sell an underlying security, and need not be exercised. However, if held to expiry, a futures contract is a legal commitment to buy or sell an underlying security. Delivery of the underlying security can only be avoided if the futures contract is closed off before delivery date.
2. This would involve either the purchase of a put option or the sale of a futures contract. In some markets, it is also possible to sell stock 'short' that is, to sell stock which is not actually owned.
3. Economic theory contends that savings essentially depend on the distribution of income over an expected lifetime. Hence savings should be a larger percentage of disposable income in the middle years of a person's life than in either the early or later years. See, for example, M.J. Farrell, 'The new theories of the consumption function', *The Economic Journal*, December 1959.
4. For a description of the different concepts involved see James Tobin, 'Liquidity preference as behaviour towards risk', *Review of Economic Studies*, February 1958.
5. Changes are differences, and differences are items of information.
6. This is a good example of what has recently become known as 'Catastrophe Theory'. See, for example, Denis Postle, *Catastrophe Theory*.

Fontana, London, 1980. This theory deals with 'discontinuities' in systems which otherwise change only gradually. The discontinuities allow a system to move to a new status without necessarily changing the structure of the system. Catastophe Theory postulates the existence of only a limited number of discontinuity 'types', and has therefore been seen as providing a possible insight into evolutionary changes.

8.

The Shape of the Bull/Bear Cycle

Introduction

We are now in a position to be able to look at the internal dynamics of a complete bull/bear cycle in more detail. We have seen that the objective of any crowd is to change the environment for its own ends. The objective of a crowd in a financial market is to *change* prices in a particular direction: the bullish crowd will try to force prices up, while the bearish crowd will try to force them down. Each crowd has its own life cycle. During periods when the market is in the process of reversing direction, the two crowds may co-exist. However, once a trend has become established, only one crowd may dominate (see Figure 8.1).

Hence within a full cycle, first the bullish crowd will dominate, then there will be a period of uneasy co-existence with the bearish crowd, then finally the bearish crowd will dominate. This means that between any two given points in time, there will be a successful crowd and an unsuccessful one. Individuals within one of these crowds will experience different emotions from individuals in the other crowd. Members of the successful crowd will be motivated by greed (or fear of missing *further* profits), will obtain pleasure from their success, and will feel integrated with like-minded investors. Members of the unsuccessful crowd, on the other hand, will experience fear (either of losing capital, or of not making *any* profits), will be prone to feelings of displeasure, and will ultimately feel divorced from other members of the same crowd. Eventually the stress becomes unacceptable, and members of the unsuccessful crowd desert to the successful crowd.

The limit cycle between prices and sentiment

The final arbiter of success, of course, is whether prices are moving in the 'right' direction. We have already seen that price *movements* are the outcome of the conflict between the bulls and the bears, and that price *trends* (once started) tend to continue because price

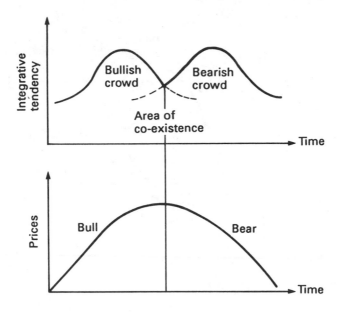

Figure 8.1. *The bull/bear life cycle*

movements transmit information and contribute to the leadership function. We have also seen that price *reversals* tend to occur when the investment community as a whole is more or less fully committed (financially) to one of the two points of view.

Essentially, therefore, there is a limit cycle relationship between changes in prices and investor sentiment. Investor sentiment has two aspects: expectations about the future trend in prices and the volume of activity which is generated. However, for the moment, we shall use a very simple proxy for sentiment — namely, a ratio of the number of bullish people to the number of bearish people. In Figure 8.2 this index is shown on the horizontal axis. A move to the right reflects a relative increase in the numbers expecting prices to rise; while a move to the left reflects a relative increase in the numbers expecting prices to fall. This index is directly influenced by both the *direction* and the *size* of the change in prices. The former has already been discussed. The latter follows because crowds are more influenced by large price changes than by small ones.

The bias in the limit cycle

Figure 8.2 shows the *percentage change* in prices against an index of sentiment. Hence, the absolute price level will be rising above the zero

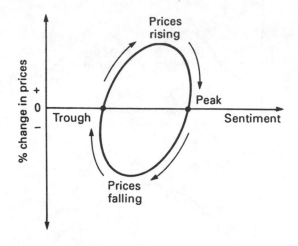

Figure 8.2. *Stock market limit cycles*

per cent line, and falling below the zero per cent line. As presented, the limit cycle is biased to the right. This reflects an important fact, which is particularly useful as an indicator of an imminent turning point: namely, sentiment *usually* turns *prior* to price reversals. Hence, just prior to market peaks, sentiment will begin to deteriorate as the percentage increase in prices falls. On the other hand, just prior to market troughs, sentiment begins to improve as the percentage fall in prices decreases. It is, in fact, possible to relate this rightward biased price-sentiment limit cycle directly to the relationships expressed in Figure 8.1. Figure 8.3 therefore shows the bull and bear life cycles, the associated periods of rising and falling prices, and the limit cycle itself. All that remains to be done is the translation of the cycle of absolute price changes into the cycle of percentage price changes. Turning points in the percentage changes precede turning points in the absolute price level.

The influence of 'external' factors

The limit cycle between the prices of financial assets and sentiment does not, of course, exist in isolation: market prices are determined by the physical supply of, and demand for, assets, which in turn are dependent on general financial conditions. In addition, sentiment in financial markets is very dependent on the general mood which pervades the economic, social and political environment.

In particular, changes in financial markets reflect, and create, a general change in wealth within the whole community. Equity prices,

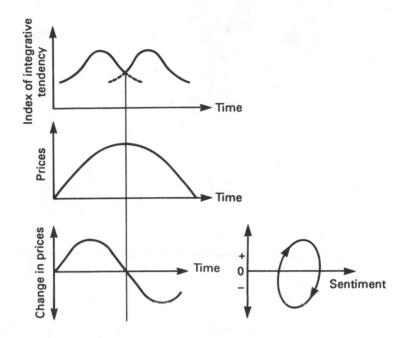

Figure 8.3. *Limit cycle relationships*

for example, may rise because of improved economic circumstances, but economic circumstances may then be improved because of the wealth effect of higher equity prices. Quite simply, more people have more capital which can be converted into current spending. Hence, rising stock prices become associated with optimism because they suggest improved employment and income prospects for the future. However, falling stock prices create general feelings of pessimism because they have adverse implications for future employment and incomes. In this way, the emotions of one area of activity spill over into another.

The limit cycle between equity markets and the economy

We can express these interrelationships, if only in part, through limit cycles which correlate financial asset prices with general economic trends. Such a correlation is shown in Figure 8.4. Since it is usual to analyse economic activity in terms of *changes*, the limit cycle relates percentage changes in Gross National Product (GNP) with percentage changes in equity prices.[1]

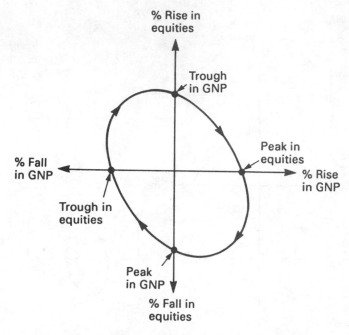

Figure 8.4. *Limit cycle relating equities to the economy*

The limit cycle could take one of a number of different shapes. As shown in Figure 8.4, however, it is biased to the left. This bias reflects the important phenomenon to which we have already referred briefly, which is that security prices effectively *anticipate* the future by turning before fundamentals. When the investment community as a whole is fully committed to a particular point of view, it can no longer respond to news items which confirm that point of view. The emergence of profit-taking after a price rise, or of 'bear-closing' after a price fall, then creates the initial phases of a price reversal. Economic fundamentals will turn at a later stage.

The influence of shocks

This analysis confirms that the price-sentiment limit cycle operating in a financial market is also integrated with limit cycles relating that market to the wider economic, social and political environment. Although accurate as far as it goes, however, the analysis implicitly assumes that financial markets are in complete harmony with their environment, and that therefore there is nothing new to learn about that environment. As we have already seen, this assumption is ultimately incorrect:[2] fluctuations which are intrinsic to a particular level of the hierarchy are inevitably modified by fluctuations imposed from a higher level. Equity and bond prices therefore have to respond to *new* information about the environment at all levels of the hierarchy. In other words, they have to respond to *shocks*.

Shocks occur because of a sudden divergence between current price movements and expected price movements, and may derive from two sources: first, they may be triggered by an unexpected movement in prices themselves; second, they may be precipitated by unexpected changes in the social, political or economic environment. Furthermore, the shocks may either be of a *pro-trend* nature or a *contra-trend* nature. Let us look at each set in turn.

Pro-trend shocks

The influence of pro-trend shocks need not concern us for long. For whatever reason, market participants suddenly find that expected prices are *further* away from the current levels than was originally thought. Pro-trend shocks are therefore *often* sufficient to destroy the unsuccessful crowd, and are *always* adequate to stimulate the integrative tendency of the successful crowd. Such shocks also involve a reduced lag between changes in sentiment and changes in prices, so that the associated price movements are particularly dynamic.

Contra-trend shocks

Contra-trend shocks, on the other hand, are altogether more interesting. First, an unexpected[3] contra-trend movement in prices will undermine existing trends by weakening the integrative tendency within the successful crowd. The shock creates a sudden divergence between actual and expected price movements. As a result, there is a revision to expected price movements. These are, of course, part of the belief system of one of the two competing crowds, and consequently there is a change in sentiment. There is thus the beginning of a process of adjustment.

The second way in which a contra-trend shock may impact on a financial market is where an unexpected item of information emerges concerning economic, social or political circumstances. Market participants suddenly realise that expected price movements are in the opposite direction from that which was originally thought. Prices therefore begin to move in the same direction as the (now revised) expected price movements, the integrative tendency of the crowd that was successful is weakened and, again, a process of adjustment begins.

The pattern of adjustment: the shock

Whatever the source of the shock (whether it is an unexpected price movement or an unexpected item of information), the response of the market is essentially the same. Specifically, the process of adjustment adopts a standard profile. In the first place, the shock itself is reflected in a change in the direction of price movement. Hence, the shock occurs as the change in prices moves either from positive to negative, or from negative to positive. The question of what happens to sentiment just prior to this shock depends, of course, on the shape of the limit cycle.

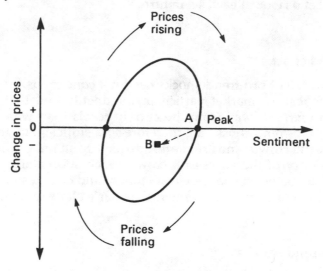

Figure 8.5. *The effect of an information shock*

However, if we show the effect in terms of Figure 8.2, initially the rate of change in prices alters and sentiment responds appropriately. Subsequently, the shock occurs. The shock itself would be represented by a 'jump' inwards from the path of the limit cycle as the change in prices moves across the zero per cent change line. Hence, in the case where a market is moving from bullish to bearish (see Figure 8.5), the position on the phase plane would jump from point A to point B as the change in prices moves into negative territory. In other words, there would be both a fall in prices *and* a drop in sentiment.

The pattern of adjustment: the response to the shock

Since the limit cycle is essentially *stable*, however, it follows that behaviour will try to return to the solution path. The sequence of events is then basically as follows (see Figure 8.6). Initially prices may fall further after the shock, and this causes sentiment to fall further. However, the fall in prices begins to slow, and eventually lower prices encourage 'bear closing'. This, in turn, causes prices to rise. The rise in prices then stimulates a reversal in sentiment. Indeed, the improvement in sentiment can be quite dramatic in relation to the change in prices. The rise in prices *may* be sufficient to take them to a new high [4] but, in the absence of other influences, the shock itself should be sufficient to preclude this. Meanwhile, it is highly unlikely that either the *rate* of change in prices or the level of sentiment will achieve their previous highs. Eventually, higher prices encourage some profit taking, and prices begin to slip again. At first, sentiment may actually continue to *improve* slightly, as investors search for 'cheap' stock in anticipation of the 'next' rally. Unfortunately, however, the vast majority of investors now hold stock, and so their ability to buy any more is strictly limited. Indeed, the subsequent price collapse is thereby assured. It is this collapse which brings prices back to the solution path of the limit cycle.

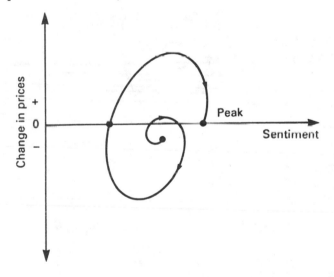

Figure 8.6. *The price-sentiment spiral after a peak*

Practical implications

There are three important conclusions which we can draw from this analysis. The first is that the adjustment process following a shock takes the form of a *spiral*. The second is that the price peak which occurs just prior to the shock is *re-tested* during the operation of the spiral. The re-test is 'successful' if market prices move to a new high, and 'unsuccessful' if they do not. The third conclusion is that sentiment *appears* to improve dramatically during the re-test, but in most cases it falls short of that which was attained during the original peak.

The pattern of adjustment after troughs

Obviously, the whole analysis can be repeated for the situation where a market is turning from being bearish to being bullish. In Figure 8.7, the position on the two-dimensional phase plane 'jumps' from C to D as the change in prices moves from being negative to being positive. The market then spirals back to the path of the limit cycle. During the spiral, absolute prices are normally unlikely to make a new low, but nevertheless may do so.

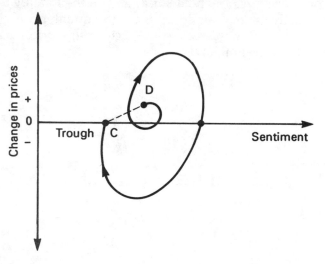

Figure 8.7. *The price-sentiment spiral after a trough*

The reversal process: (1) The shock

We have thus established an ideal model for the way that financial markets behave, and from this model we can isolate three distinct stages to a price reversal. The first development is that as a market approaches a turning point the vast majority of investors will have the same view about the future trend in prices, thereby leaving the market either *overbought* or *oversold*. However, some individuals will either recognise adverse developments in fundamental trends or may at least feel a lessening of the crowd's ability to stimulate their integrative tendency. They will therefore neutralise all or part of their commitment to the market. Hence an overbought market will encounter profit taking and will fall, while an oversold market will encounter a bear squeeze and will rise. Such price movements will undoubtedly provide a shock to the majority of market participants.

The reversal process: (2) The re-test

The second development consists essentially of the re- assertion of the sentiment of the previously successful crowd. The first stage is seen as being technical rather than fundamental by market participants.[5] It is, however, a trap for the unwary. Very often the only way to recognise that this is part of a reversal pattern rather than part of a fully-fledged bull or bear move, is to analyse the actual behaviour of the crowd in terms of underlying commitment to the market (that is, to analyse their behaviour in terms of the volume of transactions, their willing-ness to deal in the majority of securities trading in the market, their ability to open up new trading positions, and their ability to stimulate fast changes in prices). During this second stage of a reversal pattern, these technical indicators of crowd behaviour (which we shall consider in more detail in Chapter 16), will almost certainly *not* confirm either the apparent dynamism of the price movements or the sense of invincibility exhibited by traders.[6]

The reversal process: (3) The new trend

The third and, in a sense, final stage of a reversal pattern is the actual *change* in crowd sentiment as the fundamental news itself begins to alter. It is this stage that finally begins to trigger more members of the previously successful crowd into changing their minds and their trading positions. The stress and tension of seeing fundamentals confirm the move in prices is finally reflected in an acceleration of buying (in a bull market) or of selling (in a bear market). This third stage therefore generates a sharp change both in price movements and in the volume of transactions. It establishes the *trend* of the market, until a change in fundamentals is once more on the horizon.

The idealised three-stage reversal pattern

This analysis generates the concept of a *three-stage* reversal process. Idealised patterns are shown in Figure 8.8. The important point to grasp is that the derived patterns are reflections of the influence of a spiral. Stage 1 of the pattern (which may in practice be more complicated than shown in Figure 8.8) reflects the influence of a shock, and stages 2 and 3 reflect the spiral generated by that shock.

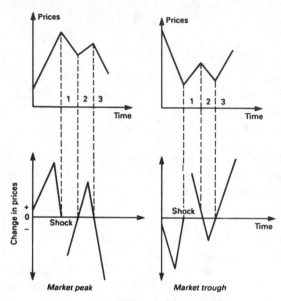

Figure 8.8. *Idealised reversal patterns*

Figure 8.8 highlights the relationship between actual price levels and price changes. The lower part of the diagram makes explicit that (a) the rate of change in prices turns before the actual change, (b) the reversal from an overbought or oversold condition creates a shock, and (c) re-tests of the initial reversal point are achieved at *less extreme* rates of change in prices.

The influence of fear

It is interesting to note the extent to which fear plays a role in these patterns. Fear is associated with feelings of isolation, inadequacy and uncertainty. It develops suddenly when expectations diverge from actual events, and is only relieved by evasive action. In financial markets, therefore, fear persists until unsuccessful trading positions are neutralised. Hence, in stage 1 of a reversal pattern, markets initially become overextended either because of fear of missing *further* profits (in a bull market) or because of fear of making *any* losses (in a bear market). There then follows the shock of an unexpected price change. This creates an atmosphere of fear, but generates only a limited degree of evasive action.

In stage 2, of course, the re-test of the former peak or trough tends to assuage the fears created by the shock, but always leaves a residue of intangible doubts. However, in stage 3 prices move *persistently* against the beliefs of the majority until naked fear triggers a widespread neutralisation (and/or reversal) of bad trading positions. It follows from this, of course, that the main indicators of investor sentiment (such as price momentum and volume) will show strong increases during periods when fear is being heightened, and will subside when fear is being reduced.

The bias in the bull/bear life cycle

This analysis of fear implies that the disintegration phase of either a bull life cycle or a bear life cycle will occur very quickly. The relevant life cycle is therefore biased to the right because the decline phase is most closely associated with fear. However, it is obvious that the fear of not making profits is of a different order of magnitude from the fear of actually losing money. This implies, therefore, that the *whole* bull/bear cycle is biased to the right.

Asymmetric investment attitudes

This rightward bias is assisted by another aspect of the effects of fear. The intensity of the fear of losing money means that most investors actually have an asymmetric attitude to investment positions: they prefer to hold stock rather than short positions.[7] If something goes wrong with a purchase of stock, it is at least possible to regard it as a long-term investment which will eventually come right. However, if something goes wrong with the sale of something which is not even owned, the short-term pressures to try again when the circumstances are more favourable are irresistible. This whole process is, of course, exacerbated by the stock-based investment policies of the savings institutions.

Bull markets therefore develop on the back of a gradual accumulation of stock, and a consequent reduction in liquidity. Furthermore, top patterns often take a long time to develop, because investors will continually take advantage of weaker prices to buy stock. However, when a bear market begins, not only do very few investors actually anticipate the fall, but also there are insufficient bear positions to be closed. There is therefore very little resistance to falling prices – indeed, liquidity can only be raised by selling, and this by definition forces prices down further. Bear phases therefore generally take a shorter period of time than do bull phases, and are very effective in destroying wealth. Not surprisingly, bottom patterns tend to develop quickly because so few investors actually have stock.

The price pulse

We are now in a position to combine the two reversal patterns shown in Figure 8.8 above into one single pattern representing a complete cycle. This is done in Figure 8.9. The pattern is asymmetric: 'stage 1' of the pattern is longer than 'stage 2' because bull markets generally take longer to develop than do bear markets. From our knowledge of the operation of limit cycles, we know that the peaks and troughs will occur on a regular basis. This implies that the basic three wave pattern of Figure 8.9 will repeat itself continuously, thereby representing an embryonic 'heartbeat' for a given hierarchical level in a particular financial market. We propose to call this the 'price pulse'.

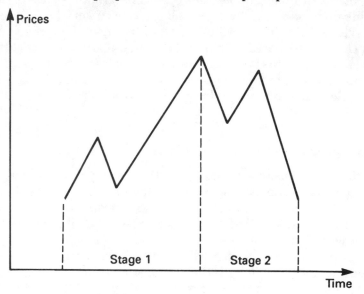

Figure 8.9. *The price pulse*

The price pulse, by definition, occurs at *all* levels of the stock market hierarchy. This means that there will, in an ultimate sense, be a 'mega-pulse' which will coincide with, and therefore trace out, the life cycle of the whole stock market. The existence of such a pulse is the inevitable deduction from the theory of growth via evolutionary shocks. Eventually there will be a stock market crash which will be associated with the termination of the currently accepted methods of production, distribution and exchange. At present, however, the concept is purely hypothetical, and is not meant to be a *specific* forecast of the demise of the capitalist system. Its purpose is purely to help illustrate the interdependence of the relationships which we have so far established.

Price-sentiment limit cycles

The concept of an identifiable life cycle for the whole stock market also implies the presence of an identifiable metabolic cycle of price-sentiment. Once a life cycle has begun, it will trigger off a whole series of metabolic cycles in exactly the same way as the birth of a human being triggers off the rhythmic metabolic processes in the body. Life cycles are separate concepts from metabolic cycles, but they are dependent upon one another. Hence, the movements of prices through time will reflect the influence of both the life cycle *and* natural fluctuations in price-sentiment.

Limit cycles and the transmission of shocks

The important point is that the highest-level cycles have an impact at the lower levels of the hierarchy. Natural metabolic cycles will therefore transmit shocks to the lower levels at turning points. Each such shock will create a specific lower-level bull or bear life cycle, and each such cycle will then have its own internalised metabolic rate. This process continues down through the hierarchical levels until we reach the smallest of daily fluctuations. Hence, metabolic fluctuations at a higher level create life cycles at a lower-level. Simultaneously, however, the combination of all lower level cycles through the hierarchy constitute the 'mega-pulse' of the highest level cycle. In this way, the system becomes completely integrated.

The hierarchy of fluctuations

From these comments we can make three deductions. First, the movements in prices will consist of both an hierarchy of metabolic cycles and an hierarchy of shock-induced fluctuations. Second, we can confirm that all oscillations will *harmonise* with one another, both because the lower-level oscillations are triggered by the highest-level oscillation and because the highest-level oscillation is constructed from the effects of all the lower-level oscillations. Third, the patterns traced out by shock waves are reflected in the pattern registered by life cycles.

Conclusion

Let us now summarise the conclusions of this chapter by re-drawing Figure 8.1 to include the greater detail which we have since uncovered (see Figure 8.10). The top part of the diagram again consists of two life

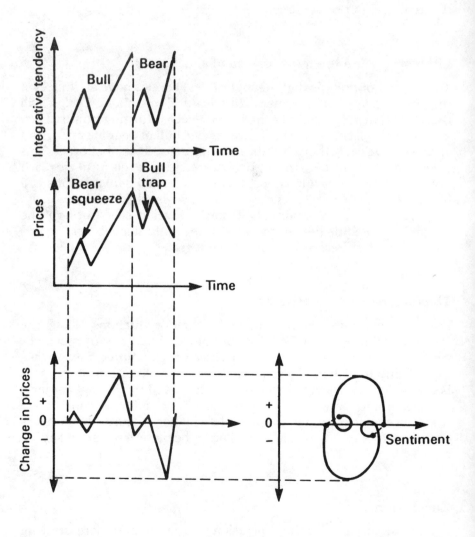

Figure 8.10. *The bull/bear cycle*

cycles – that of the bullish crowd and that of the bearish crowd. Now, however, the early stage of each life cycle is adjusted to reflect a three-stage reversal pattern, and each life cycle is biased to the right. The second part of the diagram focuses attention on absolute prices. It incorporates the three-stage reversal pattern at both the bottom and the top of market movements, and the bear phase is shorter than the bull phase. The third part of the diagram converts the absolute price changes into percentage price changes. The final part of the diagram shows the controlling influence of the limit cycle. This cycle is the metabolic cycle which is 'handed down' from a higher level of the hierarchy. As the rate of change in prices turns from negative to positive, or from positive to negative, a shock is delivered to the system. The result is the emergence of a lower-level spiral adjustment at the point of inflection of the absolute price level.

We thus have a graphical representation of the basic features of crowd behaviour in financial markets. These are:

(a) bull phases alternate with bear phases;
(b) each reversal pattern at the peak or trough of an oscillation consists of three phases;
(c) rates of change in prices oscillate between upper and lower limits; and
(d) rates of change in prices oscillate rhythmically through time.

We have already dealt in some detail with the fact that the bull and bear phases alternate with one another. We shall develop each of the other three features throughout the rest of this book. The next few chapters will deal with the shape of the oscillations in more detail. Then we shall deal with the information provided by the technical indicators of investor sentiment. Finally, we shall deal with the implications of rhythmic oscillations.

Notes

1. Among other things, it is also possible to construct a limit cycle relating the *bond* market to economic activity. This implies the existence of a limit cycle between bonds and equities. Generally speaking, reversals in the bond market tend to lead reversals in the equity market by between three and six months within the context of the $3^1/_4$-year business cycle.
2. It is valid only if it is applied to (relatively) high levels of the hierarchy over (relatively) short periods of time.
3. Unexpected, that is, by the majority.
4. Mathematically, absolute prices will rise above the previous high if the rate of change in prices *above* the zero per cent line is greater than the negative rate of change implicit in the shock.
5. In truth it is essentially the other way round. The first stage of a reversal pattern is often the sign of changing fundamentals, while the second stage is a technical response to fundamentals being discounted far too early.

6. This conclusion adds weight to the argument that market peaks do not necessarily occur at points of extremes in sentiment. Sometimes they do, but mostly they do not. Usually, sentiment will deteriorate before prices start to fall. The idea that market peaks occur at points of massive euphoria is probably created from an illusion. During re-tests of market peaks, market traders are always *very* confident – particularly as the market moves into new territory. The market has now finished 'climbing its wall of worry'; it has had a correction, and has thereby satisfied the fears of the traders; now the latter can relax in the face of apparently improving fundamentals – even to the extent of buying into weakness. The error, however, has been to mistake the *change* in sentiment (which is quite noticeable) for the *absolute level* of sentiment (which remains depressed). The majority of investors will therefore fail to recognise that the structure of the market is changing, and it is usually this error which virtually guarantees the destructive nature of the subsequent bear market.

7. This is obviously not true of foreign exchange markets where a long position in one currency automatically involves a short position in another currency.

9.

The Spiral and Fibonacci

Introduction

We have seen that the price adjustment process following an information shock can be represented by a spiral. The adjustment spiral occurs through time; hence, it can be viewed as occurring in three dimensions. In a financial market, these dimensions may be described as the rate of change in prices, the level of sentiment, and time. As an example, Figure 9.1 reproduces the theoretical adjustment process during the movement from a bull market to a bear market. The left-hand diagram represents the spiral relationship between the change in prices and sentiment but with no 'time' dimension; while the right-hand diagram represents the corresponding 'shock wave' adjustment of prices over time, but with no 'sentiment' dimension.

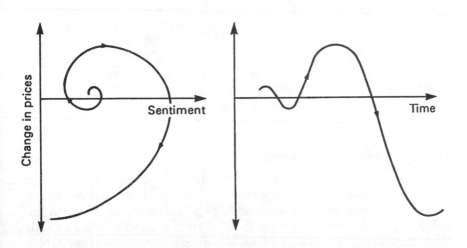

Figure 9.1. *The price-sentiment spiral in two dimensions*

The mathematics of the spiral

From this it follows, of course, that price patterns should reveal the presence of the spiral. We shall discuss this in more detail in Chapters 10 and 11. However, there is another implication which is of profound importance. This is that price movements *should be mathematically related to one another*. The reason is that the spiral itself can be defined using mathematics.

The source of all spirals is a geometric expansion of some form. Each number in a geometric expansion is obtained from the number which precedes it by multiplying it by a constant ratio. The most obvious is the so-called 'doubling sequence' where each term in the series is double that of its predecessor, namely,

$$2, 4, 8, 16, 32, 64, 128 \text{ etc.}$$

Here, the constant ratio is 2. It is readily apparent, even from this simple example, that the higher the ratio the more explosive will be the result. It therefore follows that if a spiral is actually a 'natural' phenomenon (in the literal sense of being a part of nature), the ratio must be relatively small, although greater than unity.[1]

The Fibonacci Number Sequence

Of all the geometric expansions which can, and do, occur in nature, there is one in particular which stands out above the others as being important. This is the *Fibonacci Sequence*, which is based on the ratio 1.618. This sequence is named after Leonardo of Pisa who, writing under the name of Fibonacci, published his famous *Liber Abaci* (or *Book of Calculations*) in 1202. This book introduced the decimal system (which includes zero as the first digit in the sequence and which is sometimes referred to as the Hindu-Arabic system) to Europe. Although Fibonacci was undoubtedly the greatest mathematician of the Middle Ages, it is perhaps ironic that he is remembered today mainly because the nineteenth century analyst Edouard Lucas attached his name to a sequence that appears in a trivial problem that appeared in *Liber Abaci*.

Fibonacci's rabbit problem

The problem was presented in terms of the reproductive capabilities of rabbits – namely, how many pairs of rabbits could one pair produce in a year?[2] The first pair are allowed to produce in the first month, but subsequent pairs can only produce from their second month onwards. Each birth consists of two rabbits. Assuming that none of the rabbits dies, then a pair is born during the first month, so there are two pairs. During the second month, the first pair produces another pair. During the third month, both the original pair and the firstborn pair have produced new pairs. Consequently, there are three adult pairs and two young pairs. If the analysis is continued the results are as shown in Table 9.1, and it is apparent that the basic sequence (ie the Fibonacci Sequence) is:

1, 1, 2, 3, 5, 8, 13, 21, 34, 55, 89, 144 etc.

Table 9.1. *Growth of rabbit colony*

Month	Adult pairs	Young pairs	Total
1	1	1	2
2	2	1	3
3	3	2	5
4	5	3	8
5	8	5	13
6	13	8	21
7	21	13	34
8	34	21	55
9	55	34	89
10	89	55	144
11	144	89	233
12	233	144	377

The Fibonacci Sequence and nature

Now, on the face of it, this Sequence is of no interest to anyone other than a student of mathematics or a rabbit breeder! However, mathematicians and scientists have discovered that the Fibonacci Sequence can be found throughout nature, defining both the *appearance* of physical structures and the *progress* of change in dynamic structures. Indeed, it appears that human beings find those phenomena which are overtly related to the Sequence intrinsically pleasing both to sight and hearing.[3] Before pursuing these observations any further, however, it is necessary to have a closer look at the properties of the Fibonacci Sequence.

The properties of the Fibonacci Sequence

There are, in fact, three important properties to the Sequence. The first is that each term in the sequence (after the second) is the sum of the two terms that immediately precede it. That is:

$$2 = 1 + 1$$
$$3 = 2 + 1$$
$$5 = 3 + 2$$
$$8 = 5 + 3$$

$$13 = 8 + 5$$
etc.

Such sequences, in which every term (after a certain point) can be represented as a linear combination of preceding terms, are called *recursive* sequences. The Fibonacci Sequence is the first-known recursive sequence.

The second important feature is that each term in the Sequence, when divided by the term before it, approximates the ratio 1.618. To be more precise, the ratio of successive terms *oscillates around* the limit of 1.618. The divergence from 1.618 is much greater for earlier values than for later ones. The inverse of 1.618 is 0.618. Not surprisingly, therefore, the ratio of each term in the Sequence, divided by the term after it, approximates 0.618.

The third feature of the Sequence is that *alternate* terms are related to one another by the ratio 2.618 and by its inverse, 0.382. Hence if any term in the Sequence is divided by the next-but-one number before it, the result is 2.618, while if it is divided by the next-but-one after it, the result is 0.382. Again, the ratio is more accurate for calculations applied to later terms in the Sequence rather than to earlier ones.

Finally, the same procedure can be repeated between numbers which lay increasingly further away from one another. For example, numbers which are three terms away from one another in the Fibonacci Sequence yield the ratio 4.236 and its inverse 0.236; numbers which are four terms away from one another produce the ratio 6.853 and its inverse 0.146; and so forth.

The important Fibonacci ratios

There are thus a number of ratios which can be derived from the Fibonacci Sequence, and there are a number of ways in which these ratios are related. For example,

$$0.618 \times 0.618 = 0.382$$
$$1.618 \times 1.618 = 2.618$$
$$2.618 \times 1.618 = 4.236$$
$$1 - 0.618 = 0.382$$
$$1.618 \ / \ 0.618 = 2.618$$
$$0.618 \ / \ 1.618 = 0.382$$
$$0.382 \times 0.382 = 0.146$$

It is apparent, however, that the two primary ratios are 1.618 and 0.618. The others are essentially derivatives.

The Golden Ratio

The number 1.618, and its inverse 0.618, are both known as the Golden Ratio, and are usually denoted in the literature by the Greek letter phi (=

Ø). As we shall see later, it is of some significance that the Golden Ratio is functionally related to $\sqrt{5}$, which is equal to 2.236. Specifically,

$$1.618 = \frac{\sqrt{5} + 1}{2}$$

$$0.618 = \frac{\sqrt{5} - 1}{2}$$

The Golden Ratio in geometry

The important role of 1.618 becomes even more explicit when the idea of the Golden Ratio is extended to geometry. In the first place, any straight line may be divided in such a way that the ratio of the larger part to the smaller part is equivalent to the ratio of the whole to the larger part. That ratio is always 1.618. This is shown in Figure 9.2, where

$$\frac{AB}{BC} = \frac{AC}{AB} = 1.618 = \frac{\sqrt{5} + 1}{2}$$

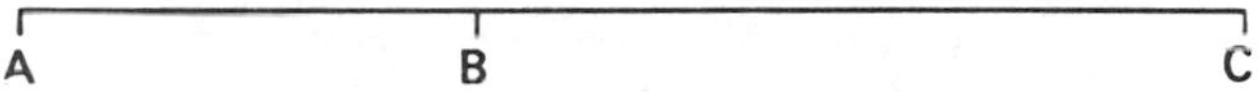

Figure 9.2. *The Golden Ratio*

The Golden Rectangle

Second, it can be shown that a rectangle ACDF, constructed from this straight line such that FA = AB, is a 'Golden Rectangle' whose sides are related to one another by the ratio 1.618. The rectangle is shown in Figure 9.3. By assumption, we know

$$\frac{AC}{AB} = 1.618$$

However, by construction,

$$FA = AB$$

and

$$AB = CD$$

therefore

$$\frac{AC}{CD} = 1.618$$

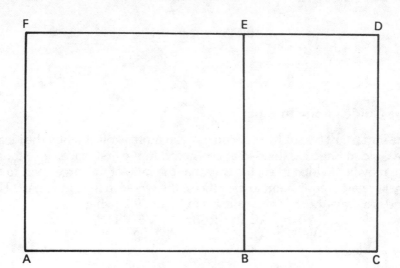

Figure 9.3. *The Golden Rectangle*

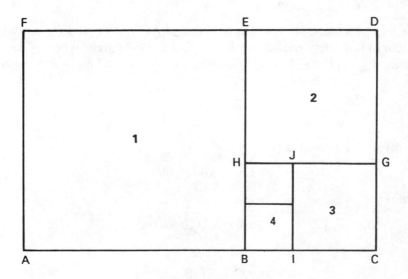

Figure 9.4. *Golden Rectangles*

Third, it may be shown that the rectangle BCDE in Figure 9.3 is also a Golden Rectangle. By assumption, we know

$$\frac{AB}{BC} = 1.618$$

However, by construction,

$$AB = CD$$

Therefore,

$$\frac{CD}{BC} = 1.618$$

The interesting feature of the Golden Rectangle is that it can be divided into a square and a smaller Golden Rectangle as in Figure 9.3. This means that rectangle BCDE in Figure 9.3 can be divided into smaller parts HGDE and BCGH. Then, in turn, BCGH can be divided into CGJI and BIJH (see Figure 9.4). Note that, as the process continues, the ratio of the sides of *alternate* rectangles and squares is equal to $(1.618)^2$ – that is, to 2.618. As we shall shortly see, this particular relationship is of some importance to our analysis.

The Golden Rectangle and the Golden Spiral

Theoretically, this process can be continued into infinity. The result is a sequence of ever-decreasing squares (marked as 1, 2, 3, 4, etc in Figure 9.4), the area of each being proportionally related to the area of the square after it, by the ratio 1.618. The series of squares literally *spirals* towards infinity. This spiral effect can be more clearly exposed by drawing a continuous line joining the point where adjacent squares meet one another on their common boundary. The result, which is shown in Figure 9.5, is a 'Golden Spiral'.

Properties of the Golden Spiral

The Golden Spiral is a *logarithmic* spiral and as such, it has two distinctive features. The first is that it starts and ends in infinity – therefore it has no boundaries, and its centre can never actually be reached. The second is that it does not change shape – any straight line drawn from the centre intersects the spiral at the same angle.[4] In Figure 9.6, therefore, the angle between the tangent at any given point and the radius drawn from the centre is a constant.

Because the Golden Spiral is defined by the ratio 1.618, there are three further characteristics which are worth highlighting. First, at any point on the spiral the ratio of the arc to the diameter of the spiral is 1.618.

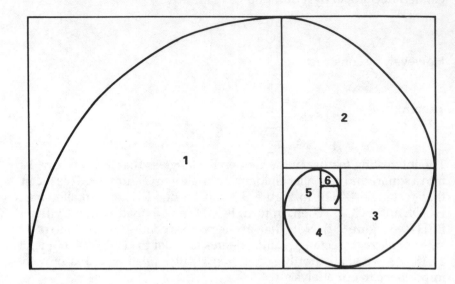

Figure 9.5. *The Golden Spiral*

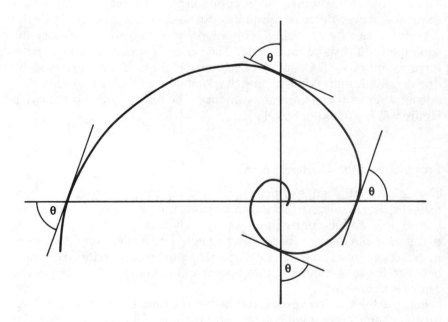

Figure 9.6. *Constant angles and the Golden Spiral*

Second, each radius drawn from the theoretical centre of the spiral is related to the radius which precedes it at 90° by 1.618. Third, each diameter of the spiral is related to the diameter which precedes it at 90° by the ratio 1.618.

The Fibonacci Sequence in the human body

Because logarithmic spirals begin and end in infinity, they have attracted a great deal of attention from philosophers over the centuries. Logarithmic spirals are the ultimate definition of growth and decay, where everything returns to its source and is then regenerated in a new form. However, whatever one's philosophical beliefs, the importance of the Fibonacci Sequence in the physical world is undeniable.

For a start, Fibonacci numbers are to be found in the structure of the human body.[5] The body has *five* bony appendages (two arms, two legs, and one head); each of the arms and legs has *five* appendages (five fingers and five toes); the head has *three* protubrances (two ears and one nose), and *three* distinguishing features which are flush to the face (two eyes and one mouth). Human beings also have *five* physical senses. In a statistically significant sample of people, the height of the navel from the ground will be found to be 0.618 of the total height. Furthermore, logarithmic spirals can be found *within* the human body: the inner ear, for example, assumes a spiral shape, and it has also been found that the heart muscle of the left ventricle is made up of a series of spirals.

The Golden Ratio in art and architecture

Not surprisingly the natural balance, or aesthetic beauty, of the Golden Ratio has long been recognised. Indeed, it has been shown that if people are presented with a large number of four-sided shapes ranging from a square to a very long, thin, rectangle, most of them will choose the shape which corresponds to the Golden Rectangle.[6] Leonardo da Vinci (1452-1519) used the ratio quite freely in his painting. Botticelli (1446-1510), a contemporary of da Vinci, also used the Ratio, as did Dürer (1471-1528) and Poussin (1594-1665). Furthermore, there is now a large volume of literature which demonstrates quite clearly that the Golden Ratio has been used regularly through the ages to create harmonious perspective within important buildings. The Ratio was, for example, used in the design of the Great Pyramid of Cheops at Giza;[7] it was used in the Parthenon in Greece;[8] and it was used in the design of those cathedrals which are now referred to as 'Gothic.'[9]

The Fibonacci Sequence in trees and plants

However, the Fibonacci Sequence can be seen quite clearly in other aspects of nature. It is reflected in the phenomenon known as *spiral phyllotaxis* which occurs in a large variety of trees and plants. In the case of trees, spiral phyllotaxis refers to the physical structure of branches in relation to the trunk of the tree. Specifically, it will be found that the branches will naturally develop around the trunk in a spiral fashion. The number of branches between a particular branch and the next branch which is directly above it will be a Fibonacci number.[10] Furthermore, the number of circuits of the tree, which occurs when tracing the spiral between the two branches, will also be a Fibonacci number. The resulting data points (ie the number of circuits and the number of branches) can be used to specify the exact form of the spiral phyllotaxis. Hence, oak, apple, and hawthorn trees have a phyllotaxis of 2/5; beech and hazel trees have a phyllotaxis of 1/3; plantain, poplar and pear trees have a phyllotaxis of 3/8; and willow and almond trees have a phyllotaxis of 5/13.[11] In the case of plants the analysis is identical, except of course that the concept refers to the relationship between leaves and the stem of the plant.

The Fibonacci Sequence in flowers

Second, the Fibonacci Sequence may be found in the structure of flowers. The sunflower[12] is a good case in point – not only does it exhibit spiral phyllotaxis, but its seeds are distributed over the flower's disc in logarithmic curves. One set of curves winds in one direction and one set winds in the opposite direction. The number of curves in each set is invariably a Fibonacci number. Consequently, the total number of curves is also a Fibonacci number.

The Golden Spiral in shells

Third, and in a sense more familiarly, the Golden Spiral can clearly be seen in the shells of soft-bodied molluscs such as snails and oysters. The patterns on their shells explicitly reflect the changes in their annual growth rate, and the clear message is – the bigger they are, the faster they grow!

The Fibonacci Sequence and the universe

There are, of course, many other examples: each arm of a galactic spiral has a logarithmic shape, and it has even beeen found that the radio signals generated by pulsars conform to Fibonacci numbers.[13] There are *five* regularly spaced occultations[14] of the planet Venus during an exact *eight*-year period. The measured periodicity of the 11.1/11.2-year sunspot cycle lies between $5 \times \sqrt{5}$ and $(1.618)^5$.[15] The list is, in fact, endless.

However, the important point to grasp is that Fibonacci numbers and logarithmic spirals are a fundamental part of the mathematics of nature.[16] The question now is: why is this so?

The role of the Fibonacci Sequence in nature

The simple answer is, in fact, that nature finds it easiest both to structure itself, and to grow, in a manner specified by the Fibonacci Sequence. It is not that nature actually plans its final shape, or that it has the Fibonacci Sequence implanted in all its relevant DNA molecules; it is merely that the Sequence is an automatic by-product of a simple growth system.

Let us take spiral phyllotaxis as an example. Trees and plants which exhibit this phenomenon grow their branches and leaves one at a time, and each branch or leaf will simply grow in the largest available gap between existing ones. This gives each part, and therefore the whole, the greatest chance of survival. It incidentally yields a pattern defined by the Fibonacci Sequence.

In the case of snail shells, however, the needs are somewhat different. It is obviously necessary that the shell grows with the organism, but it would also be totally impractical for the shell to grow as a tall cone on the snail's back. Nature's solution is to allow the outer surface of the shell to grow more than the inner surface. The difference in growth rates between the two surfaces automatically allows a logarithmic spiral to develop. Again, the end result is not the consequence of a pre-programmed plan; it is merely the response to different growth rates.

Finally, it is obviously in nature's own interest for 'successful' species to spread as quickly as possible. Logarithmic growth, as in the case of Fibonacci's rabbits, is consistent with this. Nevertheless, it is important to remember that logarithmic growth exists *because* success breeds its own success. It does not seem that logarithmic growth is, in itself, the *cause* of success.

Notes

1. If the ratio is less than unity, the series will consist of progressively *smaller* numbers.
2. Quoted in N.N. Vorob'ev, *Fibonacci Numbers*. Pergamon, New York, 1961.
3. See, for example, the analysis by H.E. Huntley, *The Divine Proportion*. Dover Publications, New York, 1970.
4. For this reason, the logarithmic spiral is sometimes called the 'equi-angular spiral'.
5. The presence of the Golden Ratio in the human body is discussed, for example, in Matila Ghyka, *The Geometry of Art and Life*. Dover Publications, New York, 1977.
6. M. Borissavlietch, *The Golden Number*. Tiranti, London, 1958

7.   See, for example, John Michell, *The New View Over Atlantis*. Thames and Hudson, London, 1983.

8.   See, John Michell, *The Dimensions of Paradise*. Thames and Hudson, London, 1988.

9.   See, for example, Louis Charpentier, *The Mysteries of Chartres Cathedral*. Robert Laffont, London, 1966.

10.   The number is calculated as including *one* of the two corresponding branches.

11.   Peter S. Stevens, *Patterns in Nature*. Penguin, Harmondsworth, 1976.

12.   See Jay Hambridge, *Practical Applications of Dynamic Symmetry*. Yale University Press, New Haven, 1938.

13.   See Walter E. White, 'Mathematical Basis of Wave Theory', in *Supplement to the Bank Credit Analyst*. The Bank Credit Analyst, London, 1970.

14.   An occultation means that the planet (in this case Venus) is hidden from earth's view as it passes behind the sun.

15. $5 \times \sqrt{5} = 11.18$ and $(1.618)^5 = 11.09$. The periodicity has actually been refined to 11.2 years using spectral analysis. See, for example, John Gribben with Stephen Plagemann, *Beyond the Jupiter Effect*. MacDonald and Co, London, 1983. It seems possible that the correct periodicity for the sunspot cycle is therefore exactly 11.18 years.

16.   Recent research into natural crystals reveals that many of them contain the Golden Ratio, particularly in the form of pentagons and pentagrams. Dr John Penrose, of the Institute of Mathematics in Oxford, speculates that the Golden Ratio may provide a crucial link between the sub-atomic and supra-atomic worlds. See 'Many-sided Penrose', in *The Economist*, 17 September, 1988.

10.

The Mathematical Basis of Price Movements

Introduction

It follows from the analysis of the previous chapter that the Fibonacci Sequence is intricately linked to the growth of dynamic systems. Since a crowd is a dynamic system, and since financial markets exhibit crowd behaviour, it follows that the Fibonacci Sequence should be found in financial markets. So the next question is: how does the Sequence actually reveal itself in financial markets?

We have already confirmed that all the points along a logarithmic spiral are mathematically related to one another. It therefore follows that spiral adjustments in financial markets should exhibit the same relationships. It will be remembered that when a financial market spiral is translated into two-dimensional space, the result is an 'unstable' cycle. Each swing of this cycle is related to its predecessor by a logarithmic ratio. In the case of the Golden Spiral, to which we have paid special attention, the relevant ratio will be 1.618 and its derivatives.

In Figure 9.4 of the previous chapter, where rectangles were used to construct a Golden Spiral, it was shown that the ratio of the sides of the *alternate* rectangles was 2.618.[1] The important point is that the length of each rectangle measures a 'width' of the spiral, and that alternate rectangles reflect opposite 'swings' of the spiral. Hence, if we transfer the spiral into the two dimensions of price and time , it follows that *successive* swings will be related to one another by the same 2.618 ratio.[2] This relationship is shown in Figure 10.1, where:

$$\frac{CD}{AB} = 2.618$$

The calculation of price targets

This implies that if we can identify the presence of the 'unstable' cycle in price movements, we should also be able to calculate *precise* price

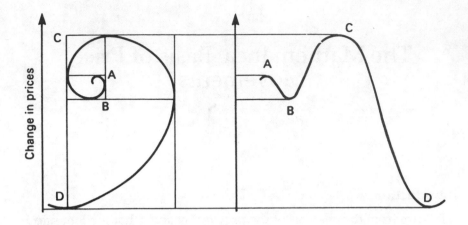

Figure 10.1. *The Golden Ratio in price fluctuations*

targets from the number 2.618. Initially, the market responds positively to a shock (which may be suggestive of either a new trend or a resumption of an old one). It then reverses direction under the influence of the spiral mechanism. Finally it jumps in a dynamic move, the extent of which is determined by the Fibonacci ratio 2.618. In other words, the target level for the thrust is 2.618 times the length of the last wave of the base or top pattern which precedes it. Hence in Figure 10.2 the target price (P_t) is given as

$$P_t = P_2 + (P_1 - P_2) \times 2.618 \text{ for rising markets}$$

and

$$P_t = P_2 - (P_2 - P_1) \times 2.618 \text{ for falling markets}$$

It is worth noting that, in the case of *bond* markets, these calculations often need to be conducted in terms of percentages. Bond markets are particularly susceptible to the psychological influence of percentage (or 'point') changes. It is a simple exercise to conduct a few calculations on historical data to see if a particular market is responding to percentage changes or to absolute changes.

The application of the target formula to bond markets

In order to demonstrate the validity of the 'spiral' targeting formula, we shall first use examples taken from the US and UK Treasury bond markets. Treasury bonds are fixed-interest bonds issued by governments to fund their borrowing requirements. Because these borrowing requirements have historically been very large in the US and UK, their respective Treasury markets are very substantial. They are highly liquid in the sense that willing buyers and sellers can be matched in large amounts within a relatively narrow range of prices, and they are efficient insofar as information is transmitted very quickly. Furthermore, bond markets are particularly applicable to the subject matter of this book because they are also very responsive to a wide range of economic, political and social influences.

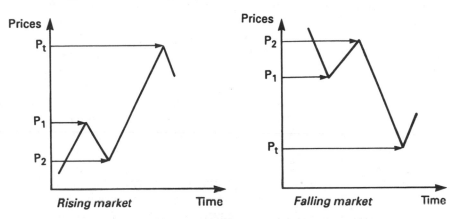

Figure 10.2. *The 2.618 calculation*

Bond markets are also useful markets to monitor for purely practical reasons. They can be very simply represented by a general index, by the price of a single bond, or by the yield of a single bond. First, apart from slight nuances with regard to coupon and maturity, one Treasury bond is much the same as any other within a particular market; second, in all fixed interest markets, yields are inversely related to prices. Therefore, provided that prices exclude accrued interest, [3] a chart history of any bond price over any given period would not only be representative of the whole market, but would also be a mirror-image of a chart history of yields over the same period.

Examples from the UK gilt-edged market

Let us first look at the UK Treasury market. This is usually referred to as the gilt-edged market. (For convenience, at this stage, we shall discuss the examples in terms of prices rather than yields, and the stock we shall use is the Treasury 8.75% 1997). The first example relates to the price 'crash' which occurred during the early 1970s, when Chancellor Barber (under Prime Minister Heath) injected a massive dose of inflation into the UK economy. Between January 1972 and December 1974, the net price of Treasury 8.75% 1997 fell from 107 to 50.2, which was a fall of 53.1 per cent (see Figure 10.3). However, the price action prior to the collapse is important. Between mid-1969 (not shown) and early 1972 prices rallied in a three-wave zigzag. The third wave of this zigzag from August 1970 to February 1972 involved a rally in the net price of Treasury 8.75% 1997 of 20.2 per cent.[4] The incredible thing is that 53.1/20.2 is almost exactly equal to 2.618. In other words, the Heath-Barber débâcle was foreshadowed by market behaviour in the period 1969-1971.[5]

The second example (see Figure 10.4), occurred not long after the major price low at the end of December 1974. Between January 1975 and the end of February 1975, stocks such as Treasury 8.75% 1997 rose by as much as 25 per cent. This rally was sufficient to convince even the most committed bears that a change in trend had taken place. However, the following month the market fell by 9 per cent in the longer-dated maturities, and delivered a traumatic shock to investor perceptions. Consequently, the market remained volatile until November 1976 when a sterling exchange rate crisis finally precipitated remedial action on the government's borrowing requirement. In retrospect, the period between February 1975 and November 1976 constituted a five-wave corrective pattern within a longer-run bull trend. The fifth wave of this corrective pattern, which developed during the eight[6] months from the end of February 1976 to the end of October 1976, was a vicious bear market during which the net price of Treasury 8.75% 1997 fell by just over 21 per cent.[7] If the spiral hypothesis is correct, then the subsequent rally should have amounted to 21 × 2.618 = 55%. Between the end of October 1976 and the major peak in October 1977, the market did indeed rally by 55 per cent.[8]

The third and final example, involving the gilt market relates to the four-year bear phase which followed the October 1977 peak. This, too, was a five-wave affair, the internal bull/bear swings of which were devastating in their volatility. The fifth, and final, wave downward was forced by a credit squeeze as the government sought to regain control of the monetary aggregates (see Figure 10.5), and Treasury 8.75% 1997 fell by 20.6 per cent.[9] Using the spiral formula, we should expect the rally which subsequently took place to amount to about 54 per cent.[10] In fact, the net price of Treasury 8.75% 1997 rallied from 61 to 93 between October 1981 and November 1982. This rise was equivalent to 53 per cent!

Examples from the US Treasury bond market

These findings can be confirmed by an analysis of the US Treasury bond market. Indeed, the period between Autumn 1981 and Autumn 1987 is so replete with examples that it is worth analysing it in a little

Source : Datastream

Figure 10.3. *The gilt-edged market, 1970-1975*

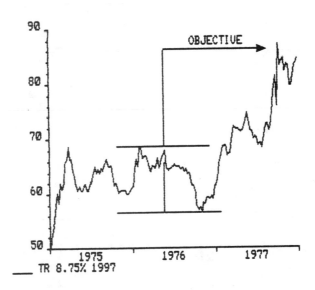

Source : Datastream

Figure 10.4. *The gilt-edged market, 1975-1977*

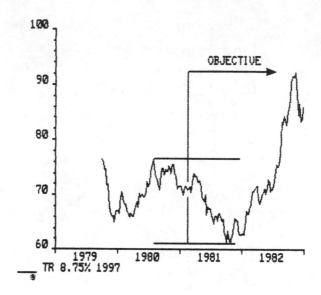

Source : Datastream

Figure 10.5. *The gilt-edged market, 1979-1982*

Source : Datastream

Figure 10.6. *The US T-Bond market, 1981-1987*

detail. For simplicity, we shall use the prices of the nearby Treasury bond future (known as the T-bond future), which is traded on the Chicago Board of Trade futures market. This contract reached a secular low point in late September 1981 at a level (marginally over) 55.[11] There then followed a prolonged base-building pattern which finished in mid-1984. This, in turn, was followed by the massive 1984-86 bull run. At the peak of the market in Spring 1986, the T-bond future was almost double its 1981 low value. The overall profile is shown in Figure 10.6. The chart is 'continuous' – ie no adjustment is made for the switch from expiring contracts to the next one every three months.

The preliminary stage of the base pattern began during October and November 1981 (see Figure 10.7). This rally occurred in three stages: the first was a rise of 8.6 per cent, the second a fall of 8.3 per cent, and the third a rally of 19.6 per cent. The rise in the third stage was not significantly short of the 21.6 per cent rally which was predicted by the spiral hypothesis.[12]

There then followed a 14.4 per cent[13] fall in the T-bond future, thereby completing the preliminary phase of the long-term base pattern. The low occurred in February 1982 at a level of 57 (see Figure 10.8). Using the spiral hypothesis, a rally of 37.7 per cent would have been predicted.[14] This corresponded to a price objective of almost 79 on the future. The market hit this target in November 1982 thereby completing the major rally phase within the 1981-4 base pattern.

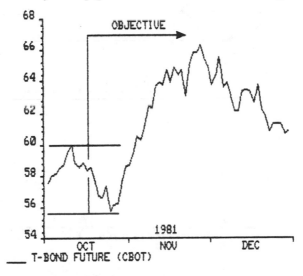

Source : Datastream

Figure 10.7. *The US T-bond market, October–December 1981*

Source : Datastream

Figure 10.8. *The US T-bond market, October 1981 – November 1982*

Source : Datastream

Figure 10.9. *The US T-bond market, November 1982 – July 1984*

The subsequent bear market actually took another six months to begin. The top pattern which developed between November 1982 and March 1983 had a final rally phase amounting to almost 10 per cent (see Figure 10.9). From this, the calculated fall using the spiral hypothesis was 25.9 per cent.[15] In the event, the T-bond contract actually fell by 25.4 per cent, bottoming at a level of 59.5 in June 1984.

The end of the bear market completed the major 1981-1984 base formation which was the prelude to the 1984-86 bull run. The objective for this rally could have been calculated from the 1983-84 bear market. Hence, the likely rise was $25.4 \times 2.618 = 66.5\%$. This was equivalent to a level of 99 on the T-bond future. Would anyone have believed such a forecast at the time? In the event, the market actually overran the objective slightly, as shown in Figure 10.10(a), peaking at 105.5 in April 1987. However, this was by no means a major discrepency, having used a *single* stock within the context of a 21 month bull market which generated a substantial rise in prices.[16] Indeed, the Dow Jones Home Bonds Index (which is a representative bond market average and which is a very useful supporting indicator in the context of forecasting US bond markets) rose by almost exactly its targeted amount (as illustrated in Figure 10.10(b)). The May 1983 to July 1984 fall in the Dow Jones Bond Index amounted to 16.7 per cent, and the calculated rally was therefore $16.7 \times 2.618 = 43.7\%$. This was equivalent to a level of 93.1 on the Index. The actual high was 95.5 in early 1987 an error of only 2.5 per cent!

Between April 1986 and January 1987, the T-bond contract traced out a top pattern. The last upwave of this pattern (see Figure 10.11)

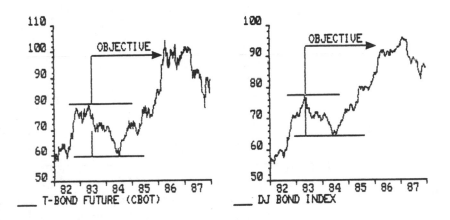

Figure 10.10. *The US bond market, 1982-1987*

Source : Datastream

Figure 10.11. *The US T-bond market April 1986 – October 1987*

amounted to 10.5 per cent. According to the spiral hypothesis, the likely fall was 27.5 per cent. In the event the actual fall was only 25 per cent. There was, however, another aspect of the calculation which was important: the target was almost exact when the price movements were measured in *arithmetic*, rather than percentage, terms. The last upwave of the top pattern had been 9.7 points. Hence the spiral formula suggested that the fall should be (9.7 × 2.618 =) 25.4 points. The actual fall was 25.5 points, with the market reaching a significant low in October 1987 as the equity market began its crash. This highlights the importance of keeping an eye on alternative possibilities when conducting the calculations.

Examples from other markets

In case there are any lingering doubts about the validity of the 2.618 spiral effect, a number of other important examples from different markets can be shown. It would take very little effort to fill the rest of this book with examples, but we shall confine ourselves to four.

The most important of these examples is probably the one involving the American stock market. The 1929-32 collapse in the Dow Jones Industrial Average Index from 386 to 42 amounted to 344 points. This gave an initial upside target for the Index of just under 1000. This target was achieved almost 34 years[17] later in 1965-6, after which

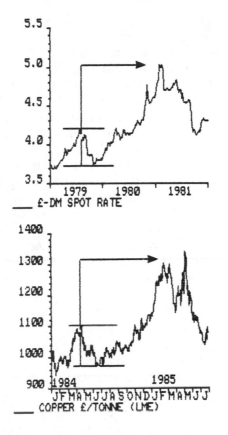

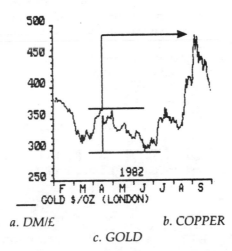

Source : Datastream

a. DM/£   b. COPPER

c. GOLD

Figure 10.12. *The 2.618 ratio in practice*

followed a multi-year correction. The level of 1000 was not seriously penetrated until early 1983.

Other examples are shown in Figure 10.12. The first of these concerns the foreign exchange markets. The sharp fall of Sterling against the Deutschemark from DM 4.24 to DM 3.70 in the summer of 1979 gave an upside target of just over DM 5.00 to the Pound.[18] This target was reached in early 1981 and marked the beginning of a two-year collapse in sterling. The next example concerns the price of copper. Between April and June 1984, the price of high-grade copper (as traded on the London Metal Exchange) fell from £1100 per tonne to £970 per tonne – a fall of £130.[19] The target following this fall was £1310 per tonne, which was achieved in February 1985. The final example involves the price of gold in 1982. The last phase of the 1980-1982 bear trend in gold occurred in April-June 1982. It amounted to a fall of $69 per ounce, from which it was possible to project a rally of just over $180. This rally was completed by the late summer of the same year and was followed by a significant correction.

Notes

1.   This is mathematically equivalent to saying that each diameter is related to the one that precedes it at 180° (ie the next smaller diameter along the same straight line) by the ratio 2.618.
2.   Note that the first wave is excluded from the calculations because it does not involve a full diameter.
3.   In the gilt-edged market prior to February 1986, all securities with maturities of over five years contained accrued interest within the price. The accrued interest therefore had to be *subtracted* in order to obtain a *net* price.
4.   That is, almost 21 per cent. The number 21 is a Fibonacci number. It is an interesting fact that many of the most significant movements in gilt prices in recent years have been of this order of magnitude.
5.   To be precise, $20.2 \times 2.618 = 52.9$.
6.   The number 8 is a Fibonacci number.
7.   The number 21 is a Fibonacci number.
8.   The number 55 is a Fibonacci number.
9.   Almost the Fibonacci number, 21.
10. $20.6 \times 2.618 = 53.9$.
11.   This is a good example of a price which is also a Fibonacci number (ie 55) being associated with a price reversal.
12.   More precisely, $8.26 \times 2.618 = 21.6$. All calculations for the US-T bond future are based on intra-day highs and intra-day lows.
13. $14.4 \times 10 = 144$, a Fibonacci number.
14. $14.4 \times 2.618 = 37.7$.
15. $9.9 \times 2.618 = 25.9$.
16.   We shall re-examine the problem of apparent errors in the target formula in Chapter 20. However, accuracy in long-term futures charts can be adversely affeted by the regular change over from expiring contracts to new ones every three months.

17.   The number 34 is a Fibonacci number.
18.   The number 4.24 is close to the Fibonacci ratio 4.236. The number 5 is, of course, a Fibonacci number.
19.   13 × 10 = 130. The number 13 is a Fibonacci number.

11.

The Shape of Price Movements

Introduction

In the analysis of the last chapter, a definite price pattern emerged. Let us demonstrate this pattern by comparing the fluctuations shown in our three gilt examples (see Figure 11.1). To facilitate the comparison we have made one change – the chart relating to the 1970-1974 period has been *inverted* by converting it to a yield basis. When the three charts are placed side by side, the message is startlingly clear. If we ignore some of the relatively minor oscillations, the patterns are virtually identical.

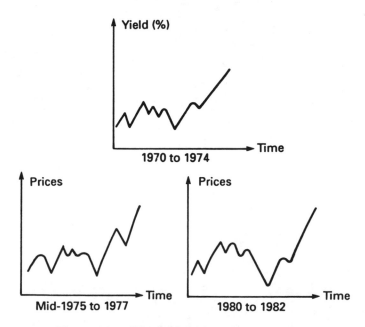

Figure 11.1. *Gilt-edged market patterns compared*
(Not to scale)

Furthermore, similar profiles emerge if we use the patterns derived from the US Treasury bond market. Figure 11.2 shows the patterns of the price movements from January 1982 to November 1982, from November 1982 to July 1984, and from January 1982 to April 1986. Since the November 1982 to July 1984 period was a bear market, the price chart has been *inverted* by converting it to a yield basis. This renders it comparable to the other charts.

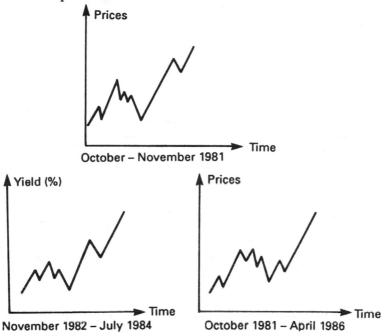

Figure 11.2. *US Treasury bond market patterns compared*
(Not to scale)

A stylised price pattern

Some leeway has obviously been taken with the omission or inclusion of some of the lower-level fluctuations. However, the comparisons confirm that prices and yields (and therefore market psychology) all follow a similar repetitive pattern. In general terms, a series of price oscillations creates a 'base pattern', which is then followed by a dynamic impulse wave. Since yields are inversely related to prices, it follows that this basic formation applies to both bull and bear markets. Consequently, and as a first approximation, we can postulate a symmetric price pattern which is applicable to a complete bull/bear cycle. This pattern is shown in stylised form in Figure 11.3.

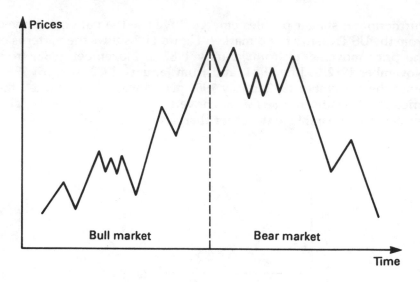

Figure 11.3. *Stylised Treasury bond price cycle*

The stylised price pattern and the price pulse

This stylised cycle is, in fact, a direct confirmation of the concept of the price pulse which we defined in Chapter 8. If the two constructs are compared (see Figure 11.4), it can be seen immediately that the overall patterns are essentially similar.

The hierarchical nature of the price pulse

It can also be seen that the stylised Treasury bond cycle contains more fluctuations within its overall structure than does the simple price pulse. The main reason for this is that any pattern which is fundamental to a market will be repeated at all levels of the hierarchy. Hence, for example, the 'base' formation in a price pattern will be a smaller version of the larger pattern of which it is a part.[1]

The up-wave

Let us denote the three primary waves of the 'up' phase of the original theoretical construct as being (α), (β), and (δ),[2] and the primary waves of the 'down' phase as being (x), (y) and (z). Now it should be readily apparent that the (α)-wave and the (β)- wave of the 'up' phase *themselves* represent a full cycle, although at a lower hierarchical level. Consequently, the (α)-wave should subdivide into three waves (ie α, β

and δ), and the (β)-wave should subdivide into three waves (ie x, y and z). Hence, the *underlying* structure of the 'up' phase now appears as shown in Figure 11.5(a).

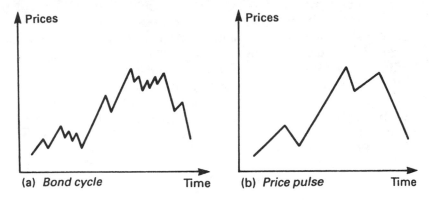

(a) *Bond cycle*   Time   (b) *Price pulse*   Time

Figure 11.4. *The stylised bond cycle and the price pulse*

The difference between theory and practice

This still leaves us with the need to account for the 'extra' fluctuations in Figure 11.5(b) – that is, the fluctuations within the y-wave of the (ß)-wave, and the fluctuations within the (δ) wave. There are a number of possible explanations, of the former but the most obvious is the *bias* inherent in the bull/bear cycle. In practice, there is usually a noticeable difference both between bull and bear markets, and between top patterns and bottom patterns. The difference arises because of the *asymmetric* influences of fear which we discussed in Chapter 8:

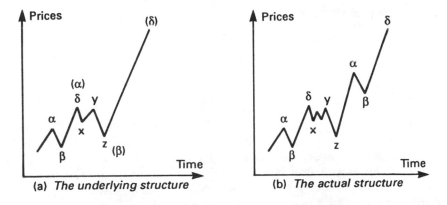

(a) *The underlying structure*   Time   (b) *The actual structure*   Time

Figure 11.5. *Theoretical Treasury bond up-wave*

impulse waves in bear markets tend to be fast because of the fear of losing money; top patterns tend to be slow because of the fear of missing further profits. Hence, during each complete cycle, z-waves will tend to be faster than δ-waves. Quite obviously, waves which develop quickly will tend to suppress lower-order waves, while waves which develop slowly will allow lower-order waves to become apparent. This specifically implies that y-waves will tend to subdivide according to the influence of lower degree pulses.

The reasons for the 'extra' wave(s) during the (δ)-wave are also simple. Specifically, the continuous unfolding of lower-level price pulses during the progress of the (δ)-wave will inevitably allow for the influence of at least one ß-wave of a lower-order pulse. This will appear as a contra-trend correction.

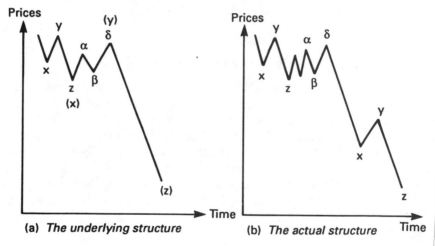

Figure 11.6. *The Treasury bond down-wave*

The down-wave

This same argument can be expanded to include the down phase of a complete primary cycle. The results are shown in Figure 11.6. Again, the underlying structure essentially consists of three-phase wave patterns. However, the (y)-wave takes some time to develop, and thereby allows lower-level waves to become more clearly apparent. Furthermore, the (z)-wave is superimposed on lower-level price pulses. This means that at at least one y-wave will appear as a contra-trend rally.

Conclusion

It is apparent from this analysis that the actual shape of the price pulse will be distorted by higher order trends. We shall demonstrate later how these distortions not only give the illusion of randomness to a regular process, but also yield the price patterns which have long been recognised as central to technical analysis. In the meantime, our purpose has been to explain the fundamental patterns which are experienced in financial markets. In practice, *any* price movement subdivides into three phases. The first two phases constitute either a top pattern or a base pattern. The third phase consists of a dynamic impulse wave. Subsidiary fluctuations occur because this three-wave pattern is repeated at all levels of the hierarchy.

Notes

1. The idea that lower degree details of a natural phenomenon are identical to higher degree details of the same phenomenon has received a great deal of support from the scientific community in recent years. For example, Professor Benoit Mandelbrot of the IBM Research Laboratories has pioneered a technique known as fractal geometry. This suggests that no matter how much an object is magnified, the new details appearing on the smaller scale are always identical to the old details on the larger scale.
2. In the Greek notation, α = alpha, β = beta, δ = delta. The Greek alphabet has been used for the up-wave to distinguish it clearly from the Elliott notation which will be used in Chapter 15. It is also worth mentioning that the introduction of the letter 'δ' helps to keep the idea of *change* in the analysis.

Part III:

Forecasting Turning Points

12.

Price Patterns at
Turning Points

Introduction

The intriguing aspect of the price pulse is that the interaction of pulses
at different levels of the hierarchy result in a limited number of easily
identifiable *price patterns*. Some of these patterns are of particular value
because they are associated with significant turning points in the
market, and can therefore be used to predict subsequent price
movements. These predictive price patterns have long been recognised by market analysts, although the essential reason for their
presence has hitherto been difficult to explain. We shall now explain
exactly how the various patterns emerge, and how they can be used to
generate profitable buy and sell signals.

Price patterns at peaks

Let us first see what happens to the shape of the pulse if we assume
that it straddles a *peak* reversal in a higher-order pulse. We shall
assume, for simplicity, that the up-trend which is being reversed is
particularly strong. Hence, the α-wave[1] of the price pulse being
examined will reach a peak at a *higher* level than the top of the previous
price pulse of the same degree. Figure 12.1 illustrates the point. This
assumption enables us to focus our attention entirely on one complete
price pulse. For the moment therefore we shall be analysing the form
of the *second* pulse shown in Figure 12.1.

   The first point to be made is that the reversal of the high-level trend
can occur during *any* part of the lower-level pulse. Since there are six
phases to each complete pulse (ie waves α, β, δ and x, y, z), it follows
that a reversal can occur in any one of six places. Figure 12.2 isolates
the possibilities.

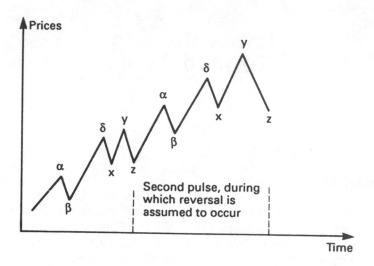

Figure 12.1. *The trend assumption*

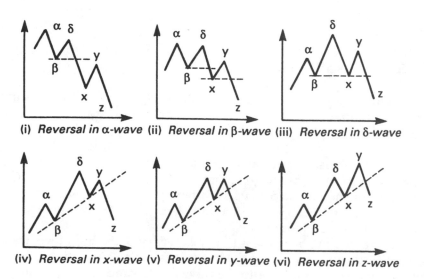

Figure 12.2. *Pulse patterns at market peaks*

Sell signals at market peaks

We know (by assumption) that the underlying trend in the market will change during the development of these patterns. The question now is whether we can isolate the point during each of these patterns when the behaviour of prices *themselves* tells us that the trend has changed. If we can, it should be possible to sell stock at that point, and virtually guarantee that the market will subsequently fall. Looking at the diagrams in Figure 12.2, we can in fact confirm the existence of three very simple trading rules.

The first sell signal applies to case (i). The signal is given when the market price falls below the trough of the β-wave. The early impact of the downtrend suggests that the subsequent y-wave rally will not travel above the level of the sell signal.

The second sell signal applies to case (ii), but is slightly complicated. A *short-term* sell signal is triggered as the x-wave falls below the bottom of the β-wave. However, the subsequent y-wave rally may abort the signal by rallying back above it; indeed, it may even retrace close to the peak levels established by the α-wave and the δ-wave. A *longer-term* (or regenerated) sell signal is given when the z-wave penetrates below the bottom of the x-wave.

The third sell signal applies to the remaining situations (ie cases (iii), (iv), (v), and (vi)). Here the sell signal is given when the extension of a straight line joining the base of the β-wave with the base of the x-wave is broken by the z-wave. The only difference between the different situations is that in cases (v) and (vi) the base of the x-wave is likely to be well above the peak of the α-wave.

Price patterns at troughs

Hence we can derive three sell signals from our original six price pulse formations which occur at market peaks. Not surprisingly, a similar situation can be found at market troughs. Let us assume that the trough of a high-level trend is straddled by a lower-order price pulse. As before, this implies that the turning point can occur during any one of six sections of the pulse. All the possibilities are shown in Figure 12.3.

Buy signals at troughs

As in the case of top patterns, there are in fact three trading buy signals which can be derived from this set of charts. The first signal applies to cases (i) and (ii) of Figure 12.3. It is triggered as the δ-wave rises above the peak of the α-wave. Because of the inherent dynamism of the δ-wave, the signal should not be aborted by the subsequent x-wave.

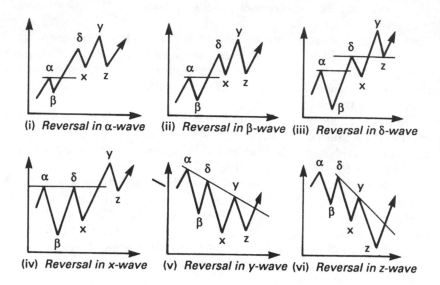

(i) *Reversal in α-wave*   (ii) *Reversal in β-wave*   (iii) *Reversal in δ-wave*

(iv) *Reversal in x-wave*   (v) *Reversal in y-wave*   (vi) *Reversal in z-wave*

Figure 12.3. *Pulse patterns at market troughs*

The second buy signal applies to cases (iii) and (iv). A *short-term* buy signal may occur if the δ-wave rises above the peak of the α-wave. However, the signal is likely to be aborted, or at least strongly re-tested, by the subsequent x-wave. This is because the δ-wave has not been able to move market prices significantly away from the area where bearish sentiment prevailed. A *longer-term* (or regenerated) buy signal is therefore given as the market rises above the peak of the δ-wave.

The third buy signal applies to cases (v) and (vi). This signal is given as the market crosses above the extension of a line drawn across the peaks of the δ-wave and the y-wave. The success of this buy signal rests, of course, on the impetus of the *next* price pulse; the δ-wave of this next pulse should provide the main upward thrust to prices.

The patterns from two price pulses

We have thus arrived at a very simple conclusion: within the context of a *single* price pulse, there are only three basic sell signals at market peaks and three basic buy signals at market troughs. However, at least one of the signals which we observed is only triggered when a *second* price pulse emerges. This raises the question of whether or not our conclusions would be substantially changed if the analysis was extended to include the influence of an additional price pulse. In fact the conclusions to be drawn from such an extended analysis are virtually identical to those which we have already obtained. A moment's reflection should reveal that we can still conduct the analysis using six waves, even if they are taken from two adjacent price pulses. It will not matter from the point of view of analysing *patterns* how the waves are split between the two pulses: the last wave of one pulse will be followed by the first five waves of the next pulse, or the last two waves of one pulse will be followed by the first four waves of the next, and so forth. In consequence, the patterns isolated in Figures 12.2 and 12.3 are applicable to *all* circumstances.

The influence of higher-order trends

So far, we have merely assumed that a peak or trough in a higher-order trend occurs as a *deus ex machina*. Obviously, however, this trend will be part of a higher-order price pulse, and will therefore have its *own* patterns identical to those shown in either Figure 12.2 or Figure 12.3. Hence, the actual higher-order trend reversal may itself occur during any one of the six sections of a higher-order price pulse. Obviously, the same sets of trading rules will still apply, but a complication has now been introduced. This is because sell or buy signals generated at the lower level may be quickly overruled by developments at a higher level. This is demonstrated in Figure 12.4. In this example, it would be important to respond to trading buy signals at the bottom of the higher-level (β)-wave.

The importance of perspective

This highlights a very important rule. It is vital that the trader/investor is broadly aware of the time frames which are applicable to the decision being made. To this end, there are a number of simple guidelines which should be implemented:

(a) Use as much historical data as possible. The more historical data available, the greater is the possibility of isolating the longer-term trends.
(b) Do not exclude fundamental analysis entirely. Fundamental analysis has a definite role to play insofar as it should help to isolate the broad thrust of the long-term trend.
(c) Pay very close attention to *short*-term market movements in order to pick up signals that *longer*-term trends are reversing.

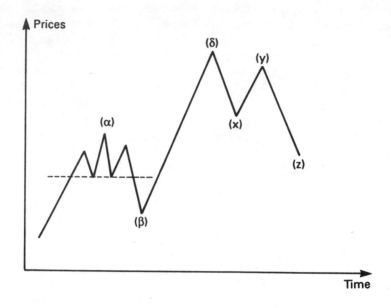

Figure 12.4. *Low-level signals and high-level trends*

Conclusion

The analysis in this chapter has been a little complicated, but it should have been rewarding. Specifically, we have been able to isolate a limited number of price patterns which can be used to *forecast* future price action. As it turns out, *all* turning points are associated with one of a very limited number of price patterns. Within these price patterns the number of trading signals, which are triggered just as market prices begin a trend move, may be reduced to six: there are only three buy signals and three sell signals. We have thus moved a very long way towards establishing the basic tools for trading profitably in financial markets.

Note

1.   We shall continue to use the price pulse notation which was established in Chapter 11.

13.

Price Patterns in Traditional Technical Analysis

Introduction

Many traders will already have recognised that the patterns presented in Figures 12.2 and 12.3 of the previous chapter correspond to patterns which have long been used in 'traditional' technical analysis. In essence, they correspond to three categories of price configuration which yield profitable trading signals, the most simple of these being the *trend line break*, the best-known being the so-called *head-and-shoulders* top or bottom, and the most difficult to interpret being the *multiple* (usually 'double' or 'triple') top or bottom.

The trend line break

The signal which is called the trend line break is given when the market price level penetrates the extension of a straight line drawn through successive troughs (in a rising market) or successive peaks (in a falling markets). Hence this particular signal is derived from case (vi) in Figure 12.2 after a rising market, or from case (vi) in Figure 12.3 after a falling market (see Figure 13.1).

Guidelines for trend lines

Because the signal is so simple, there has been a tendency among technical analysts to draw straight lines linking *any* two low points in a rising trend, or any two high points in a falling trend, and call such lines 'trend lines'. They may well be trend lines, of course, but if used indiscriminately they may well give false signals. If there is any doubt as to the validity of a trend line, there are two guidelines which can be used. The first is that if the market has bounced off a particular line three or more times, it is probably a valid trend line. The market itself has implicitly accepted the line as being a reflection of the trend. Obviously, the more times the market bounces off a line before penetrating it, the greater is its validity (see Figure 13.2).

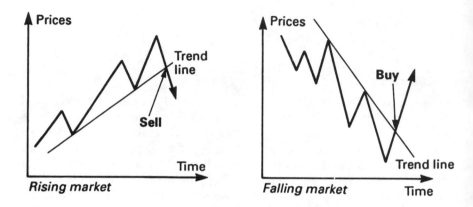

Figure 13.1. *The trend line break*

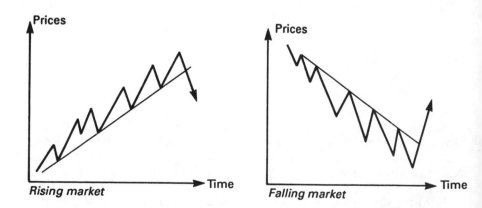

Figure 13.2. *Multiple tests of a trend line*

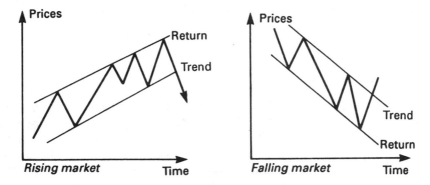

Figure 13.3. *The return line*

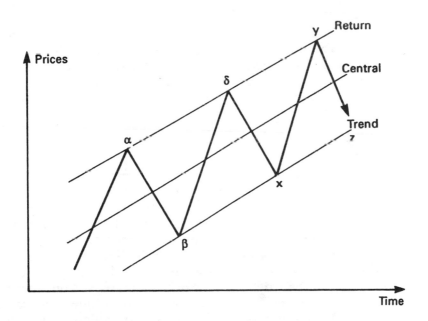

Figure 13.4. *Divergences from central trend lines*

The return line

The second guideline involves the use of what is called a 'return line'. A return line is a line drawn *parallel* to the proposed trend line. If the market has bounced off the return line at least twice then, again, the proposed trend line is almost certainly a valid one (see Figure 13.3).

The cause of trend lines

The fact that market prices tend to fluctuate *between* pairs of lines derives from a very simple phenomenon. Basically what happens is that any given price pulse has a very limited ability to diverge from the trend of the price pulse of a higher degree. This is particularly true when the higher-order pulse is basically in its third wave (ie the δ-wave in a rising market, or the z-wave in a falling market). Consequently, the lower order price pulse is forced to centre itself on the trend of the higher-order pulse, and divergences above this trend will be approximately equal to divergences below it (see Figure 13.4).

Straight and curved trend lines

There are two points that are worth making about parallel trend lines. The first is that although they are shown as being *straight* lines in the above Figures, they may actually be *curved*. Straight lines are usually a good approximation of the trend, but curved trends may nevertheless occur where a higher-level cycle is oscillating slowly through time.

The irrelevance of time

The second point, however, is that parallel trend lines can occur *independently* of time. These trends are usually straight-lined ones, because the speed of change is not a factor. Such trends can be found in point and figure charts which are used to plot price *patterns*. The standard procedure is to use squared graph paper, and to represent rising prices by crosses (Xs) and falling prices by zeros (0s). If the chart reverses direction by more than a given number of price units (however such units are defined), the price plot is moved one column to the right and the new trend is plotted until a new reversal is encountered. Such 'box reversal' charts do not therefore register the passage of time.

An example of the occurrence of parallel trend lines in point and figure charts is shown in Figure 13.5. Diagram (a) shows the price performance of the UK gilt-edged market during the period June 1980 to December 1981. Diagram (b) shows the same price action, but using a *'three*-box reversal' point and figure chart so that time is eliminated. In both diagrams there is a very clear trend defined by a trend line and a return line which run parallel to one another. Within the context of the price pulse, therefore, it appears that parallel trend lines are a fundamental part of the price pattern.

Triangles

A variation on the theme of prices oscillating between a trend line and a return line involves the presence of triangles, where the two lines converge on one another. Essentially there are two types of triangle which are important (see Figure 13.6). The first occurs at the *end* of a trend, when the long-term trend is just beginning to come into conflict with the short-term trend. Such triangles signal an immediate reversal in the higher level trend, once market prices break out of

Source : Datastream

(a) *Price and time*

Figure 13.5. *Parallel trend lines*

```
                           FT GOVT SECURITIES INDEX

BOX REVERSAL 3 BOX SIZE £ 0.25              DAILY DATA           2/ 7/80 TO 30/12/81

  73.75.................................................................................


  72.50.X.............................................................................
        XO
        XO
        XO         X
        XO     X XO
  71.25.XO....XNXO.................................................................
        XO  X XOXO
        X8   XOXOXO
        XO   XOXOXO     X
        XO   XOXO D     XO
  70.00.XO..XOO..O....XO.............................................................
        XOX XO   O     XO
        XOXOX    O     X4
        OXOX     OX 2 XO
        OXOX     OX1X3XO
  68.75..O.OX....OXOXOX5........................................................
        OX    OXOXO O
        OX    OXO   O    X
        O9    O     O    XO
        O         *-O  6 XO
  67.50.........O..XOXO.............................................................
                 OX XOXO
                 OXOXOXO
              1  OXOXOXO
              9  O O OXO
  66.25.......8......OXO...........................................................
              1      OXO
                     OX7
                     OXO
                     OXO
  65.00.............O.O..X........................................................
                 OX XO
                 OX8XOX    X
                 OXOXOXO   XD
                 OXOXOXO   XO
  63.75.........OXO.9XO..XO.....................................................
                 OX  OXO   XO
                 OX  OXO   XO
                 OX  OXO   XO
                 O   OXO   XO
  62.50..........O.O..XO........................................................
                     OX XO
                     OXOXO
                     OXOX
                     OXOX
  61.25...........OXON..........................................................
                     OXOX
                     OOOX
                     O OX
  60.00.............O..........................................................
```

(b) *Price only*

Figure 13.5. *Parallel trend lines*

the triangle. The second type occurs during a *correction*. Such triangles are a reflection of the conflict in sentiment which can emerge during a correction: the longer-term trend is still trying to drive the market in one direction, while the short-term trend (caused by an information shock) is trying to force the market in another. The conflict is usually resolved by a break-out in the direction of the dying long-term trend, which is then followed by serious reversal. The reversal occurs when the inevitable δ-wave, or z-wave, materialises. We shall comment on the nature of triangles in more detail when we come to deal with the Elliott Wave Principle (see Chapter 15).

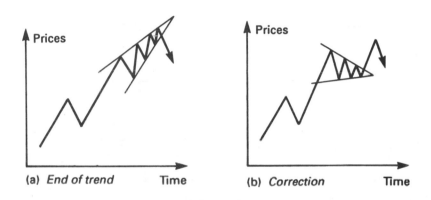

Figure 13.6. *Triangular formation*

The head-and-shoulders top pattern

The next pattern which generates a valid sell or buy signal is the so-called 'head-and-shoulders' formation. (It is recognisable as such because of its similarity to a silhouette of a person's head and shoulders). Hence, in the case of a top formation, the 'left shoulder' is formed by the period of price weakness just prior to the market moving to a new high; the 'head' is formed by the new high itself; and the 'right shoulder' is formed by a period of price strength just after the new high. The base of both the left and right shoulder occur at approximately the same level of prices.[1] It is therefore possible to draw a 'neckline' between the two. A sell signal is generated when prices finally penetrate an extension to the neckline (see Figure 13.7).

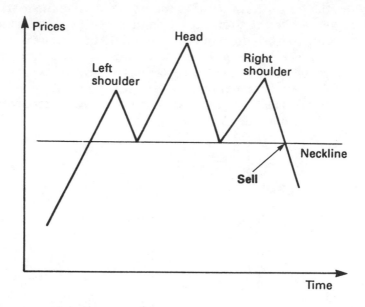

Figure 13.7. *The head-and-shoulders top formation*

The head-and-shoulders top and the price pulse

Within the context of a single price pulse, a head-and-shoulders top may occur in two ways. First, it will occur as a result of a trend reversal in the δ-wave. This corresponds to case (iii) of Figure 12.2 in the previous chapter. The formation is unmistakable (see Figure 13.8): the peak of the α-wave forms the left shoulder, the peak of the δ-wave forms the head, and the peak of the y-wave forms the right shoulder. The z-wave will provide the profits on any sales transacted as prices penetrate the notional neckline drawn across the troughs of the β-wave and the x-wave.

Second, such a formation may occur as a result of a reversal in the x-wave. This corresponds to case (iv) of Figure 12.2 in the previous chapter (see Figure 13.8). Such a formation is not *inevitable* in this situation: it depends on the position of the trough of the β-wave in relation to the trough of the x-wave. In essence, the trough of the x-wave ought to be reasonably close to the price range spanned by the β-wave in order for it to be classified as a head-and-shoulders top. However, even if there is uncertainty about the validity of the neckline, a sell signal is still generated as the z-wave penetrates below the trough of the x-wave.[2]

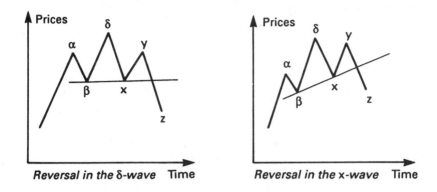

Figure 13.8. *The price pulse and the head-and-shoulders top*

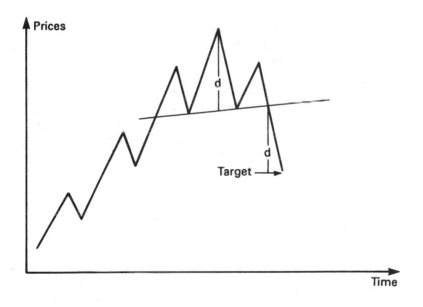

Figure 13.9. *Head-and-shoulders target*

The traditional measuring formula

One of the important aspects, if not *the* most important aspect, of the head-and-shoulders top formation is the fact that it can be used to forecast the *extent* of the subsequent price fall. The established formula is that after penetrating the neckline, prices will fall by an amount equivalent to the distance between the top of the head and the neckline itself. This is shown in Figure 13.9, where d is the calculated distance from the top of the head to the neckline.

The validity of the measuring formula

Despite the fact that the validity of the target has long been recognised, [3] no-one has hitherto been able to explain *why* it works. This gap in our knowledge can now be filled. In most cases, the right shoulder of the formation is essentially the first reaction to an information shock. The extent of the subsequent down-swing should therefore be 2.618 times the extent of the rally. Let us take an example to see how this works in practice. Assume that the peak of the market is reached at a price of 100 units and that the distance from this peak to the neckline is 10 units. Under normal circumstances (and for reasons which we shall discuss in Chapter 16) we could expect the right shoulder to rally between 38.2 per cent and 61.8 per cent of the fall. [4] Hence, the rally would terminate between 93.82 units (at the lowest) and 96.18 units (at the highest). In the first case, the projected target for the subsequent fall would be 83.8 units, [5] while in the second case, it would be 80.0 units. [6] Hence, the average projected target would be 81.9 units. Now, under the standard head-and-shoulders formula, the target is 10 units down from the neckline. If we assume that the neckline is basically horizontal, the target is therefore 80 units. The results of the 2.618 formula and the head-and-shoulders formula are virtually identical, and we thus have a valid theoretical explanation for a technique which, up to now, has been inexplicable.

The traditional formula and the 2.618 formula

A 'live' example of the relationship between the traditional head-and-shoulders formula and the new 2.618 formula is shown in Figure 13.10. The chart shows the performance of the US Dollar, as measured in terms of Deutschemarks, between July 1988 and November 1988. It can be seen that during the July to September period, the market traced out a head-and-shoulders pattern. A 'sell signal' was generated in early October as the market penetrated the 'neckline'.

The distance from the top of the 'head' to the 'neckline' was approximately DM 0.083. According to the traditional formula, this amount should be deducted from the level at which the sell signal occurred (ie DM 1.852). This generated a target of DM 1.769. Meanwhile, the height of the 'right shoulder' was DM 0.041. According to the 'spiral' formula, this should be multiplied by 2.618

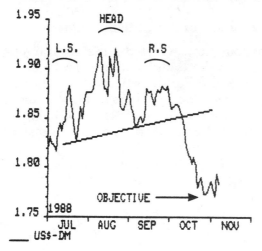

Source : Datastream

Figure 13.10. *The head-and-shoulders formulae (I)*

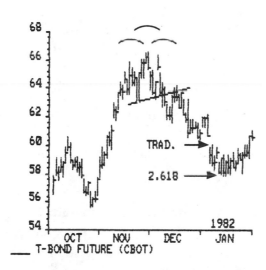

Source : Datastream

Figure 13.11. *The head-and-shoulders formulae (II)*

before being deducted from the level at which the 'right shoulder' peaked. The resulting calculation (ie 1.882 − 2.618 × 0.041) gave a target of DM 1.775. The measured targets were therefore virtually identical under *both* techniques.

The relative accuracy of the 2.618 formula

The important point, however, is that the 2.618 targeting formula is far more accurate than the traditional formula. Figure 13.11 shows the chart of the US T-bond future between December 1981 and January 1982. The chart shows the daily high and low prices over that period. The conventional formula gave the target as being 60, which turned out to be virtually in the middle of what was ultimately the breakaway gap when the market fell in early January. The correct target, calculated using the 2.618 formula, was 58.2. This level held the market in mid-January, and was the level from which the market actually rallied.

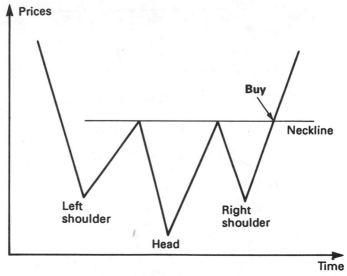

Figure 13.12. *The reverse head-and-shoulders bottom formation*

The reverse head-and-shoulders bottom pattern

In the case of a trough, the corresponding pattern is referred to (somewhat unfortunately) as a 'reverse head-and-shoulders bottom' formation. The profile is exactly the same as that which occurs at a head-and-shoulders top, except that it is inverted. The 'left' shoulder is formed by a period of price strength just prior to the market having a final sell-off into new lows, the 'head' is formed by the absolute low itself, and the 'right shoulder' is formed from a period of price weakness just after the bounce from that low. It is therefore possible to draw a 'neckline' between the two shoulders, and a buy signal is generated when prices penetrate the extended neckline (see Figure 13.12).

The head-and-shoulders bottom and the price pulse

Within the context of a single price pulse, a reverse head-and-shoulders formation can occur in two ways. First, it can occur as a result of a trend reversal in the x-wave. This corresponds to case (iv) of Figure 12.3 of the previous chapter (see Figure 13.13). The neckline is drawn between the peaks of the α-wave and the β-wave. A buy signal is generated as the y-wave penetrates the neckline. After the breakout, the neckline is 're-tested' by the z-wave, [7] but the bull market is resumed as the *next* price pulse begins to develop.

Second, a reverse head-and-shoulders can occur if the trend reversal occurs in the y-wave. This corresponds to case (v) of Figure 12.3 (see Figure 13.13). Here, the neckline is drawn between the peaks of the δ-wave and the y-wave. A buy signal is generated as the *next* pulse develops.

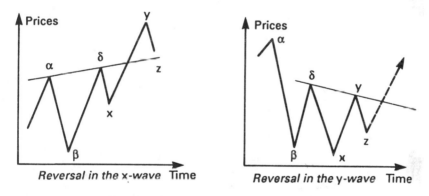

Figure 13.13. *Reverse head-and-shoulders bottoms*

The 2.618 formula

Strictly, the 2.618 formula for calculating targets cannot be used in either of these cases. Such targets can only be calculated from a β-wave. This, in turn, is only possible if *two* pulses are involved (see below) so that the right shoulder is formed from a β-wave. Then the 'average' expected movement after the penetration of a neckline using the simple head-and-shoulders formula is usually equivalent to the 2.618 result. The evidence in fact suggests that a reverse head-and-shoulders pattern normally *does* involve two pulses.

Multiple tops and the price pulse

The final set of reversal patterns which can be generated from a single price pulse involves the market bouncing away from a particular price level at least twice. At market peaks, such a formation is called a 'double top'. It is generated by a trend reversal either in the β-wave (that is, case (ii) of Figure 12.2), or during the y-wave (that is, case (v) of Figure 12.2). Sometimes, a reversal in the β-wave may be *so* slow in developing that the y-wave helps to create a 'triple top' (case (ii) of Figure 12.2). These possibilities are shown in Figure 13.14.

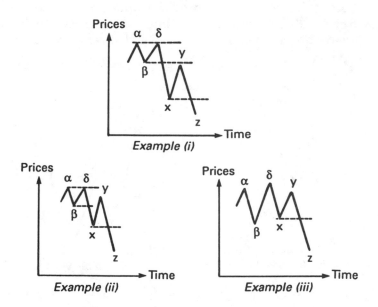

Figure 13.14. *The multiple top formation*

On the other hand, a reversal during the y-wave consists of a very much simpler pattern and gives a simple sell signal as the price falls below the level of the x-wave (see Figure 13.15).

Multiple bottoms and the price pulse

This analysis may be repeated for market lows where 'double bottoms' occur. Such reversal formations are recognisable by the fact that prices bounce *twice* off the same level before rising, and are usually generated by a trend reversal either in the β-wave (case (ii) of Figure 12.3) or during the y-wave (case (v) of Figure 12.3). In the former case, a buy signal is given as the price level moves above the peak of the α-wave; in the latter case, the signal is given as the price level rises above the level of the y-wave (see Figure 13.16).

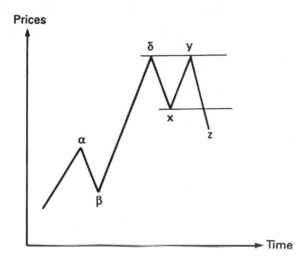

Figure 13.15. *The double top formation*

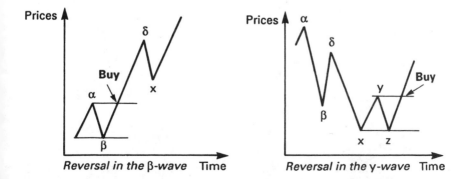

Figure 13.16. *The double bottom formation*

Other price pulse formations

This now leaves only three basic price pulse formations from Figures 12.2 and 12.3 which need to be related to traditional analysis. These include case (i) of both diagrams, and case (iii) of Figure 12.3. In each of these cases, the relevant traditional label depends on the pattern of the *preceding* price pulse. Where the price reversal occurs in the α-wave (whether at a top or a bottom), the signal will inevitably involve a head-and-shoulders pattern. Where the low occurs during a δ-wave, the signal will certainly involve a trend line break, and may involve a head-and-shoulders or multiple bottom if the trend is turning only very slowly.

The price pulse and traditional patterns

In the previous chapter, we isolated six patterns which could materialise within a single price pulse at a market peak, and six patterns which could materialise at market troughs. In the present chapter, we have noted the relationships between these twelve price pulse patterns and those recognised by traditional technical analysis. The two methodologies are compared directly in Table 13.1, which shows the traditional signals which would operate for a trend change in different phases of the price pulse. Most of the patterns derived from a *single* price pulse can immediately be related to traditional patterns, even though some variability is possible. In the case of the exceptions, the relevant standard pattern will depend on the shape taken by the *preceding* pulse.

Table 13.1. *The price pulse and technical analysis formations*

Position of pulse Reversal	Traditional Technical Analysis	
	Peaks	*Troughs*
α	See text	See text
β	Double/triple	Double
δ	H&S	See text
x	H&S/double	H&S/multiple
y	Double	H&S/double
z	Trend break	Trend break

Conclusion

This chapter has demonstrated that simple variations in a lower level price pulse, caused by developments in a higher-order price pulse, are directly responsible for *all* the major reversal patterns which have traditionally been recognised by technical analysts. The trend line break, the head-and-shoulders reversal, the double top or bottom, and even triple tops and bottoms, may all be derived from variations in the basic price pulse. There are in fact only two variables: the *point* at which the trend reverses, and the *speed* with which that trend reverses. Furthermore, the accuracy of traditional price targets following reversal patterns is accounted for by the influence of the Golden Ratio in the transmission of information shocks. The apparent mystery of technical analysis – the reason why it 'works' – is therefore finally explained.

Notes

1. An upward or downward *bias* between the two shoulders often occurs.
2. It is worth noting here that an upward bias in a head-and-shoulders pattern means that the base of the left-hand 'shoulder' will automatically operate as a potential support level as prices fall. If this level also coincides with calculated targets (see Chapter 17 for full details), then the downside after the sell signal will be limited.
3. See, for example, P.J. Kaufman, *Commodity Trading Systems and Methods*. John Wiley, New York, 1978.
4. These numbers are derived from the Fibonacci Sequence.
5. That is, $93.82 - [(93.82 - 90) \times 2.618] = 83.8$.
6. That is, $96.18 - [(96.18 - 90) \times 2.618] = 80.0$.
7. If the trend is changing only slowly, the z-wave may fall sufficiently to abort the initial buy signal. The resulting pattern may be better classified as either a double bottom, or even a triple bottom.

14.

Price Patterns during Trends

Introduction

The trading rules obtained from an analysis of distortions to the price pulse are very simple, and are consistent with traditional chart patterns. However, they do not quite exhaust all the possibilites. In constructing the analysis, we made the heroic assumption that a higher-level trend would turn at a *particular* point within the lower-level pulse. This automatically guaranteed that a buy or sell signal would be effective. Under most circumstances the signals will, indeed, be effective. However, there are certain 'grey' areas. These relate to the possibility that although a price pulse pattern may match one of the twelve possibilities outlined in Chapter 12, it may not actually indicate a serious change in the higher-level trend at all. Consequently, the associated trading signal may occur *too* late to generate a decent profit. We therefore have to distinguish between patterns which are only *consistent* with a trend change, and those which actually *confirm* such a change.

The use of fundamental analysis

One solution, of course, is to adopt a more holistic approach, and incorporate *fundamental* analysis into the decision-making process. We suggested the reasoning behind this solution in Chapter 12. However, this does not circumvent the problem that the market averages tend to anticipate fundamentals, and may therefore provide information about fundamentals which is not immediately obvious, even to the best economists.

The use of indices of investor behaviour

A second solution to the problem is to analyse the actual performance of investors as the assumed reversal pattern develops. Investor behaviour obeys certain basic rules, and will almost certainly *confirm* a reversal as it happens. In addition, knowledge of investor behaviour will enable appropriate trading positions to be opened sooner than otherwise. We shall discuss the relevant techniques in Chapter 16.

The use of the price pulse

The third solution involves reversing the analytical procedure of Chapter 12. This means trying to deduce the status of the higher-order trend *from* the distortions of the price pulse rather than the other way round. In this context, there are four rules which are important.

Rule 1: the five-phase uptrend

The first of these rules is that a price pulse will be distorted into a clear five-phase pattern if it is subjected to a dynamic up-trend. Furthermore, the middle phase will be the longest, because it is a δ-wave. This is demonstrated in Figure 14.1, which includes an excellent practical example involving the Sterling – Dollar exchange rate.

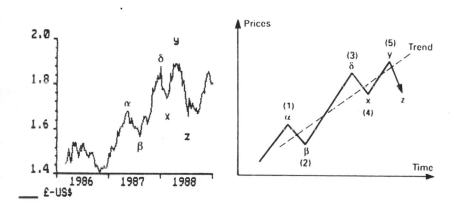

Figure 14.1. *The five-phase up-trend*

Under normal circumstances, the y-wave of a price pulse will fall short of the peak of the preceding δ-wave. If the y-wave instead makes a new high, then there is strong evidence that a higher-order trend has distorted it upwards. As a result, we may conclude that a five-phase pattern is *prima facie* evidence of a dominant up-trend.

Rule 2: the three-phase down-trend

The second rule is that the price pulse will almost invariably register some form of three-phase pattern during a down-trend. There are a large number of possibilities here. At the very simplest level, *all* bear phases consist of three phases, because of the definition of the price pulse. However, it should be clear that if we apply a downward bias to the *whole* pulse, the patterns merely become more complex versions of the same phenomenon. The most natural outcome, in fact, appears to be a 'double-three' structure, with a pair of three-phase movements linked together by a contra-trend δ-wave rally. Normally, the third phase will be the longest because the higher-level trend and the lower-level trend are synchronised with one another. This is demonstrated in Figure 14.2, which includes an example from the futures market for the Commodities Research Bureau Price Index.

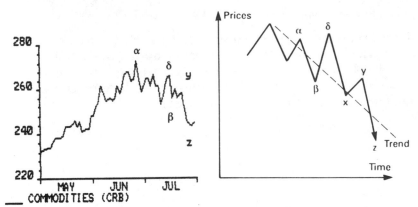

Figure 14.2. *The three-phase down-trend*

Source : Datastream

Rule 3: the impact of the z-wave

These two rules (involving a five-wave up-trend and a three-wave down-trend) are very simple, but extraordinarily accurate. In particular, they should help investors to stay with the trend. However, there are two final rules which can help to confirm the presence of price *reversals*. The first of these derives from the fact that every y-wave is followed by a z-wave. The latter is, theoretically, the most dynamic downward phase of a price pulse. Hence, during an up-trend, it follows that a significant correction will *always* follow the fifth phase (see Figure 14.1).

Rule 4: the price pattern following a market low

The last rule is that since a five-phase count confirms an up-trend, the emergence of such a count *immediately after* a market low is strong evidence that the trend is turning upwards (see Figure 14.3).

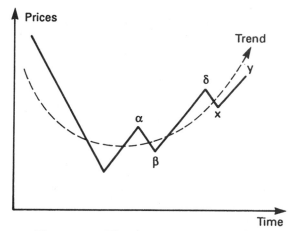

Figure 14.3. *The emergence of an up-trend*

The implications of double tops and bottoms

These rules relating to the five-phase up-trend, the three-phase downtrend, the importance of the δ-wave, and the emergence of a five-phase up-move after a trough are the most important. However, there are two subsidiary guidelines (which are extensions of the main rules), which provide valuable insights into possible *future* trends. The first of these relates to double tops and double bottoms. Where a double top involves an abnormally strong y-wave, the conclusion is similar to that where the y-wave actually makes a new high: the underlying trend is *up*wards (see Figure 14.4). Similarly, where a double bottom involves an abnormally weak β-wave, the implication is that the higher-order trend is still *down*wards.[1] These conclusions follow because under normal circumstances the y-wave and β-wave usually *fail* to retrace to the previous turning point (see Figure 14.4).

False trend line breaks

The second subsidiary guideline is that since a strong y-wave usually reflects the influence of a higher-level uptrend, a trend line break during the subsequent z-wave may prove to be false. In practical terms, the trend line break creates sufficient short-term extremes of sentiment to provide the basis of the subsequent rally. This is demonstrated in Figure 14.5. The correct trend line to use is therefore that which links the last wave of the base pattern to the trough of the z-wave. A break of this line *would* represent a change in trend.

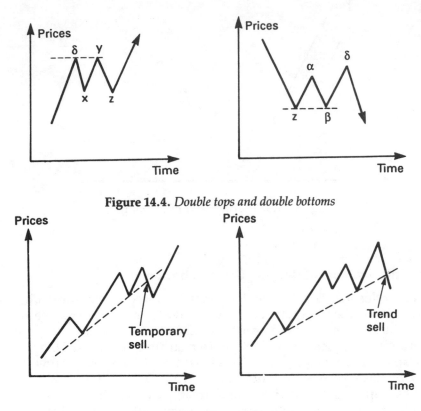

Figure 14.4. *Double tops and double bottoms*

Figure 14.5. *The use of trendlines*

Ralph Nelson Elliott

The fact that a rising five-phase count is indicative of a bull market, and a falling three-phase count is indicative of a continuing bear market, was the perceptive insight of the great American stock market theorist, Ralph Nelson Elliott.[2] Writing in the 1930s, Elliott concluded that the resulting 5-3 profile was essentially a 'law' of nature. He saw that the associated price patterns usually involved a dynamic impulse movement in the third phase of either a bull market or a bear market, and he deduced that the patterns obeyed certain clearly defined rules which could be used in trading. He observed, however, that not all patterns actually matched the basic profile, and he accordingly went to great lengths to show that any aberrations were caused by distortions to the underlying 5-3 pattern. In particular, he argued that the fifth phase of an impulse movement could 'fail', so that the whole movement essentially looked like a three-phase movement.

As we have indicated, the essential truth concerning the number of phases in an impulse movement is in fact the other way round. The laws of nature demand a 3-3 profile in price fluctuations, and the 5-3 pattern emerges as a result of the influence of higher-level trends. Nevertheless, Elliott's findings are a valid and practical philosophical approach to the stock market phenomenon. There is *no* known pattern which falls outside his framework, and his 'Wave Principle' invokes rules which are valid interpretations of the implications of the price pulse. Traders who use the Elliott Wave Principle will generally obtain exceptionally good results. We shall therefore analyse Elliott's conclusions in a little more detail in the next chapter.

Notes

1. Note that this can involve the apparent emergence of *five* waves in a downward direction. Consequently, a falling five-wave count implies that the higher-order trend is downwards. However, this phenomenon is not essential to a bear market.
2. Ralph Nelson Elliott, *Nature's Law – The Secret of the Universe*. Elliott, New York, 1946. Reprinted in Robert R. Prechter (ed.), *The Major Works of R.N. Elliott*. New Classics Library, New York, 1980.

15.

The Elliott Wave Principle

Elliott's Discovery

The Elliott Wave Principle is a widely used, but little understood, philosophical approach to stock markets. During a long period of convalescence in the early 1930s, Elliott occupied himself by undertaking a detailed analysis of stock market movements. In the process he discovered a unique formula which 'defined' stock market movements. This formula was based on the premise that the stock market averages rise in five 'waves' and fall in three 'waves', and it subsequently enabled Elliott to predict price movements with a degree of accuracy which astounded contemporary commentators. In 1938, he published his findings under the title of 'The Wave Principle'.[1]

The Elliott Wave Principle has been popularised by Robert Prechter in the United States in recent years, and its enviable record of success has created a large following. Nevertheless, it is fair to say that the Wave Principle suffers from two specific problems: the first is that it is an extraordinarily complex system to apply, and the second is that no-one (including Elliott himself) has actually been able to explain *why* the central formula 'works'.

The price pulse as the basis of the wave principle

As we demonstrated in Chapter 14, the key to understanding Elliott's formula is the price pulse. Once this is recognised the whole of Elliott's analysis becomes an acceptable method of analysing, and forecasting, stock market prices. Quite simply, price pulses from different levels of the hierarchy *combine* with one another, thereby creating the different patterns which Elliott found conformed to certain simple rules. Let us therefore survey Elliott's findings in more detail.

The basic wave pattern

Elliott's primary assertion was that all bull markets consist of five waves and that all bear markets consist of three waves. These are shown in Figure 15.1. Each bull phase therefore consists of three *impulse* waves (1, 3 and 5 in Figure 15.1), interspersed with two *corrective* waves (2 and 4). The bear phase consists of two impulse waves (A and C in Figure 15.1) interspersed with one contra-trend corrective wave (B in Figure 15.1).

Corrections

In this simple formulation, waves A, B and C of the bear phase can be broken down into easily identifiable patterns. Waves A and C are impulse waves. Elliott considered that both would therefore consist of five waves. Wave B, on the other hand, is a corrective wave (that is, it corrects during a correction!). It therefore consists of three waves, and is an *inverted* version of the whole A-B-C correction itself (see Figure 15.2).

A universal phenomenon

An important feature of the Elliott Wave Principle is that it applies to *all* degrees of movement. Hence waves 1, 3 and 5 of any five-wave impulse movement each consists of five waves themselves, while waves 2 and 4 of that movement each consists of three waves. Hence, each complete 5-3 bull/bear cycle becomes part of the cycle of the next higher degree. For example, the bull/bear formation shown in Figure 15.1 could constitute either waves (1) and (2), or waves (3) and (4), of a higher-order cycle' (see Figure 15.3). In this sense, Elliott's Principle embraces a theory of growth: ultimately, bear market price falls will be completely reversed, and the previous bull market price peak will be exceeded.

The Wave Principle as a natural phenomenon

Elliott therefore made the important observation that stock market behaviour was a natural phenomenon that contained its own intrinsic patterns. This, of course, had fundamental implications for the process of *forecasting* stock market behaviour, because in principle the patterns of the lower levels should regenerate themselves at a higher level.

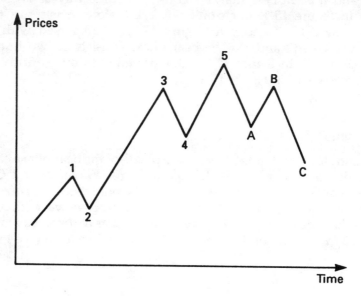

Figure 15.1. *The Elliott Wave*

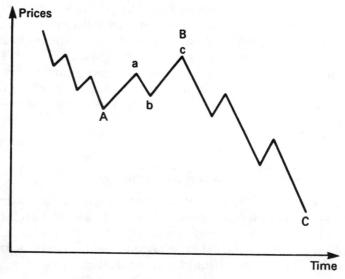

Figure 15.2. *Basic Elliott corrective wave*

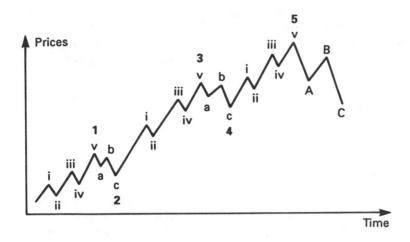

Figure 15.3. *The complete Elliott Wave*

Derived rules: trend indications

Elliott, in fact, established certain rules by which it would be possible both to establish the direction of the main trend in the market and to determine when a market reversal, or turning point, was in the process of occurring. First, he noted that the emergence of a five-wave impulse pattern, either upwards or downwards, would provide a strong indication of the *direction* of the longer-term trend. Hence, a rising five-wave pattern after a sharp fall in the market would be suggestive of further rises; while a falling five-wave pattern after a sharp rise would suggest that further falls would take place.

Derived rules: impulse waves

Second, within each five-wave movement, three basic rules would apply:

(a) wave 4 will not penetrate below the peak of wave 2;[3]
(b) wave 3 is often the longest, but is *never* the shortest, of the five impulse waves which constitute the whole movement;
(c) two of the three impulse waves will be equal in length.

Derived rules: corrections

Third, on the question of corrections, Elliott noted three basic guidelines:

(a)   no A-B-C formation will ever *fully* retrace the preceding five wave formation of the same degree;
(b)   each correction will be at least as large in price, and as long in time, as all lower-degree corrections that preceded it;
(c)   each correction tends to return to the price range spanned by a corrective wave of one degree lower – that is, either to wave 2 or 4.[4]

Complications within the system

Elliott's basic 5-3 formulation, together with its associated guidelines, provided a unique view of the way that stock markets operate. Unfortunately, however, the formula is not totally comprehensive. Elliott himself found that although the basic 5-3 pattern applied to a large number of situations, there were nevertheless certain variations which had to be taken into account. When these variations were included, then indeed the analysis is complete: there is no known stock market price pattern which falls outside Elliott's framework.

Fifth wave variations: failures and extensions

The first set of variations which Elliott dealt with were those which apply to the fifth wave of an impulse movement. The basic formulation suggests that the fifth wave will travel *beyond* the end of the third wave of the same degree. However, in practice the fifth wave can either fall short of the end of the fifth wave (a *failure*), or extend itself in an additional dynamic five-wave movement (an *extension*). These are shown in Figures 15.4 and 15.5 respectively.

Behaviour following failure or extension

The occurrence of either a failure or an extension in the fifth wave of a movement gives a very clear indication of the subsequent behaviour of the market. A fifth-wave failure is obviously the sign of great weakness at the end of a bull run, or of great strength at the end of a bear phase. Corrections following a fifth-wave bull market failure will

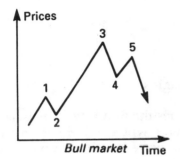
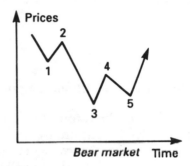

Figure 15.4. *Fifth-wave failures*

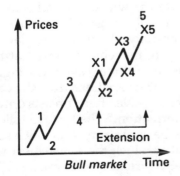

Figure 15.5. *Fifth wave extensions*

therefore be very deep in price terms; rallies following a bear market failure will be very sharp. These are shown in Figure 15.6. On the other hand, extensions signal a very dynamic impulse movement.[5] Consequently, in a bull market, prices will move to new high ground even after the apparent peak of the fifth wave; in a bear market, prices will drop to new lows after the apparent end of the fifth wave. These are shown in Figure 15.7. Elliott called this price action the 'Double Retracement Principle', since prices would *twice* cover the ground traced out by the extension itself. The first retracement would return to the beginning of the extension (ie X2 in Figure 15.7), and the second retracement would move the market back past the end of wave 5.[6]

Fifth-wave variations: diagonal triangles

In addition, Elliott found that sometimes the fifth wave consists of a diagonally-sloping triangular formation where (a) the formation consists of five waves, where (b) each wave is a three-wave movement, and where (c) the fourth wave may penetrate *below* the peak of the first wave.[7] This pattern is relatively uncommon, but is always followed by a dramatic move in prices in the opposite direction to the slope of the triangle. Two examples are shown in Figure 15.8.

Variations in corrections: the three-phase A-wave

The second set of variations analysed by Elliott relates to the form of the corrective patterns. The basic pattern, which was reflected in Figure 15.2 above, is called a *zigzag*; that is, it consists of two declining waves interspersed with a contra-trend rally. As already explained, both the A- and the C-waves of a zigzag movement consist of five declining waves, and the B-wave consists of three waves. The zigzag correction is therefore a 5-3-5 formation. The variations from the basic zigzag pattern relate to the fact that the A-wave often consists only of *three* waves, thereby yielding a 3-3-5 formation.[8] The B-wave following such a 'truncated' A-wave tends to be very strong – so much so in fact that it travels at least to the point at which the A-wave started. Elliott actually found three possible 3-3-5 formations. These he called the *regular flat* correction, the *irregular flat* correction, and the *running correction* respectively.

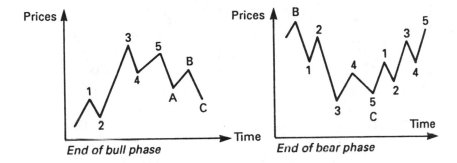

Figure 15.6. *Movement following fifth-wave failure*

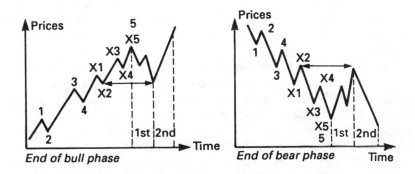

Figure 15.7. *Movement following fifth wave extension*

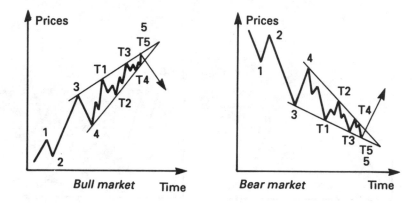

Figure 15.8. *Fifth-wave diagonal triangle*

The flat correction

With a regular flat correction (see Figure 15.9), the B-wave takes prices back to the level at which the A-wave started, and the subsequent C-wave returns prices to the level at which the A-wave ended. In other words, prices fluctuate within a trading range before resuming their trend.

With an irregular flat, however, there are two distinct alternatives: first, the B-wave may take prices back *above* the level at which the A-wave started; second, the C-wave may either fall significantly short of the bottom of the A-wave or it may significantly *exceed* the bottom of the A-wave. Two of the possible combinations are shown in Figure 15.10.

In extreme cases the relatively rare running correction occurs. Here, the B-wave substantially exceeds the start of wave A, and the subsequent C-wave also leaves prices above the start of wave A (see Figure 15.11). Elliott's basic rule concerning both flat and running corrections was that they are all indicative of the fundamental trend in the market. Specifically, the strength of the B-wave is an important indication that market prices will rally very sharply following the end of a correction, and that prices will *probably* exceed the peak of that B-wave.

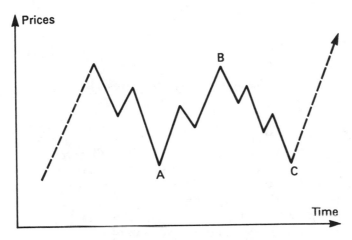

Figure 15.9. *Regular flat correction*

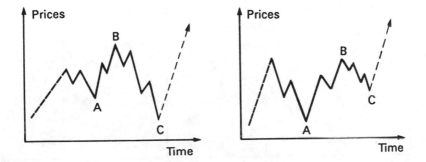

Figure 15.10. *Irregular flat corrections*

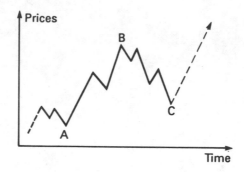

Figure 15.11. *Running correction*

Complex corrections

Obviously, therefore, corrections are potentially complicated movements. Their essential purpose is to counteract the excesses of the previous rising impulse wave of the same degree, and to prepare the conditions for the next rising impulse wave. Sometimes, however, a simple zigzag or flat correction is insufficient for this task. Consequently, the market extends the correction by *combining* two or more corrective patterns. In principle any number of such patterns may be strung together, and the only restriction on the resulting complex formation is that each A-B-C pattern is separated from the next one by another A-B-C pattern. This latter intervening pattern is usually called an X-wave (not to be confused with the x-wave of the price pulse). Two examples of complex corrections are shown in Figure 15.12.

Triangles

One of the complex corrections which Elliott considered to be particularly important was a triangular formation. Such a formation

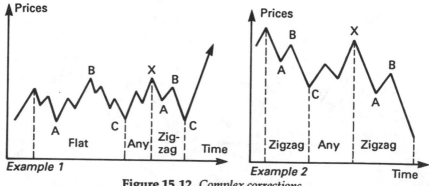

Figure 15.12. *Complex corrections*

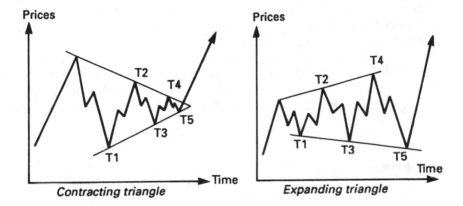

Figure 15.13. *Triangular corrections*

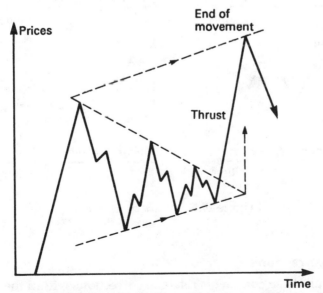

Figure 15.14. *Price movement after triangle*

essentially consists of five Λ-B-C waves or, more precisely, three A-B-C waves interspersed with two X-waves – and the extent of travel of each successive A-B-C movement is contained by boundary lines which are either contracting or expanding.[9] Relevant examples are shown in Figure 15.13.

The implications of a triangle

The importance of the triangle lies in the fact that it gives a unique indication of the subsequent behaviour of market prices. First, market prices exit the triangle in the same direction as wave 2 of the triangle; second, the resulting impulse wave is the last such wave in the direction of the main trend;[10] third, in the case of contracting triangles, prices tend to move by an amount equal to the widest part of the triangle and tend to change trend in line with the apex of the triangle.[11] These rules are reflected in the example shown in Figure 15.14.

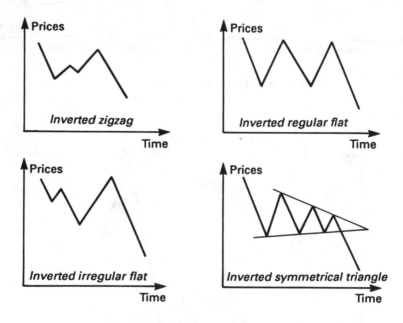

Figure 15.5. *Inverted corrections*

Inverted corrections

Although all these comments relate to corrections within the context of a rising market, they also apply to contra-trend movements within a *falling* market. Hence, they apply to waves 2 and 4 of a falling impulse wave and to the B-wave of an ordinary correction. It is usual to apply the term 'inverted' to the relevant formation. Examples of an inverted zigzag, an inverted regular flat, an inverted irregular flat, and an inverted symmetrical triangle are shown in Figure 15.15.

The 'rule' of alternation

In his book *'Nature's Law'*, Elliott argued that an essential feature of the Wave Principle was the 'rule of alternation'. At its simplest level, alternation can be taken to mean that bear markets alternate with bull markets. More importantly, however, Elliott argued that *successive* corrective patterns will be different from each other. Hence, within a five-wave impulse movement, wave 2 will differ from wave 4 both in type and complexity. Within a complex correction, adjacent three-wave patterns will also differ from one another both in type and complexity. Accordingly, for example, a zigzag might be followed by a flat, and a simple correction will be followed by a complex correction consisting of two or more three-wave patterns. However, Frost and Prechter[12] suggest that the tendency for corrections to alternate should be regarded as a probability rather than an inviolable rule. There are actually numerous examples where alternation does not occur.

The problems with the Elliott Wave Principle

Despite the fact that the Elliott Wave Principle provides a complete catalogue of price patterns, many analysts find it very unsatisfactory. There are three interrelated reasons for this. First, there has previously been no satisfactory explanation of the 5-3 formation. Elliott himself considered that the formation was a 'law of nature'[13] and left it at that. Unfortunately – and apart from the fact that the numbers derive from the Fibonacci Sequence – the 5-3 pattern does not appear as a regular phenomenon anywhere else in nature. It is difficult to believe that something which is supposedly *so* fundamental is both totally inexplicable and without parallel. Second, the integrity of the central theorem of a 5-3 pattern for each bull/bear cycle is only maintained by the use of the concepts of *failures* and *irregular corrections*. This suggests the absence of a unifying cause and effect. Third, the complexity of the Elliott wave (particularly insofar as extensions and complex corrections are concerned) means that it is often impossible to establish a unique future out-turn for market prices: it is possible to isolate alternatives (and therefore probabilities) in the knowledge that any actual out-turn will be a valid expression of the Elliott Principle, but precise forecasts are difficult to make prior to the event.

Furthermore, even those analysts who accept the basic validity of the Principle, and therefore make substantial use of it, have noted some additional problems. The first is that the Principle is more difficult to apply to some markets than to others. It is, for example, difficult to apply to commodity markets because wave 4 of a rising impulse wave often penetrates below the peak of wave 1 of the same degree. It is also difficult to apply to foreign exchange markets where a 5-3 pattern for one currency in a particular cross-rate constitutes a 3-5 pattern for the other currency in that cross-rate.[14] A second problem is that the Wave Principle suggests that the stock market will *always* rise: each upward wave is always part of a larger upward wave, and all corrections will terminate above the start of wave 1 of the preceeding bull run. This conclusion implies that dynamic systems *grow*, but do not *change*, which is at odds with the basic principles of natural development. All these difficulties disappear once the implications of the price pulse are understood.

Notes

1. Ralph Nelson Elliott, *The Wave Principle*. Elliott, New York, 1938. Reprinted in Robert R. Prechter (ed.), *The Major Works of R.N. Elliott*. New Classics Library, New York, 1980.
2. In differentiating between movements of differing degrees, it is conventional to use different notations. For example, the lowest-level waves are usually numbered using the lower case Roman numerals i, ii, iii, iv, v, followed by a, b, c. The next level is (i), (ii), (iii), (iv), (v), followed by (a), (b), (c). Then comes 1, 2, 3, 4, 5, followed by A, B, C. Then (1), (2), (3), (4), (5), followed by (A), (B), (C). And so forth.
3. Except in the case of relatively rare triangular formations, and in the case of commodity markets.
4. Indeed, Elliott found that, very often, a correction would return to the lower-degree corrective wave which bore the same relationship to the larger movement. Hence a higher degree wave (2) would return to the lower degree wave 2, while a higher degree wave (4) would return to the lower degree wave 4.
5. Elliott argued that fifth-wave extensions were likely to occur if waves 1 and 2 were short and equal in length.
6. According to the price pulse formulation, an extension during (for example) a rising market emerges during a δ-wave. The double retracement is then caused by the subsequent x-wave and y-wave, but where the y-wave itself moves to a new high. The whole pattern assumes a sharply rising trend. Conversely for a bear market.
7. In stock markets, this is the only exception to the rule that wave 4 corrections cannot penetrate below the end of wave 1 of the same degree. The evidence suggests that the rule is also sometimes violated in commodity markets.

8. This implies that *all* movements end on a five-wave count. However, Elliott himself was not entirely convinced by this, and he dabbled with the concept of an 'A-B base' which was a 3-3 construct. See Ralph Nelson Elliott, *Nature's Law – the Secret of the Universe*. Elliott, New York, 1946. Reprinted in Robert R. Prechter (ed.), *The Major Works of R.N. Elliott*. New Classics Library, New York, 1980. The A-B base is a perfect reflection of the α-β base of the price pulse.

9. The boundary lines of the triangle need not converge nor diverge in a symmetrical fashion. In an *ascending* triangle the top boundary line is horizontal, while in a *descending* triangle, the bottom line is horizontal.

10. That is, in a bull run, triangles can only occur in wave 4.

11. See Alfred J. Frost and Robert R. Prechter, *Elliott Wave Principle*. New Classics Library, New York, 1978.

12. Ibid.

13. Ralph Nelson Elliott, *Nature's Law – The Secret of the Universe*. Elliott, New York, 1946. Reprinted in Robert R. Prechter (ed.), *The Major Works Of R.N. Elliott*. New Classics Library, New York, 1980.

14. This problem does not necessarily exist where the US dollar is being used as the base currency. This is because the dollar is an international medium of exchange.

16.

The Confirmation of Buy and Sell Signals

Introduction

The greatest constraint on taking the appropriate action in any financial market is *doubt*. No matter how important a trading signal might appear to be, there is always the possibility that it might be wrong. Since important buy and sell signals almost inevitably occur at moments when the vast majority of investors are literally 'the other way', the crowd pressure to ignore the signal is likely to be *extremely* strong. The first task of any investor, therefore, is to try to reduce his or her susceptibility to such crowd pressures.

In this context, people who uses technical analysis in trading financial markets will quickly find that their ability to stand out against the herd is increased. This is quite simply because the *raison d'être* of technical analysis is to deduce what the vast majority are indeed doing, so that contrary positions can be taken at the appropriate moment. Nevertheless, it is always essential to try and *reduce* the element of doubt by applying as many techniques as possible to each particular situation. The interpretation of price patterns is only one of these techniques. Others involve the calculation of price objectives, the calculation of the timing of likely turning points, and a direct analysis of investor sentiment and behaviour. We shall deal with price objectives in the next chapter, and analyse the influence of time cycles in Chapters 18 and 19. In the present chapter we shall examine the idea that we can deduce the exact position of the market in its bull/bear cycle by analysing *investor behaviour*.

Investor sentiment and price fluctuations

The starting point to the analysis is the relationship between investor sentiment and price fluctuations (which we examined in detail in Chapter 8). It will be remembered that there is both a *limit cycle* relationship and a *spiral* relationship between sentiment and prices. While a trend is intact, changes in sentiment encourage changes in prices, which in turn stimulate changes in sentiment and in investor activity. However, at a turning point the following sequence of events occurs. First, the 'circular' relationship between prices and sentiment begins to break down. Changing prices are unable to induce additional changes in investment positions. Accordingly, the market becomes overextended. Second, investor psychology receives a shock as prices move in the opposite direction to the expectations of the vast majority. Third, prices move to re-test the levels which were reached just prior to the shock. Sometimes prices actually move into new territory during the retest; sometimes they do not. During this phase sentiment often appears to run ahead of the price changes, but it does not actually return to levels achieved prior to the shock. Finally, prices begin a proper reversal and investor sentiment reverses with it.

Overextended markets and the principle of non-confirmation

This analytical framework not only allows investors to understand exactly what is happening at each phase of a full bull/bear cycle, but also pin-points exact trading rules which can be used to take advantage of this understanding. First, it emphasises that it is possible to *anticipate* a shock when the market becomes overextended in one direction or another. Second, it highlights the fact that investor sentiment becomes *damaged* by the shock. Hence, re-tests of the price levels which were reached prior to the shock should be used to open up new trading positions in the *opposite* direction.

In both of these situations, the main indicator of an imminent reversal is a change in the level of either investor sentiment or investor behaviour. When a trend is intact, the majority of investors will open up new trading positions, increase their dealing activity, be prepared to stimulate the momentum of the price trend, and deal in all sectors of the market. However, when a price reversal is imminent, the trend is *not confirmed* by some, or all, of these factors. When the market is overextended, investors are essentially *unable* to open up new trading positions; when the market is trying to recover from the subsequent shock, investors will then be *unwilling* to open up new trading positions, even if market prices are actually able to move into new territory.

Indicators of investor behaviour

All we therefore need to know is the condition of investor sentiment, and the nature of investor activity. The most obvious indicators to use are opinion surveys and liquidity surveys. However, these can be expensive to create and usually take time to calculate. A much easier approach is to use simple mechanical indicators which are readily available from the markets themselves. These are volume indices, open interest indices, momentum indices, and auxiliary (or secondary) price indices. We shall now look at these indicators.

Volume and open interest

Because the rules applying to volume and open interest are essentially the same, we shall analyse them together. Volume is a direct measure of the amount of activity taking place in the market at a particular time. It may be measured either in terms of nominal turnover, or in terms of the number of bargains. The data may be obtained from the cash markets, from the futures, or even from the options markets. Indeed, in principle the volume figures for one market for a particular asset may be applied to any of the other markets in the same asset: all that is required is that the data be consistent and the markets be well traded. Hence, for example, in the foreign exchange markets where it is impossible to obtain volume data, it is perfectly acceptable to use volume figures generated by the Chicago Board of Trade for an equivalent futures contract.

Open interest, on the other hand, is a cumulative measure of the unclosed bull positions in a particular futures market. As a corollary, of course, it is therefore a measure of unclosed bear positions. Although the measure applies to specific futures contracts, it may be used equally to apply to the underlying security.[1] Hence, for example, the open interest for the US September long T-bond futures contract on the Chicago Board of Trade (CBOT) may be applied to the Treasury bond cash market as a whole during the June-August period. Better still, the total open interest for *all* T-bond contracts can be used in conjunction with the Treasury cash market for *any* period.

The level of volume

There are two aspects of open interest and volume which warrant discussion: the first is the general *level* of the indicators, while the second is the *direction* of change of those indicators. Let us start with the levels. The level of volume is indicative of people's *willingness* to deal. This, in turn, reflects traders' attitudes to the market. A low level of volume indicates an unwillingness to open new positions and close old ones: it therefore also indicates some uncertainty about the future direction of the market. Alternatively, a high level of volume is a direct reflection of traders' willingness to open new positions, to take profits, or to close bad positions: it therefore also indicates a high degree of confidence in the future direction of the market.

The level of open interest

In the case of open interest, the level is indicative of the efficiency, or liquidity, of the market. Specifically, it is a measure of the market's ability to absorb new deals at current prices. If open interest is low, then there are very few profits to be taken or bad positions to be closed. A new trade is likely to have a large impact on prices because prices have to adjust in order to induce another dealer to 'go the other way'. At low levels of open interest, therefore, the market is illiquid. If, on the other hand, open interest is high, there are plenty of profits to be taken and bad positions to be closed. A new trade is likely to have only a very small effect on prices because another dealer is likely to take advantage of the availability of the trade at the current price level. At high levels of open interest, therefore, the market is very liquid.

Sudden changes in the indicators

The concepts of 'high' and 'low' are, of course, relative. There needs to be a benchmark against which to measure them. In this respect, historical precedent and local market knowledge should provide some assistance. Very often, however, the most important facet of the levels of either open interest or volume is the fact that they *change suddenly*. This is a clear indication that something is altering in the price-sentiment relationship. In this context, volume is often more important than open interest, but open interest can help to determine the extent of the price reversal which subsequently takes place. Let us therefore analyse the implications of the *direction of change* in volume and open interest in more detail.

The direction of change in volume and open interest

Both volume and open interest may be taken as proxies for investor sentiment. *Rising* volume suggests a growing awareness of the higher-level trend, and rising open interest indicates a growing commitment to that trend. *Falling* volume, on the other hand, indicates a spreading inability or unwillingness to pursue the immediate trend, while falling open interest suggests some reversal of sentiment as profits are taken and bad positions are closed out.

Changing emotions during the cycle

It will be remembered that while a trend is developing, the limit cycle process between prices and sentiment will ensure that investor activity continually strengthens that trend. This implies that during the trend, volume and open interest should both *rise*. This occurs whether the price trend is upwards or downwards. At some stage in the limit cycle process, the change in prices will trigger the emotion of fear amongst investors – either the fear of being left out of the market during a rise, or the fear of being left in the market during a fall. Most emotions have a number of different dimensions, but fear is unique in closing the mind to rational thought and focusing the body's energy on physical, mental or social survival. Fearful investors will deal blindly, and both volume and open interest should rise sharply. Consequently, the market starts to become overbought or oversold.

Sharp rises in volume and open interest

A sharp rise in volume and open interest essentially undermine the price-sentiment limit cycle *in the short term*. In particular, the rise in open interest creates conditions where investors are overstretched and are easily induced to close their positions in response to relatively small changes in price. On the one hand, therefore, investors are unable to marshall sufficient resources to perpetuate the old trend. On the other hand, profit-taking or bear-closing may emerge quickly as prices start to reverse. Consequently, the reversal will become self-generating.

The reversal process

This is, however, only part of the process. Notice what happens as the reversal gathers pace. Investors close profitable positions and cut out losing ones. Not all of them will do so, of course, but many will. This means that open interest will either not rise or will actually *fall*. At the very least, therefore, the immediate price trend is not being confirmed. At some stage, prices will begin moving in the same direction as the old trend again, and will re-test the levels at which the market became overbought or oversold. It is this re-test which provides the true indication of the future direction for the market.

Volume and open interest during 'successful' re-tests

As we have already seen, a re-test is considered to be successful if prices are able to move into new territory. There are then four possibilities with respect to the associated movements in volume and open interest:

(a) volume *and* open interest rise into new ground;
(b) volume and open interest rise, but not into new high ground;
(c) volume rises, but open interest falls;
(d) volume *and* open interest fall.

It follows from the nature of the price-sentiment cycle that if volume and open interest both respond strongly to a successful re-test, the higher level trend remains intact. Consequently, the damage inflicted by the earlier overbought or oversold condition will have been overcome, and the price reversal will have been no more than temporary. If, however, volume and/or open interest do not manage to rise into new high ground, then a *non-confirmation* takes place (see Figure 16.1). The damage inflicted on sentiment by the initial price reversal was serious, and an important trend reversal is about to emerge. This conclusion is even more true if open interest falls during a volume non-confirmation. The implication here is that traders are taking advantage of new price levels to *close* positions. Sentiment has therefore already altered, and the subsequent price reversal will be strong. Finally, and in potentially the worst case of all, if prices move into new ground but volume *and* open interest fall, then the subsequent price reversal could be quite dramatic. The limit cycle has obviously already broken down completely, and investors are in a position to respond with vigour when a new price trend emerges.

Volume and open interest during 'unsuccessful' re-tests

In terms of the price pulse, the re-test of a previous peak is carried out by a y-wave, and the re-test of a previous low is carried out by a β-wave. By definition, sentiment during either of these waves is likely to fall short of that which occurred during the preceding impulse waves.[2] The only exception is where a higher order pulse is indeed causing the market to move steadily into new ground. This means that the implications of an *unsuccessful* re-test of a previous price high or low will be compounded by the internally weak technical position of the market. An unsuccessful re-test occurs when the y-wave fails to make a new high, or the β-wave fails to make a new low. Then there are three relevant combinations of volume and open interest:

(a) volume *and* open interest rise;
(b) volume rises, but open interest falls, or vice versa;
(c) volume *and* open interest fall.

Volume and open interest may well rise together as the sentiment of

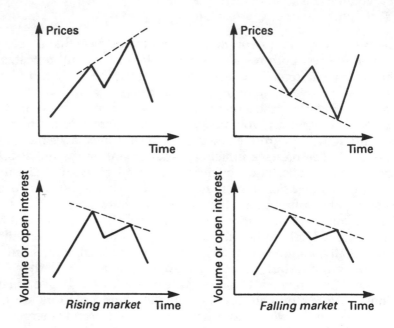

Figure 16.1. *Volume or open interest non-confirmation*

the previous trend reasserts itself. Usually, however, one or both remain subdued, and will not reach the levels attained during that trend.[3] The real clue to future price movements may, in fact, be given by the performance of open interest. If open interest falls, the evidence suggests that investors are *closing* positions. This is, of course, true whether volume is rising or falling. If investors are closing positions then the implication is that the damage done by the previous shock to the market has not been overcome. The greater is the fall in open interest, the less the market is subsequently able to cope with changes in the supply of, or demand for, stock and consequently, when an impulse wave materialises, the effect will be dramatic.

The wider implications of falling open interest

The foregoing analysis highlights the fact that *falling* open interest (particularly if accompanied by rising volume) can provide a very accurate warning of an impending *reversal* in prices. In fact, falling open interest can also warn of an impending *acceleration* in prices just after a price reversal. It is as well to be clear about the difference between the two situations. Remember that falling open interest essentially restricts the flexibility of the market: the subsequent move is likely to be large because small changes in demand or supply have a large effect on prices, and large changes in prices then induce a significant change in sentiment so that the process becomes self-generating. Table 16.1 shows the likely fluctuations in open interest during the course of a theoretical bull/bear cycle. Put bluntly, falling open interest occurs when the 'winners' are squeezing the 'losers'. Hence, generally speaking, a *sharp* fall in open interest marks the 'death' stage of the life cycle of either a bull market or a bear market. It therefore marks the *beginning* of a significant reversal. Alternatively, a *moderate* fall in open interest may mark the 'birth' stage of a new bull or bear trend. It therefore often *precedes* an acceleration into the main thrust of that trend. Figure 16.2 shows these possibilities (without taking account of high level trends) within the context of a price pulse.

Table 16.1. *The bull/bear cycle and open interest*

Prices	Open interest
1. Bear squeeze	Sharp fall
2. Re-test of low/new low	Rise, but not to new high
3. Beginning of bull	Fall
4. Bull	Rise
5. Overbought set-back	Sharp fall
6. Re-test of high/new high	Rise, but not to new high
7. Beginning of bear	Fall
8. Bear	Rise

Momentum and overextended markets

The third analytical tool which can be used to judge the internal strength of a market is a *momentum* index. Such an index is basically a measure of the speed of change of the market. The value of using a momentum measure is actually twofold. First, the price-sentiment limit cycle suggests that during the δ-wave of a rising market and the z-wave of a falling market, momentum will *accelerate*. Furthermore, momentum will be at an *extreme* at the end of these waves, and analysts use the term 'overbought' or 'oversold' to indicate these extremes. Having reached an extreme, the market should reverse itself. If the price pulse is a high level pulse, the reversal will be immediate, sharp, and long-lasting.[4] If, however, the pulse is of a lower order, the reversal will be only temporary.

Momentum and non-confirmation

Second, and if the reversal is only temporary, a momentum measure can be used to judge the strength of the renewed trend. The principle

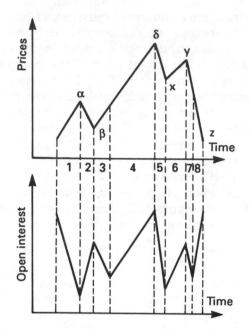

Figure 16.2. *The price pulse and open interest*

of non-confirmation relies on the idea that the momentum of a market (whether upwards or downwards) will slow appreciably during the final wave which precedes an important reversal. Indeed, this can often be seen in the form of a change in the *slope* of price movements on the price-time charts during the final wave. Momentum non-confirmations occur both because the short-term limit cycle relationship between prices and sentiment is biased (see Chapter 8), and because this limit cycle is, in any case, being gradually overridden by longer-term forces. If higher prices are unable to encourage buying, or lower prices are unable to encourage selling, a reversal may be imminent.

Measures of momentum

There are three different measures which can be used as a momentum index. The first is a simple *percentage rate of change*, where the current price is expressed as a percentage of the value of an earlier price. The 'earlier' price is always a constant time period (which may be expressed in terms of hours, days, weeks, months, etc.) away from the 'current' price. The second measure is the *deviation from a (long-term) moving average*. This index is calculated as the difference between the current price and the moving average. The moving average has a constant number of data points in it, and includes the current price as the last such data point. The third momentum measure is known as a *relative strength indicator* (RSI). This indicator, developed by Wells-Wilder in the USA, measures the relationship between the sum of the daily price increases during a given recent period (usually the last nine days) and the sum of the daily price decreases during the same period. The formula for the measure is given as

$$\text{Current RSI} = 100 - \cfrac{100}{1 + \cfrac{\text{Sum of positive changes}}{\text{Sum of negative changes}}}$$

If the sum of all the *positive* changes during the chosen time period is zero, the ratio in the denominator is also assumed to be zero. However, if the sum of the *negative* changes is zero, the ratio in the denominator is assumed to be equal to the sum of the positive changes (ie the sum of the negative changes is assumed to be unity).

Rates of change

Each of the different momentum measures has its own advantages and disadvantages. The percentage rate of change index, for example, is certainly very easy to calculate. Furthermore, it is possible both to utilise indicators with very short time periods (such as five days) to isolate the momentum of lower degree price pulses, and to use measures with long time periods (such as twelve months) to analyse higher degree pulses. In order to obtain some idea of what constitutes overbought and oversold, however, it is necessary to have a long history available. Extremes of momentum can then easily be determined by inspection (see Figure 16.3).

Deviations fom a moving average

The use of deviations from a moving average is almost as popular. We shall be looking at some of the other implications of moving averages in Chapter 18, but in the meantime it need only be said that moving averages are used as a proxy for the market trend. The theory behind using the deviation from the moving average implicitly relies on the fact that lower degree price pulses cannot deviate too dramatically from the trend imposed by higher degree pulses. Consequently, it is possible to test the historic data to find out what constitutes overbought or oversold. Furthermore, a narrowing of the deviation when the market reaches new highs or new lows is taken to mean a reduction in the power of the lower degree pulse *vis-á-vis* the (gradually reversing) higher degree pulse.

Although the system works reasonably well, it is not without its imperfections. Specifically, the calculated value of a moving average applies to the data at the mid-point of the time period over which it is calculated. Consequently, it is not possible to know the 'correct' value of a moving average which is applicable to *today* until some time in the future. The system actually works partly because of the idiosyncracies of the moving average technique itself. The moving average will *lag*

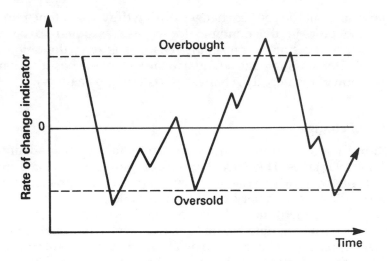

Figure 16.3. *Overbought and oversold momentum*

the current price quite significantly. Hence overbought and oversold conditions occur simply because the moving average has not 'caught up', and non-confirmations occur simply because slowly-moving final waves actually do allow the moving average to catch up. The moving average system does not, therefore, necessarily say anything useful about the relationships between different levels of the price pulse.

The relative strength index

The beauty of the Wells-Wilder RSI, on the other hand, is that it requires only a very short history, needs no testing to find out what constitutes overbought or oversold, and is easy to present graphically. The RSI can oscillate only between values of 0 and 100. Generally speaking, if the value is 20 or less then the market is likely to be oversold; if the value is 80 or more, the market is likely to be overbought. The RSI is also well suited to establishing divergences at market troughs and peaks. When testing for peaks, the momentum high at the top of the δ-wave should be achieved with an RSI of 80 or more. The market will then correct for the overbought condition, and the RSI will fall. Prices and the RSI will both subsequently rise again, as the y-wave (the Elliott fifth wave) comes into force. Prices will move into new high ground but the RSI will not (see Figure 16.4). The same argument applies in reverse, of course, when testing for market lows. The momentum low, usually at the end of a z-wave, should be achieved with an RSI of 20 or less. The market will then correct for the oversold condition, and both prices and the RSI will rise. The subsequent price fall will take the market to a new low, but that new low will not be confirmed by the RSI (see Figure 16.4).

It has to be remembered, however, that the RSI is essentially a short-term trading tool. Hence, a nine-day RSI implicitly assumes that it is unusual for a market to move in one direction for more than eight consecutive trading days. It is nevertheless worth checking the historical data to ensure that uni-directional movements of eight days or more are indeed uncommon. If necessary, the RSI can be calculated using longer time periods.

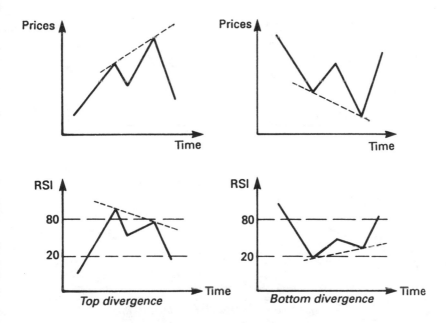

Figure 16.4. *RSI divergences*

Momentum trading rules

Whichever method is used to track momentum – whether it be rates of change, deviations from a moving average, or the RSI – there are three important rules which should be borne in mind. The first is that markets can remain overbought for quite a *long* period of time. As we have already observed, fear of missing further profits (ie greed) takes time to dissipate. Traders should not therefore react solely to an overbought condition unless there are *other* grounds for supposing that a reaction is imminent. Errors can be avoided by waiting until the price level and momentum have both started to fall from their overbought level. Second, markets tend to remain oversold for relatively *short* periods of time, because the fear of making losses tends to trigger swift corrective action. Hence, purchases based on oversold criteria will usually yield a profit.[5] Third, and most importantly, non-confirmation of new price highs or new price lows *only* occurs when prices themselves (and therefore the momentum index) actually start to reverse. Many analysts make the mistake of assuming that because prices have moved into new territory while momentum has not, a price reversal is imminent. It is, in fact, often true that either the non-confirmation persists for an extended period of time, or that momentum eventually catches up with the market (see Figure 16.5).

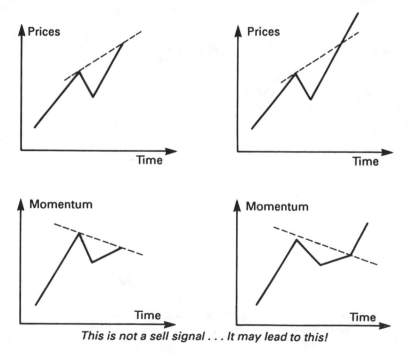

This is not a sell signal . . . It may lead to this!

Figure 16.5. *Incorrect non-confirmation*

The advance-decline index

The final set of indices is the auxiliary indices. These are used to estimate the extent to which all stocks, or all sections of the market, are participating in a trend. There are two basic auxiliary indices which can be used. The first is an index which is constructed from the daily figures for the number of stocks which have *advanced* in relation to the number of stocks which have *declined*. The most popular method of construction is simply to add the net daily advances to, or deduct the net daily declines from, a cumulative figure. the resulting index is known as the 'cumulative advance/decline indicator', or the A/D line. Obviously, such figures are not readily available for all markets, but they are available for stock markets in both the UK and the US. Since they relate to the *total* number of stocks being traded in the market, they readily provide a good proxy for the internal strength of the market. Hence if a market price index moves into new ground, but the A/D line does not follow suit, then there is a strong suggestion that trading activity is becoming too speculative and that not all stocks are participating in the movement. Such a non-confirmation does not necessarily mean that it is wrong to participate in the market, but it does mean that the life expectancy of the movement may be limited [6] and that it could be followed by relatively severe setback.

A second price index

The alternative type of auxiliary index involves the use of a *second* price index. This second index must, however, consist of stocks which are entirely different from those included in the primary index. Hence in the fixed interest markets, for example, a short-term (interest rate related) bond index may be used to complement a long bond index; in the US stock market, the Dow Jones Transportation Index may be used to complement the Dow Jones Industrial Index; in the gold market, the price of gold itself may be used to complement a gold mining share index. In all cases, it is reasonable to expect that if a trend is developing in a healthy fashion, both primary and secondary indices should perform together. A divergence between the two indices suggests that a reversal might be imminent.

The principle of direct confirmation: the Dow Theory

This chapter has so far covered the basic notion that *non*-confirmation provides a useful warning of an imminent reversal. The final stage of the analysis is to see how technical indicators can be used to *confirm* directly the validity of buy and sell signals based on price patterns.

The first technique, which involves the use of an auxiliary price index, was first introduced by Charles Dow.[7] Dow likened movements in the market to the behaviour of the sea: the primary trend in the market corresponds to the direction of the tide, the secondary reactions and rallies are the waves, and the movements of lesser degree are the ripples on the waves. The fundamental tenet of the Dow Theory is that, since two stock indices are part of the same 'ocean', the tidal action of one must be reflected in the tidal action of the other. The second tenet of the Theory is that a bull market is formed of a series of rising peaks and rising troughs, while a bear market is formed of falling peaks and falling troughs. Hence, a bull market is not signalled until both primary *and* secondary indices conform to the bull market pattern, and a bear market is not signalled until both indices conform to the bear market pattern. This is shown in Figure 16.6.

The main criticism of the Dow Theory is that the signals it provides are very late. Yet the signals are usually very accurate: first, an apparent reversal in only one index is often aborted if it is not confirmed by the other; second, a confirmed buy or sell signal is invariably correct.

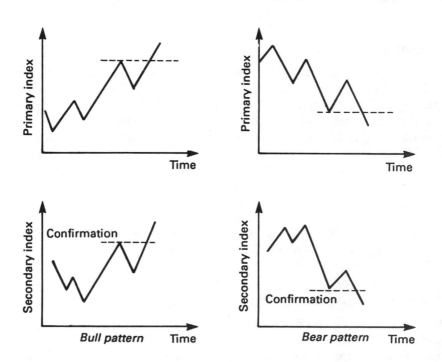

Figure 16.6. *The Dow Theory*

The principle of direct confirmation: other indices

Similar conclusions can be derived from the use of sentiment indicators. If volume, open interest and/or momentum start to confirm a price movement immediately *after* a price reversal, the reversal is likely to be important. In particular, a sharp change in momentum (to the extent of either becoming very overbought or very oversold very quickly), strongly suggests that the limit cycle relating prices to sentiment has reversed. We shall analyse the reasons why this should be so in Chapter 18.

Conclusion

Let us now summarise the conclusions of this chapter. The limit cycle relationship between prices and sentiment postulates that a price trend is essentially intact while sentiment is reflecting that trend and while the majority of stocks are participating in that trend. Sentiment may be represented by a number of different analytical tools, of which the most popular are volume, open interest and momentum. Hence a trend is intact while all these indicators are still increasing. Such changes are *beneficial*: increasing dealing activity and accelerating momentum (whether up or down) are healthy indications of profits being taken, of bad positions being closed and of new positions being opened. Sooner or later, however, the sentiment indicators will reach excessive levels (often in a surge) which cannot be sustained. Such changes are *adverse*: prices will need to undergo a correction as the overbought or oversold conditions are unwound.

Corrections may be either a temporary contra-trend correction, or they may be the first stage of a more serious reversal pattern. In either case the price levels associated with the overbought or oversold condition will always be re-tested to some degree. If the re-test is successful, then the original trend will remain intact only insofar as volume, open interest and momentum are able to respond. If, on the other hand, the re-test is unsuccessful, the market is potentially very vulnerable to a reversal. Hence, either a non-confirmed successful re-test, or an unsuccessful re-test, becomes the second stage of the reversal process. The third stage is a dramatic thrust in the direction of the new trend.

These conclusions will cover the majority of situations which investors will meet. There are, however, three other techniques which can be used to ensure against major errors. First, remember that volume and open interest are essentially *short*-term indicators. It is therefore useful to track at least one long-term indicator. Second, financial markets respond to Fibonacci influences and tend to reverse when these influences come into effect; Fibonacci analyses may be used to confirm the conclusions from other methods. Third, the impact of limit cycles implies that markets contain a rhythmic beat within their oscillation mechanisms. Cycle analyses may therefore be used to pinpoint the moments in time when excesses of sentiment may be expected to occur. It is therefore to the concepts of Fibonacci reversals and time cycles to which we now turn.

Notes

1. An alternative measure is the ratio of puts to calls in the options market. A high ratio reflects a large percentage of open bear positions, and a low ratio reflects a large percentage of open bull positions. The analysis of this chapter can be applied to the put:call ratio
2. If the re-test is unsuccessful, the concept of non-confirmation does not apply.
3. There is an important point here which is often missed. Volume and open interest analysis is only applicable to relatively short-term market conditions. It is possible therefore to pinpoint long-term reversals only because of an accurate interpretation of the short-term. It is *not* valid to compare today's open interest or volume with that which occurred (say) two years ago. The market structure is likely to alter over such a time period.
4. For example, cyclical lows in the Dow Jones Industrial Averages in 1932, 1942, 1949, 1957, 1962, 1966, 1970, 1974, 1978 and 1980 occurred simultaneously with momentum lows. See Robert R. Prechter, *The Elliott Wave Theorist*, May 1982. However, it should be added that this does not mean that the low will never be re-tested. The influence of a large cycle just means that the re-test occurs after such a significant time period that it cannot be used for short-term trading.
5. It is necessary here to be very aware of the relevant degree of pulse which is being traded. If a high level uptrend is in force, the trader should ignore short-term overbought conditions and buy short-term oversold conditions; conversely for a high-level downtrend.
6. Limited, that is, within the context of the hierarchical level being analysed. The last wave of a supercycle pulse may remain unconfirmed for years.
7. See Robert Rhea, *Dow Theory*. Vail-Ballou, Bingham, NY, 1932.

17.

Natural Reversal Points

Introduction
One of the most striking aspects of financial markets – and, in some ways, the most important evidence of the existence of 'natural' laws in the unfolding of crowd behaviour – is the presence of mathematical relationships between price movements. These relationships exist in the dimensions of both price *and* time. In this Chapter we shall discuss the nature of the relationship between the *extent* of price movements. In the next Chapter, we shall turn to the influence of *time*.

The spiral hypothesis
It will be remembered from Chapter 10 that price objectives can be calculated with reference to the 'second' wave of a reversal pattern – that is, with reference to either the β-wave or the y-wave of a price pulse. We deduced that the functional ratio was 2.618. It is appropriate therefore that we now discuss Fibonacci influences in more detail in order to present a complete picture of the relevant methods of calculating objectives.

The first point to make is that, while the ratio 2.618 is the most important ratio, it can in fact only be used to provide a *probability estimate* of the price objective. The main difficulty is that impulse waves may be damped or extended by the influence of higher level trends. However, even here, it seems to be a feature of nature that Fibonacci influences still dominate because cycles are mathematically related to one another. What happens is that when a higher level trend *counteracts* the impulse wave, then the appropriate ratio for calculating the subsequent objective is 1.618; while if the higher level trend *complements* the impulse wave, then the appropriate ratio is 4.236 – that is, $(1.618)^3$. We thus have three potential targets from β-waves and y-waves: one based on 1.618, one based on $(1.618)^2$, and one based on $(1.618)^3$. The possibilities in a rising market are demonstrated in Figure 17.1 below. Similar calculations can be made for a falling market.

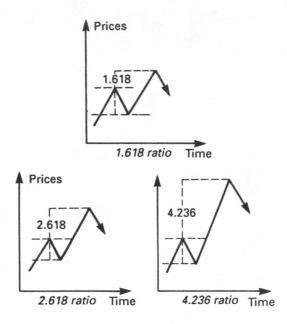

Figure 17.1. *Fibonacci targets for impulse waves*

The 1.618 formula

It is possible to illustrate these variations on the basic formula with some important examples. The first relates to the rally which took place in the 90-day US Treasury bill futures contract during 1981 and 1982 (see Figure 17.2). The rally had three phases. The first lasted from August to November 1981 and the second (the downwave) lasted into February 1982. The third and final phase, then took the market to a high in October 1982. This third phase was exactly 1.618 times the second wave.

The 2.618 formula

The next example involves the extent of the rise in Sterling against the Dollar during the second half of 1987 (see Figure 17.3). Overall, the rally extended from October 1986 to April 1988. However, between May and August 1987 Sterling fell by $0.13, as measured by the IMM nearby Sterling futures contract. The subsequent target was therefore for a (2.618 × 0.13 =) $0.34 rally, to $1.90. This objective was almost reached in December 1987, and was finally achieved in April 1988.

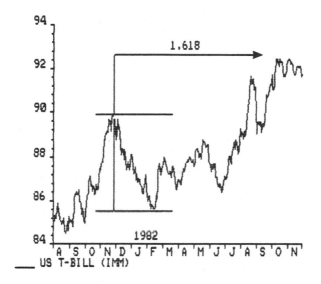

Source : Datastream

Figure 17.2. *The 1.618 formula*

The 4.236 formula

The final example (see Figure 17.4) involves the 1981 bear market in UK Treasury bonds (gilts). During the Spring of 1981, the market rallied by 2.6 points (or 38 per cent) as measured by the Government Securities Index. Multiplying the extent of this rally by 4.236 gave a potential fall of 16 per cent. This target was achieved at the bear market low in October 1981.

Further examples

Obviously these examples have been specifically chosen to highlight the argument, but a brief survey of charts of any financial market will quickly reveal numerous other examples. Figure 17.5 shows a wide variety from different markets.

Source : Datastream

Figure 17.3. *The 2.618 formula*

Source : Datastream

Figure 17.4 *The 4.236 formula*

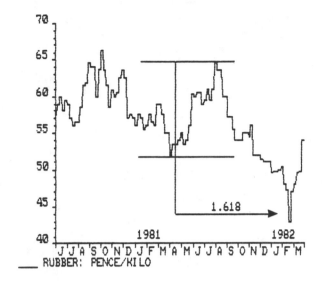

Source : Datastream

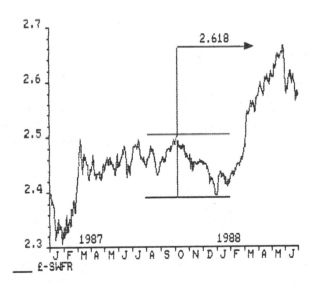

Source : Datastream

Figure 17.5(a). *The 1.618, 2.618 formulae*

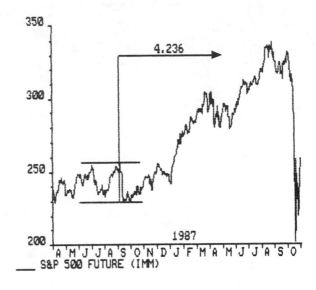

Source : Datastream

Figure 17.5(b). *The 4.236 formulae*

Fibonacci retracement targets

In addition to targets for impulse waves, Fibonacci numbers can also be used in calculating potential *retracement* targets. The seminal work on retracements was conducted in the 1930s and 1940s both by Elliott[2] (as part of his analysis of the 5-3 Wave Principle), and by the eminent US stock and commodity trader William D. Gann[3]. We have already addressed the implications of some of Elliott's work in Chapters 14 and 15, and pointed out how complex it was in its original form. Gann's work is also difficult to understand as it was originally presented. However, as in the case of Elliott, it can be shown that the theoretical basis of Gann's findings is the operation of natural systems. We have analysed some of Gann's techniques in Appendix 1.

The one-third/two-thirds retracement rule

Elliott and Gann both discovered that, following an impulse move either upwards or downwards, a contra-trend movement (or even a trend reversal) would encounter support and resistance at specific points. Gann found that these points were related to the original impulse move by one or more of the fractions in the series:

1/8, 1/4, 3/8, 1/2, 5/8, 3/4, 7/8, 1

Let us take a simple example. The rally in the gilt-edged market from January 1975 to September 1977 covered 31 points in the Government Securities Index, and peaked at a level of approximately 80 on that index. Gann's important support levels can be calculated as follows: first, multiply the extent of the rally by each ratio in the 1/8 series shown above; second, deduct each resulting number from the rally peak of 80. The final results (with all calculations rounded up) are shown in Table 17.1 and are reproduced in graph form in Figure 17.6.

Table 17.1. *Gann support during bear market 1977-1981*

Calculation	Comment
$80 - (31 \times 0.125) = 76$	Minor support after September peak
$80 - (31 \times 0.25) = 72$	Not important
$80 - (31 \times 0.375) = 68$	*Support during 1978*
$80 - (31 \times 0.5) = 65$	*Major support in February 1979*
$80 - (31 \times 0.625) = 61$	*Major low in October 1981*
$80 - (31 \times 0.75) = 57$	Not achieved
$80 - (31 \times 0.875) = 53$	Not achieved

As it turns out, not all of Gann's support/resistance levels were effective in this particular example (although it is always worthwhile looking for them). The important feature of the example, however, is that those levels which were effective are also particularly significant. Note that, in our example of the 1977-1981 bear market in gilts, the important support levels were achieved at levels which were 3/8, 1/2, and 5/8 of the preceding bull run. Hence, Gann's ratios certainly confirm the old stock market adage that a bear market retraces between one-third and two-thirds of the rise that preceded it! However, it is far from accidental that the numbers 3/8 and 5/8 are very close approximations of the Fibonacci ratios 0.382 and 0.618. The important implication is that corrections have 'natural' Fibonacci limits. This, indeed, is exactly what Elliott found.

The natural constraints on reversals

Given our analysis in previous chapters, it is now possible to deduce why the Gann/Elliott/Fibonacci retracement targets should be important. Remember that financial market patterns are based on the operation of the logarithmic spiral. The spiral is indicative of progress: it is associated

Source : Datastream

Figure 17.6. *The gilt-edged market 1976-1981*

with the *irreversibility* of change, and hence with learning and evolution through time. After receiving a shock and moving to a new hierarchical structure, a system must introduce constraints on its ability to regress. Otherwise natural structures would essentially be static rather than dynamic.

So it is with financial markets. If an information shock of sufficient power creates (for example) a bull market which lasts for a number of years, then the ability of the market to return to its starting point must become increasingly limited as the bull move 'progresses' or evolves. Contra-trend information shocks cannot significantly influence the thrust of the main trend. Some regression will be tolerated, but will not be allowed to become dominant. It is as if the market 'knows' that there are levels to which it cannot return. Consequently, prices will respond to fundamental trends, and will respond to contra-trend 'technical' factors, but they will not respond to fundamental trends that do not exist. Hence if prices are rising because fundamentals are improving – and are expected to improve, and indeed *do* improve – then prices will not suddenly start to discount Armageddon!

All evolving structures carry a record of their history in whatever it is that constitutes their 'memory' (ie in their mind, and/or their genes),[4] and they therefore 'know' where the last set of boundaries has been established. In financial markets such 'knowledge' is reflected in the tacit recognition of the *limitations* which are imposed on corrective movements. In particular, the evidence suggests that a corrective phase during any given trend is usually related to the impulse wave which preceded it either by the ratio 0.382 or (less frequently) by the ratio 0.618. The limits (or targets) set by nature are therefore even more precise than is implied by the stock market adage concerning the one-third/two-thirds retracement.

The correction relative to trend

On the basis of what has already been said in this and preceding chapters, it follows that the extent of any retracement depends on the position of the correction in relation to the higher level trend. In the early stages of a bull run, for example, a contra-trend shock will be able to excite bearish sentiment because the bullish and bearish crowds are still in open conflict. The correction is therefore likely to be quite deep. In the later stages of a bull run, however, contra-trend shocks cannot easily stimulate such sentiment because of a deeper commitment to fundamentals. The correction is likely to be relatively shallow. This has two implications. First, 0.618 retracements may be expected shortly *after* a trend reversal (this is the basis of one of the most profitable trading rule which an investor can use – see Chapter 20). Second, 0.382 retracements are likely to occur late in a trend and *prior* to the eventual trend reversal point. Furthermore, the evidence suggests that 0.618 retracements may be overshot or undershot, but that 0.382 retracements are likely to be met precisely. These observations are illustrated in Figure 17.7 below where the extent of each correction is related to the impulse wave which preceded it by one of the two Fibonacci ratios. It should, incidentally, now be clear why we used the 0.382/0.618 range when calculating the Fibonacci targets from the head-and-shoulders formations in Chapter 13.

The 0.382 and 0.618 ratios in practice

It is very easy to demonstrate the existence of these two Fibonacci ratios in the bond and equity markets. A number of excellent examples can be found in the history of the last ten years. In the case of the US T-Bond futures market, the 1986-1987 bear market retraced 0.382 of the 1981-1986 bull market. In the case of the US equity market, the 1976-1978 bear market in the Dow Jones Industrial Average retraced 0.618 of the 1974-1976 bull run. Elsewhere, in the UK gilt market, the 1982-1984 sell-off retraced exactly 0.382 of the 1982 bull run, and the 1977-1981 bear market retraced exactly 0.618 of the 1975-1977 rally.

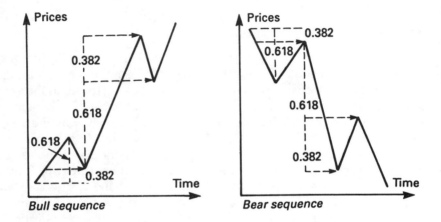

Figure 17.7. *Corrective phases*

Natural support and resistance

The idea that a market imposes implicit constraints on itself during the generation of a trend can obviously be applied to all levels of the hierarchy of trends. This may be done in two ways. First, the market will 'remember' the natural constraints which have created reversal points in previous trends. This is one of the reasons why a market will turn again at exactly the same level as it did many years previously – it is not the reappearance of ancient fund managers who have been sitting on a losing trade for twenty years and are finally managing to get out at cost! The market has established its own natural reversal points (see Figure 17.8). Second, a market will resist at 0.382 and 0.618 retracements of the *previous* trend, because the market cannot always be certain that a totally new structure is appropriate. The market is continually assimilating new information and testing old barriers. The process of moving to a new trend therefore always involves the breaking of old Fibonacci constraints.

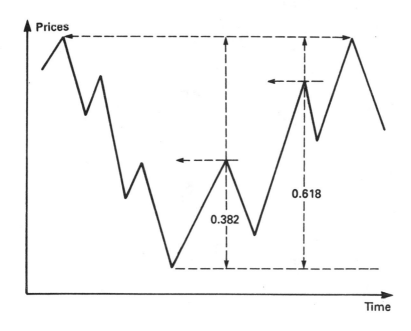

Figure 17.8. *Natural support and resistance*

Natural support and resistance levels in practice

Good examples of these phenomena have occurred in recent years (see Figure 17.9). First, in late 1982, and again in late 1986, the IMM 90-Day US Treasury bill futures contract turned away from levels that had previously represented important turning points. Second, during the bull phase in the gilt market which followed the 1972-1975 collapse, prices hesitated significantly at Fibonacci calculated levels.

Natural numbers in support and resistance

We thus owe Gann and Elliott a great deal in our understanding of how support and resistance levels can be generated using natural ratios. However, both found that natural numbers also have other applications. Gann, for example, used two other techniques to determine potential price objectives. The first was the explicit psychological effect that certain numbers can have on a crowd. Gann found that if certain numbers were included in a price, and a reversal was due, the price itself could act as a trigger. Gann's system actually allowed for a larger variety of numbers

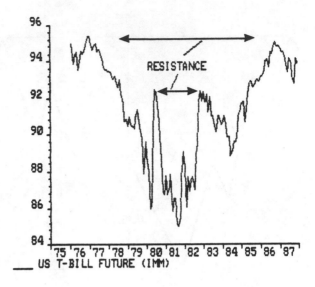

Source : Datastream

Source : Datastream

Figure 17.9. *Natural price constraints*

than those included in the Fibonacci series. However, we can find Fibonacci-related examples without too much trouble: the nearby long-dated US Treasury bond future reached an historical low at a price of 55 in September 1981, and the Deutschemark reached a secular high of 144 against the Japanese Yen in November 1979.

The second technique, which was employed by Elliott as well as by Gann, related to the *extent* of price movements. They found that if a price movement (whether measured in absolute or percentage terms) matched a number in a natural number series then a reversal could be triggered. It is fair to say that Gann's own number sets do not appear to be applicable to broad financial indices. However, if Fibonacci numbers are used, the problem is partly resolved. Indeed, it is not an overstate-ment to say that a price movement of any degree will accord to a Fibonacci number (or to an explicit multiple or derivative[5]) if at all possible. The FT Government Securities Index fell by 34 points between early 1972 and early 1975. Other examples (see Figure 17.10) include the 0.34 pfennig rise in the Deutschemark futures contract between 1985 and 1988, and the 3.82 fall in the US 90-day Treasury Bill futures contract between 1983 and 1984.

Similar Fibonacci calculations can be conducted in percentage terms. For example (see Figure 17.11) the nearby futures contract on the Commodities Research Bureau (CRB) price index rose by 21 per cent between March 1988 and June 1988, and the IMM three-month Eurodollar future rose by 13% between February 1982 and August 1986. The most stunning example of all, however, was the exact 38.2% fall in both the FTSE 100 Index and the FT30 Industrial Index during the 'crash' of October/November 1987. This technique is, indeed, very powerful.

Conclusion

In this manner, Gann and Elliott were able to isolate *constraints* on prices which would be effective for trading purposes. Generally speaking, future performance was (partly) related to past history. However, this is not the end of the story. Both analysts firmly believed that stock prices are subject to *rhythmic* fluctuations. Their basic view (which found the more complete expression in Gann's work) was that price reversals were to be expected when a particular trend had been intact for given 'natural' periods of time. Let us therefore now turn to the influence of time.

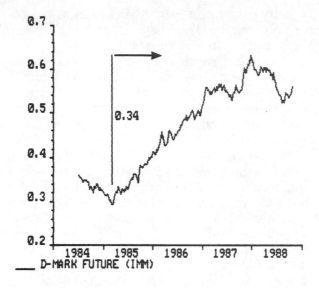

Source : Datastream

Source : Datastream

Figure 17.10. *Fibonacci numbers in absolute price movements*

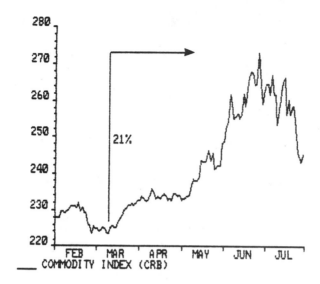

Source : Datastream

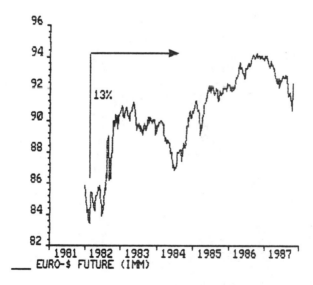

Source : Datastream

Figure 17.11(a). *Fibonacci numbers in percentage price movements*

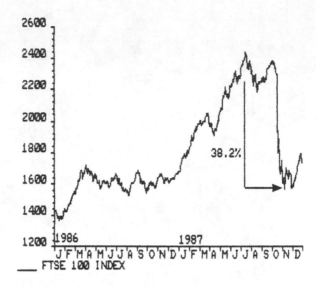

Source : Datastream

Figure 17.11(b). *Fibonacci numbers in percentage price movements*

Notes

1. Note the presence of the Fibonacci ratios 2.618 and 0.382.
2. See Ralph N. Elliott, *Nature's Law. The Secret Of The Universe.* Elliott, New York, 1946. Reprinted in Robert R. Prechter (Ed.), *The Major Works Of R. N. Elliott.* New Classics Library, New York, 1980.
3. See, for example, William D. Gann, *How To Make Profits In Commodities.* Lambert-Gann, Pomeroy, Washington, 1942.
4. See Erich Jantsch, *The Self-Organising Universe.* Pergamon, Oxford, 1980.
5. Explicit multiples and derivatives of the Fibonacci ratios include 3.82, 38.2, 6.18, 61.8, 1.382, 13.82, 1.618, 16.18, 2.382, 23.82, 2.618, 26.18 etc. They also include √5=2.236.

18.

The Use of Time Cycle Analysis

Introduction

The important point about time cycles is that their presence makes it possible to *anticipate* when the next turning point is likely to occur. Since a financial market crowd is a natural dynamic system, and since such a system exhibits *rhythmic* oscillations, it follows that cycles exist in financial markets. Therefore, it also follows that it should be possible to predict the timing of price reversals.

The relationship between cycles

Because cycles are natural phenomena, they obey certain natural laws. The first of these is that the cycles *harmonise* with one another. This harmony can either involve cycles fluctuating in synchrony with one another (such as the activity/rest cycle and the day/night solar cycle) or it can involve cycles being mathematically related to one another (such as in the case of the vibrations which make musical notes). In this way cycles integrate and co-ordinate so that the total energy being used by any overall system is conserved, and the shocks being transmitted around the system are minimised. From this follows the next law: that there is only a relatively *limited* number of cycles. If there was an infinite number, there would effectively be chaos rather than order because the cycles would conflict with one another. The final law, which follows from the other two, is that cycles which are found in one area of nature will invariably be found elsewhere in nature.[1]

The limited number of periodicities

Overall, these laws mean that the oscillations in nature may be represented by a relatively limited list of periodicities. This, indeed, was one of the findings of W. D. Gann (see Appendix 1). He deduced the existence of a series of number *sets* which could be used to define cycle periodicities. He found that if a particular date in the future was related to the date of *three* or more earlier turning points by time periods derived from one of his number sets, then that future date was likely to represent a turning point. Obviously, turning points would harmonise with one another.

There are therefore two sources of information regarding cycle periodicities in markets. The first of these is the known rhythms which exist in nature. The second is a direct analysis of any price-time series, using statistical methods, to ascertain the cycles which are actually operating in a particular market. The results can then be 'cross-checked' by reference to other cycles in other time series.

The presence of Fibonacci numbers in cycles

It is beyond the scope of this book to delve into the link between natural rhythms and oscillations in financial markets, although the theoretical possibilities cannot be ignored. We shall concentrate here on the technique of direct investigation. Before doing so, however, it is worthwhile commenting on the fact that Fibonacci numbers are frequently to be found in the elapsed time between price reversals. This was found by both Elliott and Gann, and is further confirmation – if any was needed – of the central importance of the Fibonacci Sequence to natural systems.

There are in fact two 'types' of influence in this context. The first is that a price reversal is likely to occur once a *lengthy* Fibonacci-defined time period has elapsed since an earlier important turning point. Hence, we might expect a reversal 55 days (or 55 weeks or 55 months or even 55 years) from a previous turning point. For example, the Summer 1987 equity market peak occurred 55 years after the 1932 Great Depression low. The second 'type' of Fibonacci influence occurs when three or more Fibonacci-defined time periods coincide after previous reversals. The only constraint here is that the time periods must all be defined in terms of the same units (for example, weeks, months or years). Again, a conjunction of Fibonacci time periods occurred at the equity peak of Summer 1987 (see Chapter 20). It is important, therefore, to keep a close eye on the passage of time defined in terms of Fibonacci units.

The direct search for time cycles

With respect to a *direct* search for cycles, there are a number of statistical methods which can be used. Some of them (such as spectral analysis) are very sophisticated and very accurate, but require the use of computers. Others (such as measuring the distances between successive low or high points) are very simple and can be implemented very quickly but they are obviously less reliable. There is, however, one method which is both relatively simple and reasonably accurate. The method involves two tools used in combination, namely deviations from a 'centred' moving average, and some form of rate-of-change indicator.

Deviations from centred moving averages

The use of deviations from a centred moving average is actually the traditional way of measuring cyclical fluctuations,[2] and the passage of time has done very little to undermine its essential usefulness. The basic analysis consists of two parts: first, the data in the time series is *smoothed* by calculating an arithmetic moving average series of that data; second, each number from the original series is divided by the appropriate average from the moving average series.[3] In this context, the appropriate average is the one which contains the original number as its *middle* term.[4] The result of this procedure is that the analyst has access both to a *trend* (determined by the moving average) and to a series of de-trended *fluctuations* (calculated as deviations from the moving average). If the measured period from trough to trough (or from peak to peak) in the fluctuations is constant, then a cycle is present in the data. The cycle can then be used to *predict* reversal points.

These basic procedures are shown in Figure 18.1: the top part of the diagram shows the raw data, the middle part shows the calculated moving average and the lower part shows the result of dividing the raw data by the moving average. This latter shows fluctuations with a *fixed* periodicity.

The length of the moving average

There are three points worth making here. First, in deciding on the optimum period for the moving average, it is important that the number of terms from which the average is calculated is *at least as large*[5] as the number of data points in a complete cycle. Hence, if a seven-week cycle exists in prices, the moving average should ideally be a seven-week moving average. The reason for this is quite straightforward. Oscillations derived from a limit cycle process will be very evenly distributed around a higher order trend. The total value of the

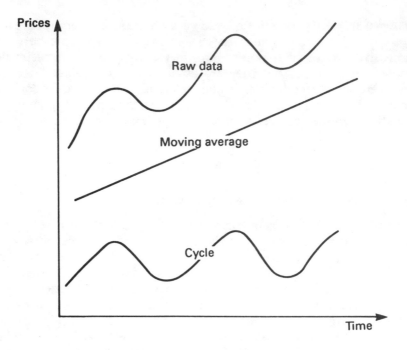

Figure 18.1. *Calculating the presence of cycles*

divergences from the trend, as measured from one low point of the cycle to the next, should be zero. Hence, a correctly specified moving average will be a perfect representation of the trend.

The presence of multiple cycles

The second point to note when de-trending a data series using moving averages is that *more than one* cycle can be present in a given time series. When searching for cycles, it is often useful to start the process with a short-term average which will damp down short-term cycles and thereby reveal the longer-term ones. Ultimately, however, it is best to use as long an average as possible. Indeed, an average which is derived from the lowest common multiple of the cycles being tracked, will eliminate them all. For example, cycles of three, five and ten weeks will be eliminated by using a 30-week average.

The importance of centred averages

The third point is that it is essential to concentrate on the term in the *centre* of the group from which the moving average is calculated. The trend at any given point in time is calculated from the data generated both before *and* after that point in time. This obviously presents the problem of a lack of immediacy when tracking cycles in 'real' time. In essence it is only possible to confirm that a cycle occurred in the past — it is not possible (using moving averages) to confirm that the low or high of a cycle is occurring in the present. Many analysts attempt to surmount this problem by using the time-honoured, but incorrect, technique of dividing the *most-recent* data point[6] from the moving average. It is therefore automatically assumed that the most recent trend will persist into the future. Such assumptions are not only false, but are also misleading. Indeed, they are at odds with the *raison d'être* of the analysis in the first place.

Some problems with cycle analysis

Moving average techniques are a simple and effective way of eliminating trends, and of thereby isolating the presence of specific cycles in a price-time series. It is true that a (sometimes lengthy) process of trial and error may be required in the early stages of the analysis in order to isolate the dominant cycles. However, it is also true that a visual scanning of graphs, and the measuring of the periods between important reversal points with a ruler, may provide very strong evidence of particular cycles. This nevertheless still leaves unresolved the problem of tracking the cycles as they develop. This might not matter so much except that there are a number of specific problems with cycle analysis, no matter what techniques are used to isolate the cycles.

The first problem is that a measured cycle may, in fact, be a composite of two cycles with periodicities which differ only slightly. As Edward Dewey has shown,[7] two cycles may start off in phase, but sooner or later they diverge from one another before eventually cancelling each other out. Consequently, the measured cycle disappears.

Another problem is that even the most comprehensive search for cycles may miss long-term rhythms which were not previously covered by the available data. Any analytical process based on cycles therefore needs a control system to warn the analyst that longer-term cycles may indeed be asserting an influence.

A further problem is that no matter how strong is the evidence for a *precise* rhythm to a particular cycle, there is always the possibility that the cycle may turn earlier or later than experience would predict. This is because the limit cycle relationships which yield rhythmic processes are inevitably subject to discontinuities. Indeed, it is sometimes better to specify a *period* of time (sometimes referred to as a 'time window'), rather than a *specific* date, during which a cyclical reversal can be expected. Hence, for example, a 39-month cycle might be expected to reverse during the period between the 38th month and the 40th month[8] since the last turning point.

The use of a momentum index

Each of these problems may be resolved to a large degree by the use of a *second* analytical tool which can be used to track a particular cycle in 'real time'. This tool is a short-term momentum indicator, which measures the rate of change in prices per unit of time. The nature and time period of such a momentum indicator is a matter of personal preference. Ideally, a percentage change indicator should be used, since a 10 point move in the market means something different if the base is 25 points rather than 100 points. However, some analysts use a simple difference, calculated by subtracting one term in the data series from another. The time period involved should be as short as is convenient, but in any case no more than 25 per cent of the length of the cycle(s) being tracked. Hence, for a cycle lasting 20 days or more a five-day rate of change should be adequate, while for a cycle lasting eight days a two-day rate of change should suffice. A general analysis of momentum indicators was presented in Chapter 15 where they are discussed in the context of price *patterns*.

Momentum and the cycle

The value of a momentum indicator lies in the fact that it can provide a good indication of the status of a cycle. There is a very good theoretical reason for this. Figure 18.2(a) shows the position of a regular cycle with respect to time. Note that the slope of the cycle varies with the stage of the cycle. At point A the slope is flat, because the cycle is in the process of reversing; at point B the slope is steep and downward (or negative); at C the slope is flat again; and at D the slope is steep and upward (or positive). Now, the steepness of the curve represents the rate at which the position changes. It is the *velocity* of the cycle, and is known to mathematicians as the first differential of the cycle with respect to time. This velocity is shown in Figure 18.2(b) below. The important point to notice is that the resulting curve is the same shape as that of the basic cycle, but that it is displaced a quarter cycle *back* from the basic cycle.

The analysis can be taken a stage further, however. The slope of the velocity curve represents the rate at which velocity is changing: that is, it represents the *acceleration* of the basic cycle. Mathematicians call this the second differential of the cycle with respect to time. This acceleration is shown in Figure 18.2(c). Note that the new cycle is displaced a quarter cycle back from the velocity cycle, and is therefore a half-cycle back from the basic cycle. As a result, the acceleration cycle is exactly opposite the basic cycle.

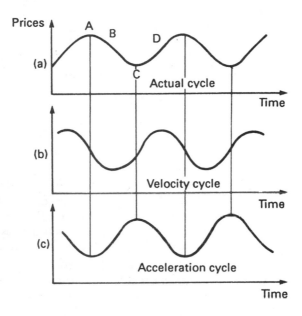

Figure 18.2. *Time cycles and momentum*

Tracking the cycle

This simple relationship between absolute prices, velocity and acceleration gives us access to some important information concerning the current status of any particular cycle. First, we obviously have a direct method of tracking the basic cycle. A 'spike' in momentum will occur a quarter-cycle *ahead* of the actual price cycle. Hence such a spike *forecasts* the timing of the absolute turning point. If we are tracking a 3.25-year cycle, and an 'oversold' reading occurs in the rate of change indicator, we can accurately predict that the absolute low in the price cycle will occur approximately 42 weeks (a quarter of the 3.25-year cycle) later. As a corollary, of course, the time lapse between the point when a market becomes 'oversold' (or 'overbought'), and the point where a reversal in the absolute price level occurs, can be used to calculate the periodicity of a *new* cycle.

Velocity and non-confirmation

Second, the relationship between absolute prices and velocity helps to explain the idea of 'non-confirmation'. It is apparent from Figure 18.2 that upward momentum is going to be weakening at price cycle highs, and that downward momentum will be fading at price cycle lows. In fact, the situation is particularly clear-cut in the case of long-term cycles. There is a preliminary spike in a short-term momentum indicator as the market becomes overextended. This is normally followed by a sharp correction in the market. Prices then move back towards the level at which they became overextended. As prices move out into new territory there will be a second spike in the momentum indicator. This spike will not usually be greater than the first one[9] (see also Chapter 15).

Acceleration and the cycle

Third, and finally, the acceleration cycle provides us with an exceptionally accurate tool for confirming when a cycle has *actually* reversed. There are occasions when momentum reaches exceptionally high levels (either positive or negative) immediately *after* a reversal in absolute prices. This reflects the cycle of acceleration which, as we have seen, occurs in opposition to the cycle of absolute prices. Such a development should be taken as *prima facie* evidence that a high level cycle has reversed direction.

Derived trading rules: closing positions

The fact that momentum reaches a spike a quarter-cycle ahead of the peak or trough in absolute prices implies that it is possible to employ certain elementary trading rules to complement those which we have already covered. In particular, a momentum index can be used to trade at the margin because it is possible to anticipate what comes next.

The first and simplest rule is that all 'sensitive' trading positions should be closed if momentum reaches levels which historically have been associated with price reversals. A reversal of some degree will almost invariably follow, and it may be very uncomfortable if some evasive action is not taken. The definition of 'sensitive' in this context is highly subjective, since it depends on the objectives of the trader. There is an old stock market adage which suggests that market participants should 'trade down to their sleeping level'.[10] This is true because sustained periods of stress ultimately lead to errors of judgement. Managers of long-term pension funds, for example, should not trade (and should not be expected to trade) 7- or 20-day cycles with anything other than marginal liquidity. It remains true, however, that the larger the cycle which is turning, the greater is the likely extent of the retracement and the greater is the volume of trading positions which can therefore be considered to be sensitive.

Derived trading rules: opening positions

The second trading rule actually follows from this. New trading positions should not be opened automatically as the old ones are closed. This is because the *terminal* juncture in the absolute price cycle still lies ahead. Indeed, as contra-trend profit taking becomes widespread around the market, successful traders can *re-open* their original positions. A genuine reversal of positions should take place only when absolute prices are finally moving into the time window which has already been calculated for the cyclical peak or trough.

Conclusion

These rules often prove to be so successful in practice that many analysts conclude that momentum is the *only* valid indicator of cycles in the absolute price level. As a corollary, they also conclude that re-tests and non-confirmations are caused by the influences of cycles which are higher than those being tracked, and that therefore peaks and troughs of *high*-level cycles themselves are neither 're-tested' nor validated by momentum 'non-confirmations'.[11] It is true that a further price movement in the direction of the original trend *may* be evidence of the influence of a higher-level cycle. However, it is certainly not true that the cycle of price momentum coincides with the cycle in absolute prices. Hence re-tests and non-confirmations will, in fact, *always* occur, but the relevant event may be beyond investors' normal trading horizons.

We now have a basis for discussing the presence of actual cycles in financial markets. This we shall do in the next chapter.

Notes

1. This implies, of course, that solar, lunar and planetary cycles have an active influence on life on Earth. One of the more notable examples is the finding of Frank Brown that the feeding rhythms of oysters are triggered by the gravitational pull of the moon. Oysters were moved inland from the coast, and it was found that their feeding rhythm adjusted from the time of full tide on the coast to the time when the moon was overhead.

See Frank A. Brown, 'Persistent activity rhythms in the oyster', *American Journal Of Physiology*, 1954.

2. See, for example, R.G.D. Allen, *Statistics For Economists*. Hutchinson, London 1949.

3. There are some slight variations on this theme. For example, it is possible to use either a geometric or a weighted moving average instead of an arithmetic one. Furthermore, some analysts prefer to *deduct* the moving average from the raw data rather than use the division method. The main criterion, however, is usually simplicity of use.

4. A *moving* average is a succession of averages calculated from a series of numbers. Having calculated the average from the first group in the series, the next average is calculated from a group which is constructed by dropping the first number in the old group and then including the first new number after that group. For each moving average, the important term is the middle one: it is this term that is divided by the moving average. Obviously there is no difficulty if the number of terms in the moving average is odd. The middle term in a three-period moving average, for example, is the second term. Nevertheless, a complication arises if the moving average is taken for an even number of terms, because there is no centre term. The simple solution is to ensure that all analysis is conducted using an odd numbered average.

5. It can be shown that a moving average will only completely suppress a cycle if the moving average is either the *same* length as the periodicity of the cycle or is an *exact multiple* of that periodicity. If the moving average has a period which is *smaller* than the periodicity of the cycle being tracked, that cycle will still be present in the moving average. If the average has a period which is *greater* than the periodicity of the cycle (but not an exact multiple), then the averaging process will reverse the cycle. On these and other relevant points see, for example, Gertrude Shirk, *Cycle Analysis – A Case Study*. Foundation For The Study Of Cycles, Pittsburgh, 1981.

6. That is, the last data point in the group from which the average is calculated.

7. Edward R. Dewey with Og Mandino, *Cycles – The Mysterious Forces that Trigger Events*. Hawthorn, New York, 1971

8. In measuring a cycle, it will often be found that the time period taken for one complete beat varies slightly from beat to beat. In such cases, it is perfectly valid to calculate the *average* length of time, taken from all the observed beats, and use this average to predict the 'time window' for the reversal point.

9. Such spikes yield the illusion of an 'echo' cycle in the data, or of a sub-cycle which does not actually exist. For short-term trading, it matters little which turning points are used, but it obviously makes a difference to long-term perspectives.

10. This adage is reported in Edwin Lefevre, *Reminiscences of a Stock Operator*. George Doran and Co, New York, 1923.

11. See Note 4, Chapter 16.

19.

The Evidence for Time Cycles

Introduction

An examination of the price history of any financial market, using the very simple techniques which are described in the last chapter, will reveal the presence of a large number of cycles. Unfortunately, we can concentrate on only one market here, and the one we have chosen is the UK gilt-edged market.

Table 19.1 shows 16 cycles which are present in this market. There are of course many others, but those shown represent a cross-section of the most easily identifiable ones.

Table 19.1. *Cycles in the gilt-edged market*

Years	Months	Weeks	Days
54			
36			
16			
9.6			
9.2			
7.2			
4.5	54		
4.0	48		
3.2	38.4		
1.8	21.6	93.6	
0.8	9.6	41.6	
0.64	7.7	33.3	
		9.6	
		7	49
		4	28
		1	7

The relationship between the time units

The first thing to notice about these cycles is that there are definite mathematical relationships between them. There are two aspects to these relationships: the first is that the periodicity values appear to be *independent* of the units of time which are used, and the second is that many of the cycles are *multiples* of other cycles.

First, let us look at the units of time. Table 19.1 suggests that there is both a 54-*year* cycle and a 54-*month* (ie 4.5-year) cycle, that there is a 9.6-*year* cycle and a 9.6-*month* cycle, that there is a 9.2-*year* cycle and a 9.2-*week* cycle, and that there is a 7-*week* cycle and a 7-*day* cycle.[1, 2] This consistency suggests that, if a particular number is found to apply to one particular unit of time, there is a high probability that it will operate in other units of time. It also confirms William Gann's view that *specific* numbers are important.

The harmony between the cycles

The second point is that each of the cycles appears to *harmonise* with other cycles. For example, it transpires that certain of the annual periodicity numbers in Table 19.1 are related to other numbers in the same table by the numbers 2.222, 2.25 or 5 (see Table 19.2). The first two are remarkably close to the Fibonacci source number 2.236, which of course is the square root of 5. Hence, it appears that Fibonacci is at work in cycle periodicities.

Table 19.2. *The influence of Fibonacci*

36/16	=	2.25
16/7.2	=	2.222
7.2/3.2	=	2.25
4/1.8	=	2.222
1.8/0.8	=	2.25
3.2/0.64	=	5.0

Furthermore, some of the numbers in Table 19.1 are related to others by the number 4 and, therefore, the number 2 (see Table 19.3). This extends the idea of a general interrelationship between all the numbers. More particularly, however, it helps to explain the similarity between the periodicities of annual cycles and the periodicities of monthly cycles because the periodicities harmonise with the number

Table 19.3. *The harmony with the number 4*

80/4	=	20
36/4	=	9
16/4	=	4
7.2/4	=	1.8
3.2/4	=	0.8
1.44/4	=	0.36
0.64/4	=	0.16

12. It also helps to explain a phenomenon which has baffled cycle analysts in the past, which is that sometimes a cycle will reach a peak when it is expected to reach a trough, and vice versa. This is because if a long cycle harmonises with shorter cycles which are a quarter or half its length, then peaks (or troughs) in the former will periodically offset the peaks (or troughs) of the latter.

The harmony with other cycles

Furthermore, it is worth observing that some of the cycles which we have identified in the gilt market are also present both in stock markets and in other areas of nature. In the US, for example, Louise Wilson[3] has noted evidence of stock market cycles lasting 28 days, 7 weeks, 34 weeks, 9.2 months, 22 months, 3.2 years, 4.5 years, 7.1 years, 9.2 years, 9.6 years, 36 years and 54 years. Furthermore, Edward Dewey[4] has noted the existence of a 9.2-year cycle in such diverse time series as grasshopper abundance, partridge abundance, pig iron prices, tree rings and new patents issued. He has also registered the presence of a 9.6-year cycle in rabbit abundance, lynx abundance, barometric pressure, wheat acreage under harvest, ozone, tree rings and heart disease. The fact that all these phenomena correlate so closely with the gilts cycles suggest *very* strongly that common forces are at work. It would be surprising if the synchrony were purely accidental. The evidence suggests that fluctuations in financial markets are literally a 'natural' phenomenon, that they are rhythmic, and that they harmonise with one another.

The 9.6-month cycle in gilts

The overall harmony between the cycles helps to confirm their validity, and we shall take a closer look at each of the gilts cycles in Appendix 2. In the present chapter we shall concentrate on just *one* of the cycles in order to demonstrate how natural rhythms can be used to predict the timing of turning points. The cycle we have chosen is the 9.6-month cycle because it is short enough to be practical for traders and long enough to be useful to investors. It also harmonises with the 3.2-year cycle. The top part of Figure 19.1 shows the actual price movements of Treasury 8.75% 1997 from the beginning of 1975 to the end of 1988. The lower part of the diagram shows the one-month percentage change in the price of the same stock. The *troughs* of the 9.6-month cycle (see Table A2.10 in Appendix 2) are shown in both charts. The actual troughs occasionally vary from the

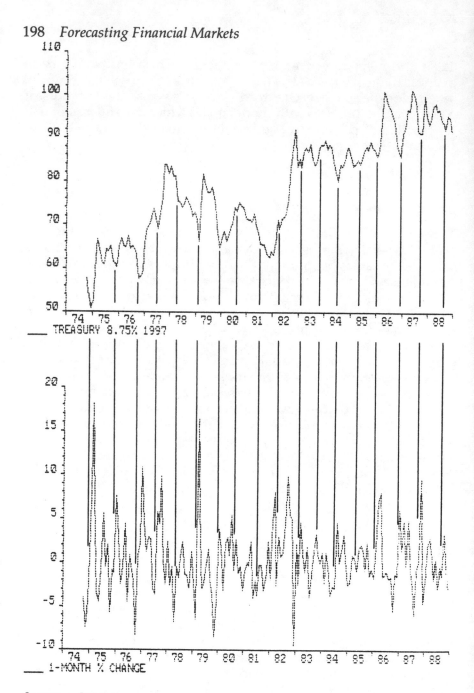

Figure 19.1. *The gilt-edged market 1975-1988*

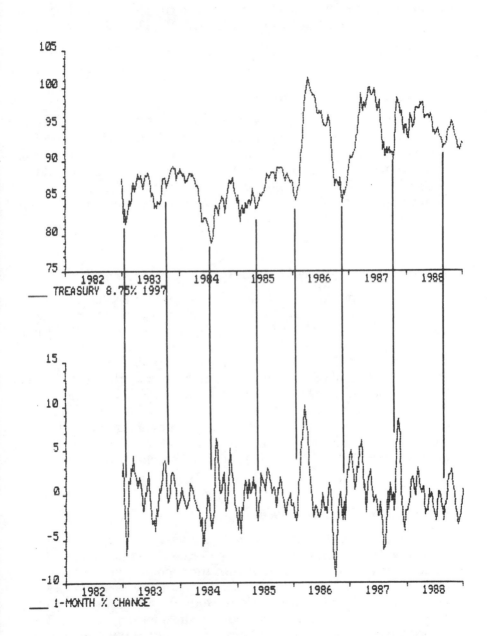

Source : Datastream

Figure 19.2. *The gilt-edged market 1983-1988*

theoretical troughs because of the 'slippage' which we mentioned in Chapter 18. However, the message of Figure 19.1 is quite clear: there is a regular 9.6-month cycle operating in the UK gilt market, and each cycle low is accompanied by a downward 'spike' of some sort in momentum.

The evidence from 1983 to 1988

The accuracy of this cycle can be seen even more clearly if we look just at the more recent past. Figure 19.2 below shows the price performance of Treasury 8.75% 1997 from January 1983 to December 1988, together with the associated one-month rate of change. All seven beats of the cycle bottomed (more or less) on schedule. Furthermore, each trough was accompanied by a downward spike in the momentum indicator.

The evidence of non-confirmation

Of some relevance to the analysis is the fact that each cyclical trough in prices is also *preceded* some weeks earlier by a downward spike in the momentum indicator (see Figure 19.2). In other words, there is a 'double' spike. In the majority of cases the first spike is greater than the second. This is entirely consistent with our analysis relating to the 'non-confirmation' of price lows, and with the fact that the momentum cycle precedes the price cycle. In the latter case, the theory would lead us to expect that the trough in the momentum cycle occurs a *quarter*-cycle ahead of the trough in the price cycle. In the case of the 9.6-month cycle, therefore, this implies that the initial warning should occur 2.4 months (or 10.4 weeks) ahead of the eventual price low.

The evidence from 1987-1988

Obviously, since the cycle is not necessarily going to develop smoothly, there will be some leeway in these figures. However, the evidence is definitely consistent with the theory. Figure 19.3 shows the price of Treasury 8.75% 1997 between January 1987 and October 1988, together with a two-week percentage change indicator. The charts therefore span *two* cycle lows. The momentum conditions associated with the price cycle lows are compared with the momentum conditions approximately 2.4 months earlier. It is quite clear that in both cases a momentum spike preceded the price low by the expected amount.[5]

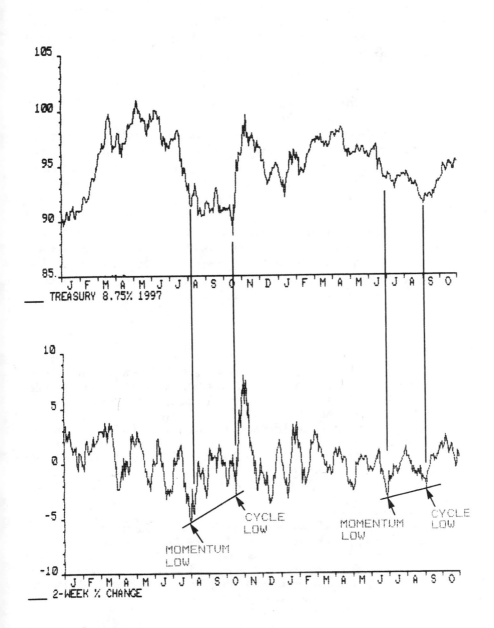

Source : Datastream

Figure 19.3. *The gilt-edged market January 1987 to October 1988*

The 9.6-month gilt cycle and the equity crash

Finally, it is worthwhile commenting on the fact that the 9.6-month cycle low in the gilt market in October 1987 coincided with the equity market crash. This means that the UK bond markets were actually scheduled to rally from mid-October. Furthermore, and as we pointed out in Chapter 10, the US Treasury bond hit an important price objective on 19 October 1987. This means that the US bond markets were also likely to rally after 19 October. It is difficult to convey the importance of these apparent 'coincidences'. Prior to 19 October, there was no obvious fundamental reason why bond markets throughout the world should rally. Indeed, most governments (especially the US Federal Reserve) were actively in the process of tightening monetary conditions. This policy was dramatically reversed by the event of the equity crash. However, it can also be shown that the equity market was scheduled to fall in October 1987. The analysis is presented in Chapter 20. In fact an important sell signal had been generated in the US equity market on Friday, 9 October. The markets were therefore participating together in an intricate dance, whose steps were perfectly harmonised and choreographed. The message of this book is that those steps could have been determined in advance by those who knew what to look for!

Notes

1. The presence of rhythms in human behaviour with a periodicity units of 7 has been recognised for thousands of years. See, for example, Steve Richards, *Luck, Chance and Coincidence*. The Aquarian Press, Wellingborough, Northants, 1985.
2. There is some evidence that there are also cycles of 7.2 weeks and 7.2 days.
3. Louise L. Wilson, *Catalogue of Economic Cycles*. Foundation for the Study of Cycles, Pittsburgh, 1964
4. Edward R. Dewey with Og Mandino, *Cycles – The Mysterious Forces that Trigger Events*. Hawthorn, New York, 1971.
5. Using a 10-day relative strength indicator to measure momentum actually gives a very precise lead time. The RSI lows applicable to Figure 19.3 occurred on 31 August 1987 and 29 June 1988. The associated price lows occurred on 19 October 1987 and 2 September 1988. The lead time in the first case was therefore 11 weeks and 1 trading day, while the lead in the second case was 9 weeks and 2 trading days. The average lead time was therefore 10 weeks and 3 trading days!

Part IV:

The Theory in Practice

20.

The Equity Market Crash of 1987

Introduction

This book has detailed all the techniques which are necessary for successful investment. It has explained *exactly* why the discipline known as 'technical analysis' works, and why it is a valid method of forecasting movements in financial markets. This assertion can, of course, only be validated by using the techniques in an actual trading environment. Nevertheless, some indication of their power can still be demonstrated by an analysis of *historical* examples. This we now propose to do by analysing the circumstances surrounding the US equity market 'crash' of October 1987.[1]

Recent history of the Dow

The last important bear market in US equities prior to 1987 occurred between the spring of 1981 and the summer of 1982. Over that period, the Dow Jones Industrial Average fell by just over 22 per cent. The closing level of the Dow on 12 August 1982 was 776.8. Five years later, on 25 August 1987, the same index closed at a record level of 2722.4. The rally had therefore amounted to just over 350 per cent (see Figure 20.1).

The overbought condition, Summer 1987

The first point to make is that the sheer momentum of the move left the market *overbought*. There had been a contra-trend correction during 1986, which had ended in late September at 1755.2 on the Dow Jones index. From this low, the market rallied by 55 per cent to its August 1987 peak. This rally compared very favourably with any other rally over an 11-month time period since the great secular low of late 1974 (see Figure 20.2). Of some importance, however, was the fact that the 1986-87 surge did *not* occur from a major cyclical trough, but from

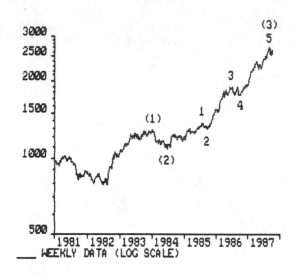

Source : Datastream

Figure 20.1. *The Dow Jones Industrial Average 1981-1987*

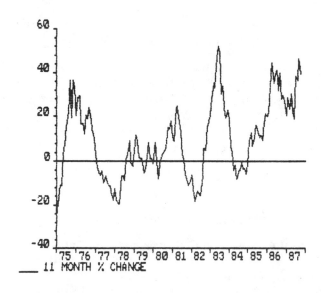

Source : Datastream

Figure 20.2. *The overbought condition August 1987*

the base of a contra-trend correction. In other words, the momentum was high, not because it had started off from a grossly oversold condition, but because it was based on genuine investor participation.

Other evidence

Over-extended momentum is not, in itself, conclusive. Bull markets generally can – and do – remain over-extended for significant periods of time. However, there were other causes for concern: price *patterns* were consistent with an imminent top, short-term investor *behaviour* was not confirming new highs, and prices had achieved calculated *objectives*.

The price patterns

The rally from the 1986 price low (see Figure 20.3) was a classic 'Elliott'-type five-wave rally. Furthermore, this rally could itself be counted as the fifth wave of a five-wave movement which began in 1984 (see Figure 20.1). As we saw in Chapter 14, however, a five wave rally is inevitably followed by a correction as a z-wave of the price pulse comes into effect. In addition, the nesting of the five-wave movements suggested that the end of the rally from 1986 would also mark the end of the rally from (at least) 1984. The problem, therefore, was to judge when the top of the final set of five waves would actually occur.

Investor behaviour

There were two lines of thought here. The first was to confirm that the final set of five waves from 1986 were following the rules of natural behaviour: that is, that the energy of the crowd (in generating, and responding to, price movements) peaked at the top of the *third* wave; and that such energy was dropping as the *fifth* wave developed. This would have simultaneously confirmed the operation of a y-wave and the imminence of a z-wave. The appropriate indicators did, indeed, behave according to theory. Stock exchange volumes, and the one-month percentage rate of change in prices, actually peaked during the third wave in early 1987. New price highs during the summer of 1987 were accompanied by lower highs both in volume and in the momentum indicator. Furthermore, open interest in the Standard and Poors futures market followed a similar profile (although, here, the high occurred during the early summer). In other words, new price highs were *not* being 'confirmed'. The internal structure of the y-wave

Source : Datastream

Figure 20.3. *The 1986-1987 bull phase*

was ensuring that rising prices were not generating a full-blooded
investor response (see Figure 20.4). A sell signal would therefore be
triggered once prices actually turned down.

Price targets: Fibonacci numbers

The second consideration, and in many ways the most important, was
the implication of the *extent* of the price movements which had already
been travelled. We highlighted the importance of Fibonacci numbers
in price movements in Chapter 17. The Dow Jones Industrial Average
is particularly influenced by such numbers (as indeed is the UK
counterpart, the Financial Times Industrial Index). At the August 1987
high, there were at least *three* Fibonacci numbers which occurred
simultaneously: first, the rally from the major 1974 low had been 377
per cent; second, the rally from the September 1986 low was 55 per
cent; third, the rise since the March 1987 low was 21 per cent (see
Figure 20.5).

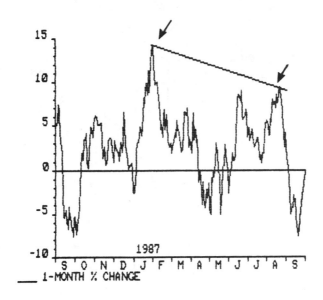

Source : Datastream

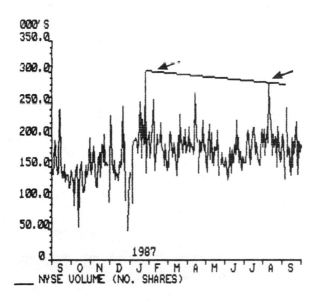

Source : Datastream

Figure 20.4. *The potential non-confirmation August 1987*

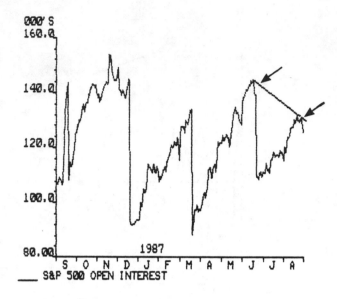

Source : Datastream

Figure 20.4. *The potential non-confirmation August 1987*

Source : Datastream

Figure 20.5(a). *Fibonacci price constraints*

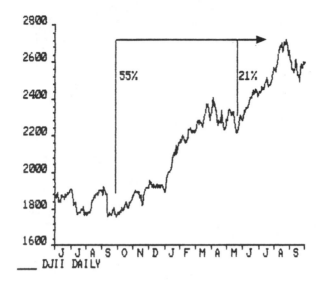

Source : Datastream

Figure 20.5(b). *Fibonacci price constraints*

Price targets: the spiral hypothesis

There were, however, other influences. According to our 'spiral' hypothesis, a rally is likely to be a Fibonacci multiple of the last phase of the base pattern which preceded it. This had been the case with the 34–year bull market following the Wall Street 'crash' of 1929–32. In this case, the relevant base pattern had ended with the 1973-1974 bear market. In 24 months, the Dow had fallen by 474.1 points, or 45 per cent, to close at a low of 577.6 on 6th December 1974. Targets from this low (see Figure 20.6) were therefore:

$$577.6 + (474.1 \times 1.618) = 1344.7$$
$$577.6 + (474.1 \times 2.618) = 1818.8$$
$$577.6 + (474.1 \times 4.236) = 2585.9$$

Over the next 13 years, the Dow moved progressively towards the higher of these targets. The first target did not, in fact, act as a constraint. The second was associated with the correction which occurred during the summer of 1986. The 4.236 objective was hit in August 1987. Obviously, the market over-ran somewhat, to peak at

Figure 20.6. *Fibonacci targets from 1974 base*

2722.4. There are, however, three points to bear in mind: first, the over-run was less than 5 per cent, within the context of a 2000 point bull run; second, the objectives could have been set as early as 1975, and certainly no later than 1983; third, no market is likely to *stay* above the 4.236 level for very long.

Short-term targets

The problem of over-shooting is, of course, important for traders. *In the short-term,* 130 points on the Dow is a large move. However, when the level of 2585 was hit in August 1987, it was already apparent that the immediate targets were somewhat higher. First, 2.618 multiplied by the setback which took place in April and May of 1987, gave a target of 2712; second, the other calculations which we have just mentioned gave a strong indication that Fibonacci constraints would not become operative until the low 2700s. (See also Figure 17.5.)

The influence of time: Fibonacci constraints

The final dimension to the analysis of the 1987 'crash' involves the influence of *time*. In this context, there were two types of influence. The first was the passage of time defined in terms of Fibonacci units. The second was the operation of cycles. Let us look at each of these in turn. Fibonacci constraints were, in fact, very important in 1987. In particular, the rise in equities since 1932 had lasted for 55 years, the bull run since 1974 had taken 13 years, the rally since the 1982 low had lasted five years, and the rise since the 1984 low had lasted three years. At the same time, the August 1987 high occurred three months after the May 1987 trading low, 13 months after the important July 1986 trading low, 21 months after the September 1985 low, and 34 months after the October 1984 trading low. It is fair to say that some of the elements in this latter grouping were easier to spot *after* the event than before it, but the former grouping undoubtedly made 1987 a particularly dangerous year! (See Figure 20.7).

The influence of time: cycles

The cycle analysis was equally important. There have been two main cycles operating in the US equity markets in recent years – these are the 4-year cycle and the 3.25-year cycle. The 4-year cycle was not scheduled to *peak* until at least mid-1988 (having previously peaked in 1976, 1980 and 1984), although its *momentum* peak (a quarter-cycle earlier) was scheduled for 1987. We have shown how markets become overbought and vulnerable to corrections at momentum peaks of a limit cycle. Meanwhile, the 3.25-year cycle was scheduled to reach a *low* in late 1987, having previously reached actual lows in late 1974, early 1978, mid 1981 and late 1984. The 'crash' therefore spanned the momentum peak of the 4-year cycle and the absolute trough of the 3.25-year cycle (see Figure 20.8).

Figure 20.7(a). *Fibonacci time constraints*

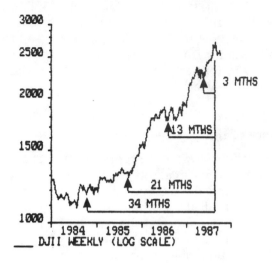

Source : Datastream

Figure 20.7(b). *Fibonacci time constraints*

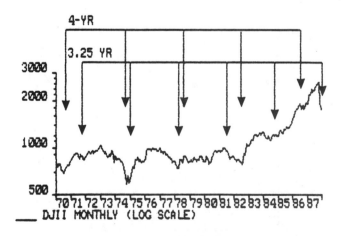

Source : Datastream

Figure 20.8. *4-year and 3.25-year time cycles*

The influence of the Kondratieff cycle

It will be remembered that both the 3.25-year cycle and the 4-year cycle also exist in the London gilt-edged market. By extension, therefore, it follows that some of the other cycles listed in Table 19.1 of Chapter 19 were also applicable to the Dow. A fall of the size registered in October 1987 suggests very strongly that a *long*-term cycle was involved. In fact, the most likely cycle appears to be the 54-year Kondratieff cycle. The analysis, however, is by no means clear cut. The important point is that downward spikes in market prices can occur during at least *three* different stages of a particular cycle (see Chapters 18 and 19). These stages are: (a) just after a top, when momentum *accelerates* downwards, (b) at the *trough* of a cycle, when velocity reaches a low, and (c) immediately after the *overbought* condition, which precedes the absolute top by a quarter-cycle.

The three Kondratieff possibilities

First, the 1987 peak in the Dow Jones Industrial Average occurred 58 years after the 1929 peak. This was four years later than might have been expected if the cycle was considered to be of an *exact* periodicity. Nevertheless, in practical terms, an error of four years is within the limits that can be tolerated for such a long-term cycle.

Second, the October 1987 low occurred 55 years after the July 1932 market *low*. Furthermore, a momentum low also occurred in late 1974, and therefore preceded the October 1987 low by almost a quarter of a Kondratieff cycle.

Third, the largest bear market in price and time, which immediately preceded the 1987 crash, occurred between January 1973 and December 1974. It was associated with severe dislocation to the economic system and could have been a Kondratieff low. In stock market terms, the previous Kondratieff cycle low would therefore have been in the early 1920s with the start of the 1921-1929 bull market. On this argument the 12.75 year bull run from December 1974 to August 1987 would have marked the initial quarter-cycle period of one complete beat of the Kondratieff cycle (since 12.75 × 4 = 51 years, which is tolerably close to 54 years).[2]

There is, of course, no way of knowing which of these possibilities is actually correct and the analysis can only be retrospective. Nevertheless, an awareness of the 54-year cycle would have made it *essential* to be wary of the market once it became overbought, and once acceptable price objectives had been reached.

The combined evidence

Whatever one's conclusions might have been about the importance of the 1987 top before it occurred, the basic facts were that:

(a) the market was over-extended,
(b) the four-year cycle 'predicted' that the market would be overbought to some degree in 1987;
(c) the wave 'count' was consistent with a setback;
(d) investor behaviour was consistent with a top;
(e) a number of important price targets had been reached;
(f) Fibonacci time constraints were operating;
(g) a 3.25-year cycle low was scheduled for late 1987.

The sell signal, 9 October 1987

Natural prudence therefore dictated that a selling programme should have been implemented when a *sell signal*, based on price patterns, was given. Such a signal occurred on Friday 9 October, when the market fell through a rising trend line which had been operating since at least January 1987 (see Figure 20.9). By the closing low of the market, six trading days later, the Dow had lost almost 38 per cent of its 25 August high value.

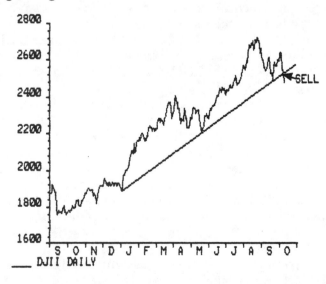

Source : Datastream

Figure 20.9. *The trend line break — Friday, 9 October*

The absence of subsequent buy signals

It can, of course, be argued that the *speed* of the fall could not have been forseen, unless the Kondratieff influences had been accurately predicted. However, the fact remains that it *did not matter* to those who had taken the appropriate action. First, the natural course of events *required* a significant fall in prices. Second, no buy signals were generated *during* the crash.

The prelude to the sell signal

In the 19 trading days after the top on 25 August, the Dow shed just under 230 points (ie it fell by 8.4 per cent) as it traced out an x-wave within the context of the emerging higher-level z-wave. At the end of this fall, the market found support both from the trend line which had been operating since August 1986, and from the fact that the drop (at that stage) represented approximately 38.2 per cent of the very last phase of the bull run from May 1987 (see Figure 20.10). However, the market had received a 'shock' from the fall, and the spiral mechanism required a further *two* waves: one up and one down.

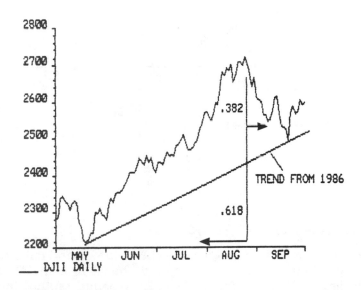

Source : Datastream

Figure 20.10. *The x-wave*

The counter-trend rally: investor behaviour

The up-wave (or y-wave) measured 148.2 points on the Dow, and lasted for nine trading days (see Figure 20.11). There were two crucial aspects of the rally. The first was the behaviour of investors. During the initial *fall* from the August top, open interest in the Standard and Poors futures contracts had *risen* (see Figure 20.12) This had certainly confirmed that the trend had turned downwards. During the up-wave, however, open interest actually *contracted* quite sharply[3] (see Figure 20.12). Furthermore, stock exchange volumes subsided noticeably. In other words, the re-test of the high was not stimulating investor participation. This definitely confirmed that the underlying trend was *still* down.

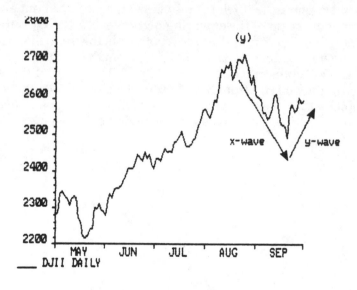

Source : Datastream

Figure 20.11. *The y-wave*

The countertrend rally: 0.618 resistance

The second important point about the counter-trend rally was that it retraced almost exactly 61.8 per cent of the fall from the August peak (see Figure 20.13). The fall had been 229.6 points. Multiplying this fall by 0.618 gave a potential rally of 141.9 points. The actual rally was 148.2 points. Once the market started to trade *back down* again, further evasive action should have been taken.

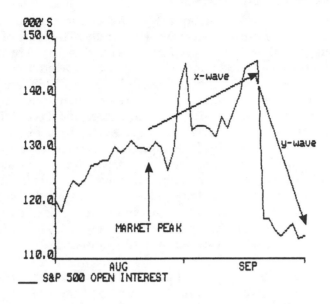

Source : Datastream

Figure 20.12. *Investor behaviour during the x- and y-waves*

Source : Datastream

Figure 20.13. *The 0.618 retracement*

Low risk trading strategies

There is a very good reason for selling at (or around) the 0.618 retracement level during a counter-trend rally. The logic of the price pulse suggests that a re-test of a previous high is made by a y-wave. The *higher* the level of the price pulse which is involved, the *less* likely it is that the y-wave will actually be forced to a new high, and the *more* likely it is that the 0.618 Fibonacci constraint will operate (see Chapter 17). This provides one of the *safest* trading rules that it is possible to use when shorting a market: sell at the 0.618 level, with a 'buy-back' order (known as a *stop-loss order*) if the market trades into new high ground. If the short position is correct – and in this case, it most certainly was! – the market is just about to move into its z-wave, where profits are the largest, and where downside targets can be calculated (see below). If the short position is incorrect, losses can be minimised by triggering the 'buy-back' order. If this strategy is used regularly across a number of markets, cumulative profits should substantially exceed cumulative losses.

(The same argument can, of course, be used for *purchases*, when markets are in a β-wave having retraced 61.8 per cent of the preceding α-wave. The balance of probabilities is that a δ-wave is just about to materialise. The stop-loss should be set at the previous low. Profits on such strategies should regularly exceed losses.)

Potential downside targets

Whether short positions were opened on the basis of the 0.618 retracement 'rule' or on the basis of the trend sell signal generated on 9 October, it was possible simultaneously to calculate potential downside targets. The four methods of doing so were: (i) to isolate previous support levels, (ii) to calculate 38.2 per cent retracement levels, (iii) to apply the spiral formulae, and (iv) to measure movements in terms of Fibonacci numbers.

The most obvious support levels were 2215.9 and 1755.2 on the Dow Jones Industrial Index. (See Figure 20.14.) Importantly, *both* levels could be read as corresponding to the bottom of Elliott–type 'fourth' waves, and were therefore valid objectives. The former (reached in May 1987) was the end of the fourth wave within the five waves from September 1986 to August 1987; while the latter (reached during the summer of 1986) was the end of the fourth wave within the five waves measured from June 1984 to August 1987.

As was pointed out in Chapter 16, however, the 'normal' limit to a correction is 38.2 per cent of the ('five wave') rally which precedes it. Given that the market had completed a whole *series* of five–waves upwards, the z–wave which was about to drive the market downwards could have come from any one of a number of hierarchical levels. This meant that a number of potential 38.2 per cent support levels could be calculated, depending on where the bull market was assumed to have begun. These levels were: 2352.9 (for the rally starting in September 1986), 2097.5 (for the rally starting in July 1984), and 1903.1 (for the rally starting December 1974). (See Figure 20.14.)

Meanwhile, targets could be calculated by applying the spiral formulae to a relevant y–wave. There were two y–waves which were appropriate. The first was the May–August rally into the peak, of 506.5 points. Here, the 1.618 target was 1902.4 (the others being too low to be considered valid). The second y–wave was the September–October re-test rally, of 148.2 points. Here, the 1.618, 2.618 and 4.236 targets were 2401.2, 2253.0 and 2013.2 respectively. (See Figure 20.14.)

Finally, it was possible to calculate 'natural' Fibonacci movements of 13 per cent, 21 per cent and 34 per cent from the re-test high. These suggested possible targets of 2297.7, 2086.0 and 1743.0 respectively. (See Figure 20.14.)

Source : Datastream

Figure 20.14. *The downside targets for the bear market*

The probable target

Unusually, none of these calculations yielded targets which satisfied more than two criteria simultaneously. However, four emerged as being possible: 2215.9/2253.0 (a fourth wave support and a 2.618 target); 2086.0/2097.5 (a 21 per cent fall and a 38.2 per cent retracement); 1902.4/1903.1 (a 1.618 target and a 38.2 per cent retracement); and 1743.0/1755.2 (a 34 per cent fall and a fourth wave target). Of these, the 1902.4/1903.1 level immediately appeared as the *most* likely. This was partly because of the power of the 1.618 target and because of the importance of a 38.2 per cent retracement of the rally since December 1974. However, it was also partly because it was *so* precise. Meanwhile the 2215.9/2253.0 level was the *least* likely — not only did it represent an insufficient correction to the 1984–1987 bull phase, it was also relatively *im*precise.

The actual experience

During the week following the sell signal, the Dow fell almost continuously. On Friday 16 October, it fell by just over 108 points to close at 2246.7. The Dow had therefore lost 235 points (or nearly 10 per cent) in a week. This was a record fall, signalling that something was wrong even to those who were not professionals in the markets.

At this stage, the market had reached the first level which could be viewed as a valid objective. However, as previously discussed, this level was insufficient to constitute a correction to the rally since 1984. There was therefore no need to close any short positions.

This logic highlights one of the huge advantages of technical analysis: it allows an investor to remain aloof from the 'herd' mentality. On Monday, 19 October, the selling panic in New York drove the Dow down by 508 points – a record one-day fall of 22.5 per cent. At the close, the Dow stood at 1738.7. This was approximately 34 per cent down from the October re-test high and was on Elliott 'fourth wave' support (see Figure 20.15).

0.382 support

The following morning, the Dow touched a level which was 38.2 per cent lower than the August high. Note, however, that this was a 38.2 per cent retracement of the rally since the Dow index was notionally equivalent to *zero*. Remember that 38.2 per cent appears to be the natural limit to a market's ability to regress in the face of *favourable* fundamentals. Even a cursory glance at the fundamentals at the time should have confirmed that the collapse of Western civilisation was not imminent.[4] In addition, the level virtually coincided with the August 1986 low, which had been the base for the *last* wave of the 1982 to 1987 bull run. It was an important support level. Not surprisingly, therefore, the market finally began to rally. At the close on 20 October, the Dow stood at 1841.0.

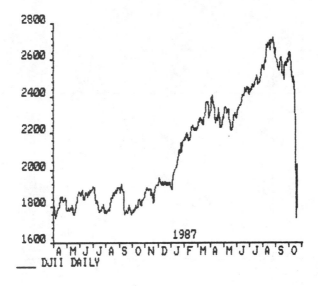

Source : Datastream

Figure 20.15. *The crash*

The overshoot on the downside

One problem in this analysis is that the market overshot the 'natural' target of 1902. Nevertheless, there are two points which are relevant. The first is that, for those investors who stayed short into 19 October, it mattered little that the market 'overshot'.

The second, and more important theoretical point, is that the calculated target turned out to be almost *exactly* the centre of gravity around which the market oscillated during the next few months (see Figure 20.16). This is an important phenomenon. It seems that the margin of error is always small from the market's own perspective, even though it may at times appear large from the investor's point of view: an error of 200 points or so within the context of a 2722 point bull run is not particularly large, even though the trader on the spot may feel otherwise! In the context of the market's own perspectives, the objectives held.

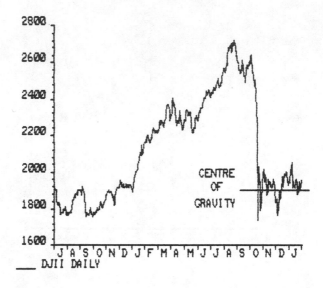

Source : Datastream

Figure 20.16. *The year after the crash*

The official response

In subsequent months, the 'crash' in the US was blamed (at least in part) on programmed trading using computers.[5] Measures were therefore introduced to suspend such trading after the indices had moved by a certain amount during any given trading period. As usual, rational people could not bring themselves to accept the widespread presence of non-rational behaviour in markets, [6] and preferred instead to blame mindless computers. This diagnosis was (and is) fallacious on two counts. First, the assumption of rational behaviour implies that the computers (even if they were guilty[7]) should have been overridden. Second, the same phenomenon occurred in other equity markets where programmed trading did not exist.

The experience in the UK

Of particular relevance here is the experience of the UK. The long-term target for the FT 30 Index (which is the Financial Times index of 30 industrial shares) was 4.236 times the extent of the 1972-1974 bear market: that is, 1830.2. This level was reached in the early days of July 1987 (see Figure 20.17), but (as in America) the index overshot its target because of the sheer momentum of the rise. However, the overshoot was only temporary, because the market became grossly overbought. The subsequent fall in prices was quite remarkable, not only because of its *extent* but also because of its *precision*. Naked fear drove the FT 30 Index down from an intra-day high of 1936.2 on 16 July to an intra-day low of 1198.1 on 10 November – a fall of 38.1 per cent! Furthermore, the broader FTSE 100 Index fell from 2455.2 to 1515.0 over the same period, thereby registering a decline of 38.3 per cent.[8] The fact that the declines were so precise in *both* indices is a tremendous confirmation of (and advertisement for) the efficacy of the 0.382 retracement rule. It also demonstrates the power of the Fibonacci Sequence.

Source : Datastream

Figure 20.17. *The FT 30 Industrial Index*

Notes

1. This chapter is an expanded version of the forecasts made in Hambros Bank *Market Monitor*, 3 September 1987.
2. The analysis obviously suggests that the craze for forecasting an imminent collapse in the capitalist system is not necessarily correct!.
3. Open interest fell sharply in September because of the expiry of the September futures contract and the move to the December contract as

being the most traded. However, this does not change either the basic fact that substantial new positions were not opened in that contract.

4. At the time, comparisons were made with the crash of 1929 which became a major bear market. However, in 1929 the economy had already peaked well ahead of the stock market. Subsequently, the agricultural recession made things worse, and the Fed made a major policy error by allowing the money supply to collapse.

5. See *Report of the Presidential Task Force on Market Mechanisms*. US Government Printing Office, January 1988.

6. Indeed, much academic research remains directed towards showing that stock market behaviour is consistent with rational behaviour even during excesses. See, for example, Behzad T. Diba and Herschel I. Grossman, 'The theory of rational bubbles in stock prices', *The Economic Journal*, September 1988. Such arguments do not provide acceptable analyses either of the actual behaviour of investors or of their motivations for dealing. (See Tony Plummer, 'The psychology of financial markets', *Market Technician*, October 1989.)

7. The view that the 'crash' was caused by computers has been strongly attacked in a report prepared by the Chicago Mercantile Exchange. See Miller, Merton, Hawke, Malkiel, and Scholes, *Preliminary report of the Committee of Inquiry appointed by the Chicago Mercantile Exchange to examine the events surrounding October 19, 1987*. Chicago Mercantile Exchange, December 1987.

8. The Fibonacci fall in the FTSE 100 Index occurred despite the fact that the Index is relatively new.

21.

Summary and Conclusions

And so, an analysis of universal laws can provide us with an explanation of stock market dynamics. The need of individuals to obey universal laws, and participate in greater wholes, is the key to a fuller understanding of all social, economic and political activity. In the current context, it allows us to 'explain' the stock market phenomenon by forcing us to adopt the assumption of *non-rational* crowd behaviour by market participants.

The important point to remember is that the ownership of investment positions, in the pursuit of stock market profits, creates a 'crowd' mentality. The decision to make an investment (or disinvestment) may have been arrived at rationally but, once a financial exposure exists, so does the potential for stress and fear. Price behaviour becomes the arbiter of investment decisions and price movements can therefore trigger responses from investors which have a large non-rational dimension. This non-rational response is the binding force of the crowd situation.

Once a crowd has been created, it has a *life cycle* of its own. In the context of a financial market, the crowd's behaviour during this life cycle can be measured by changes in *prices* and by changes in *sentiment*. The former can be tracked using price-time charts, while the latter can be judged by plotting variables such as volume, open interest or momentum.

While a crowd exists, it has natural metabolic *rhythms* which have both an internal and an external dimension. The internal rhythms are, by definition, specific to the particular crowd, and are reflected in regular cyclical fluctuations which can be found in the price-time charts. At the same time, however, the crowd has to oscillate in a limit-cycle relationship with its social and economic environment. Some of the environmental oscillations are themselves 'regular', and so the crowd oscillates in harmony with these external rhythms because it has essentially 'learnt' to do so. In both these situations, where the fluctuations are regular and continuous, it is possible to use observed cycles to forecast the *timing* of turning points in financial market prices.

Most of the environmental oscillations, however, will appear as 'shocks' to the crowd. Such shocks may consist of either pro-trend information or contra-trend information: pro-trend information merely encourages existing trends; but contra-trend information generates a three-stage fluctuation as the crowd seeks to assimilate that information. This three-wave response is the basis of what we have called *the price pulse*.

Each phase of the price pulse is defined by the Fibonacci Number Sequence. This Sequence has long been recognised as an intrinsic part of nature in terms of both the relationship between different aspects of the same spatial structure, and the growth and learning processes of that structure. It follows that price movements in financial markets are subject to the 'constraints' of the Fibonacci Sequence, and it is therefore possible to forecast the *extent* of price movements using this Sequence.

Finally, the alternating up-down movements created by the combination of rhythmic cycles and contra-trend shocks, are reflected in a limited number of price *patterns*. These patterns have long been identified by traditional technical analysis, and can be used to deduce *trading signals* which have a low risk of being incorrect and a high probability of being profitable.

No system is, of course, perfect. There will be occasions when the messages being given are either inconclusive or conflicting. On these occasions, investors should not anticipate reversals if to do so means 'moving away from base'. At the simplest level this implies that long-term investors should always stay *in* the market until definite sell signals are given, and that short-term investors should always stay *out* of the market until definite buy signals are generated. On most occasions, however, technical analysis will confirm the presence of a reversal while it is *in the process of developing*.

The most important method of wealth accumulation involves being properly positioned for *large* market movements. It is important to remember that large movements are created essentially by the failure of the majority of investors to anticipate all developments fully, and by the consequent reaction *en masse* to largely unforeseen events. Substantial price movements simply cannot occur if everybody is getting the market right all of the time. Technical analysis focuses attention on what the majority of investors are doing at any given time, while simultaneously enabling successful investors to stand aside from the crowd mentality. It is a *rational* approach to a non-rational environment.

Hence technical analysis should, at the very least, ensure that no *major* mistakes are made. When used properly, it will not give strong buy signals just prior to a price collapse, nor will it give strong sell signals just prior to a rally. More generally, there are always clear warning signals that a terminal juncture is approaching, and these signals subsequently translate into some form of appropriate buy or sell signal just prior to the *major* part of the relevant impulse wave. Technical analysis is demonstrably an accurate, and theoretically justifiable, method of forecasting behaviour in financial markets. Investors who follow the rules outlined in this book should, after a little experience, find it entirely possible to embark on a long-term programme of accumulating wealth.

Appendices

Appendix 1:

The Theories of W. D. Gann

Introduction

One of the greatest exponents[1] of the presence of natural forces in equity and commodity markets was an extremely successful American investor named William D. Gann. Operating in the 1930s, [2] Gann discovered certain truths about the way financial markets behave and he used his findings to amass a personal fortune. Subsequently, he wrote books[3] and introduced training courses, [4] in order to disseminate some of his ideas to a wider audience. Nevertheless, and as anyone who has studied his work will readily testify, his techniques often appeared to be lacking in theoretical justification and they were certainly very complicated in their application. It seems that there was a central body of theory underlying Gann's analysis which he was either unable, or unwilling, to reveal. It may be, of course, that Gann simply did not know why his techniques worked. However, it is far more likely that he considered that the underlying theories were too esoteric for general consumption.

Gann's theories and 'natural' systems

It will not be possible to provide a complete survey of Gann's findings here because they are simply too extensive. All we shall do is provide a cursory examination of his work – first, to demonstrate that his market approach is consistent with the analytical framework which we have established in the preceding chapters, and second to give a flavour of some of his findings.

The first point to make is that Gann was profoundly aware of the concept of an oscillating universe. His 'Law of Vibrations' used the notions that (a) an original impulse of any kind finally resolved itself into regular vibrations, and (b) all original driving forces themselves vibrated. The parallel between these ideas and the concept of natural dynamic systems is inescapable. Gann was, in fact, *many* years ahead of academic research and philosophical thought.

Application to stocks and commodities

Gann's techniques related primarily to the behaviour of *individual* stocks and commodities and were not specifically considered to be appropriate to financial markets taken as a whole. Nevertheless, it remains true that an individual stock is an important *part* of a complete market for stocks: the performance of an individual stock contributes to the performance of the whole market, and the performance of the whole market influences the behaviour of an individual stock. Hence, given that Gann's analysis is intellectually consistent with the concept of natural systems, the broad thrust of his techniques ought to be malleable enough to be applicable to whole markets.

The spiral of prices and the circle of time

Gann in fact employed two tools which we have already come across: namely, the spiral and the circle. He associated the former primarily with price movements, while the latter was derived from his conviction that *time* was important. Indeed, if Gann's attitude to markets could be summarised in a single sentence, it would be that a reversal can be expected when *the constraints on prices meet the constraints of time* that is, when the spiral of prices meets the cycle of time.

The importance of the historical low

It is not certain that Gann was aware of the specific relevance of the spiral to his analysis. The spiral does, however, occur in the visual presentation of his graphs and tables from which he derived potential price turning points. There were two aspects to these tables: the first was the historical low point (the 'lowest low') of a stock price;[5] and the second was the relationship of subsequent price levels to that historical low.

Gann considered that the lowest known price in any market would be of major psychological significance, and that the subsequent reversal points would be mathematically related to it.

The price square

One of Gann's main tools in this context was a price 'square'. The lowest historical price would be placed in the middle square of a piece of graph paper. Then the next price (measured in whole units) would be placed one square to the right, and the next price would be placed one square down. The process would be repeated, circling clockwise, until a full 'square' was complete. In the simplest case, the next stage of the process was to draw horizontal, vertical and diagonal lines through the middle square (ie through the lowest price), thereby dividing the whole square into quarters and eighths. Gann regarded any prices falling along the dividing line as potential reversal points. An example of such a square, using *unity*[6] as the lowest price, is shown in Figure A1.1.

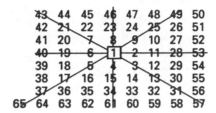

Figure A1.1. *The Gann square*

Problems with the price square

The construction of Gann's price square is revealing. First, it is presented in the form of a spiral. The prices revolve outwards around the lowest price which is at the centre. Second, the important prices occur at specific points on the resulting spiral. This should mean that the spiral can be 'specified' in a mathematical sense, because it should be possible to derive the mathematical expansion which defines the spiral from those specific points. In fact, however, there are two difficulties in putting this theory into practice. In constructing his square, Gann did not explicitly separate those points on the vertical, horizontal and diagonal lines which were *effective* reversal points from those which were ineffective. As a result there are too many numbers: they are not related to each other by a simple mathematical expansion. In addition, there is a possibility that some of the numbers which should be part of the expansion do not actually fall on the important dividing lines. The use of equiangular dividing lines might therefore be too rigid under some circumstances.

These problems are clearly revealed in the example of the price square shown in Figure A1.1. Close inspection of the square will reveal the presence of the Fibonacci Sequence. The first eight numbers in the Sequence[7] fall on the dividing lines specified by Gann. However, the ninth number (55) actually just misses a line. Hence, while the square would undoubtedly pick up Fibonacci reversals at lower price levels, it would not necessarily pick them up at higher levels. Furthermore, the observer would not easily be able to determine the presence of the Fibonacci Sequence.

The extent of price movements

A partial 'solution' to this problem was Gann's recognition that

(a) certain mathematical series and sets of numbers were independently relevant to the analysis, and (b) the circle of time could be superimposed on the price spiral.

We shall look at each of these in turn. To start with, Gann found that price reversals were likely to occur after prices had moved by certain amounts. Often these levels would be mathematically related to a common number, one of which might be the 'base' number (ie the lowest low) in the square.

Natural number series

Gann's explicit numbers were based on 'natural' number series: that is, series which appeared to be relevant to the world in which we live. Of these number series, there were four in particular which he considered to be important. The first was the series derived by 'squaring' each of the numbers from 1 to 12. In this series, particular emphasis was placed on $7^2 = 49$ and on $12^2 = 144$. The second important series is the so-called 'doubling sequence', where each number is twice that of the one before it. The third is the 'trebling sequence', where each number is three times the one before it. And the fourth series, of course, is the Fibonacci Sequence. These four series are shown in Table A1.1.

Table A1.1. *Gann's natural number sets*

Source	Derived number set
12^2	4, 9, 16, 25, 36, 49, 64, 81, 100, 121, 144
Doubling	2, 4, 8, 16, 32, 64, 128, 256, 512, 1024, etc.
Trebling	1, 3, 9, 27, 81, 243, 729, 2187, 6561 etc.
Fibonacci	1, 2, 3, 5, 8, 13, 21, 34, 55, 89, 133, etc.

The rule of three

There was one particular aspect of these number sets which Gann found to be important. This was that a price objective was more likely to be satisfied, or a price level was more likely to mark a turning point, if the relevant price was the calculated outcome of *at least three* complementary measurements. Hence, if we are using Fibonacci numbers in the measurement process, then the coincidence of three or more Fibonacci numbers at the same level would indicate a potential turning point.

A very simple example will illustrate this point. Assume that a bull market has completed four phases – two rallies, each followed by a correction – and that a fifth wave has developed which has taken the market to a new peak (see Figure A1.2). There is a high probability that a particular level in this fifth wave will mark the ultimate reversal point if it coincides with at least three Fibonacci measures taken from successive low points in the move to date. The Fibonacci measures may be either absolute changes or percentage changes (although not both, since the measurements must be from the same number set). In our example changes of 13, 8, and 5 units coincide to yield a suitable target. The rule here is that the more Fibonacci measures which coincide at a particular level, the greater will be the probability that it marks a turning point. The need for three measures is only the minimum.

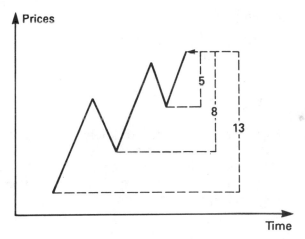

Figure A1.2. *The coincidence of three Gann numbers in prices*

Ratio analysis

The alternative source of important Gann numbers was ratio analysis. There were two different aspects to this analysis. The first was that reversal points could be expected at levels which bore a specific mathematical relationship to the lowest known price and the second was that price movements were mathematically related to price movements which preceded them.

The important ratios

Gann himself gave great emphasis to four specific ratio series. These were the series based on fifths, sevenths, eighths, and twelfths (see Table A1.2). Note that the series based on twelfths also includes the series based on halves, thirds, quarters and sixths. Each of these series could then be used to measure price objectives. First, the objectives could be measured *upwards* from the 'lowest low' by the simple expedient of adding each ratio to unity and then multiplying the resulting number by the lowest low. Second, important support levels could be calculated by measuring the extent of the preceding bull movement, and then dividing that movement into equal portions according to one of the important ratios. Hence, the extent of the bull movement could, for example, be divided into eighths. These divisions would then mark potential support levels on the way *down*. Obviously the analysis can be reversed for bear markets.

Table A1.2. *Gann's important ratio series*

Source	Series
1/5	1/5, 2/5, 3/5, 4/5
1/7	1/7, 2/7, 3/7, 4/7, 5/7, 6/7
1/8	1/8, 1/4, 3/8, 1/2, 5/8, 3/4, 7/8
1/12	1/12, 1/6, 1/4, 1/3, 5/12, 1/2, 7/12, 2/3, 3/4, etc

The influence of time

The analysis of reversal points, based solely on natural numbers which are intrinsic to the prices themselves, places Gann among the most perceptive of analysts. However, it is probably fair to say that the most influential aspect of Gann's work was his observation that *time* was a major constraint on price movements.

The circle

In the first place, Gann considered that the *circle* exerted a controlling influence over the spiral in his price square. His starting point was to break down the circle into divisions which correlated with natural cycles exprienced on earth. Since the smallest effective unit is 1°, and since there are 360° in a circle, it was natural for Gann to correlate 1° with (approximately) one day of a 365-day year. He then broke the circle down into quarters, representing the seasons of the year. This was particularly important in his analysis of commodity prices, where seasonal influences were important. Finally, he divided the circle into twelve units representing the months of the year. Gann's idea was to place the resulting diagram on to his square to represent the natural constraints of time. These external constraints would then supplement the intrinsic support and resistance levels generated by the price movements themselves.

The important task, obviously, is to set the 'clock' correctly. If each of the main divisions of the circle was going to represent a potential turning point, then the starting position had to be carefully established. One of Gann's solutions was to let each of the 90° divisions of the circle represent the beginning of one of the seasons, as defined in astrological terms. Hence 0° marked the first day of spring (21 March, the vernal equinox), the 90° line marked the first day of summer (21 June, summer solstice), the 180° line marked the first day of autumn (22 September, autumn equinox), and the 270° line fell on the first day of winter (21 December, winter solstice). The final stage in this process was to ensure that the 0° line cut through that part of the spiral in the price square which contained the actual price ruling on 21 March. If a price in the square subsequently occurred on the same day as one of the important dividing lines then a reversal could be expected. The important lines were one month, three months, six months, nine months and one year from the 'initialisation' of the square.

Natural time units

Gann's second line of approach was to use time units independently of the price square. Specifically, Gann found that prices would often reverse direction after the elapse of a time period (or periods) derived from particular *number sets*. Gann's researches led him to the conclusion that two types of number set were appropriate. First, there were those numbers which were based on the divisions of the 360 degrees of a circle by 5, 8 and 12. The numbers so obtained (see Table A2.3) include those derived by dividing the circle by 2, 3, 4 and 6. Second, there were those numbers which were derived from 'natural' mathematical sequences, such as the doubling, trebling, squaring and Fibonacci Sequences (see Table A1.3).

Table A1.3. *Gann's important 'circular' number sets*

Ratio	Numbers
1/5	72, 144, 216, 288, 360
1/8	45, 90, 135, 180, 225, 270, 315, 360
1/12	30, 60, 90, 120, 150, 180, 210, 240, 270, 300, 330, 360

The rule of three in time

Furthermore, Gann found that a reversal was very likely if three or more time periods (measured in identical units such as hours, days, weeks etc, and taken from the same number set) coincided simultaneously. That is, measuring forward from successive historical turning points (whether they be highs or lows), the coincidence of three or more time divisions from *one* of his number sets on a particular date would be likely to mark an important reversal point. Hence, if we are using Fibonacci numbers we could expect a reversal at time *t* in Figure A1.3. Obviously, the more Gann numbers which coincide on a particular date, the more likely it is that a reversal will occur on that date.

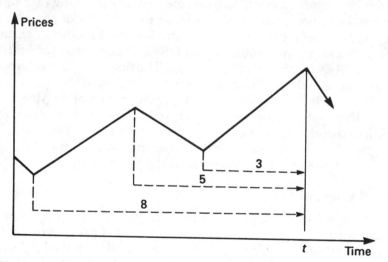

Figure A1.3. *The coincidence of three Gann numbers in time*

The divisions of the circle and time units

In theory, Gann's number sets are applicable to *any* time unit, whether measured in terms of hours, days, weeks, months or years. This is certainly true of the 'natural' series, such as the Fibonacci Sequence and the doubling sequence. It is not, however, immediately obvious that the same is true of numbers derived from the divisions of a circle. As we have already mentioned, there is an obvious relationship between the number of days in a year and the 360° of a circle. This would seem to imply that the Gann numbers relate primarily to days, and relate to other time units only where products or factors of 360 are concerned. In fact, the important consideration is the cycle of time which is correlated with the circle: if the cycle is one calendar year then each degree of the circle can be correlated with (approximately) one day, while if the cycle is 360 calendar years, then each degree can be correlated with one year. If, however, the relevant cycle is 30 days (ie approximately one calendar month), each degree of the circle will correlate with two hours. Hence Gann's numbers relate directly only to the degrees of a circle; it is necessary to translate them into the relevant time units.

Gann's belief in planetary cycles

One of the important questions now, of course, is what actually determines the relevant time units. To some extent, the cycles must be considered to be *intrinsically* determined; that is, each oscillating unit contains cycles which are determined by its own 'internal' metabolism. However, Gann's own analysis suggests that he considered some of the cycles to be *extrinsically* determined; that is, he considered *planetary* cycles to be one of the important controlling influences. The most obvious cycle in this context – and one on which we have already commented – is the annual cycle created by the orbit of the earth around the sun. Another cycle would be the rotation of the earth on its own axis which yields the day/night cycle; a further would be the tidal cycles created by the orbit of the moon around the earth. In all cases, there appears to be a *de facto* correlation between terrestrial cycles and those observed in the heavens.

Conclusions

We can therefore draw the following conclusions from Gann's use of time cycles:

(a) there is only a limited number of time cycles (*vide* the impact of only a few number sets);

(b) the cycles bear a mathematical relationship to one another (because of the importance of using numbers from the same set);

(c) the cycles appear in harmonic clusters (because of the importance of the coincidence of three numbers from the same set).

Notes

1. The other major exponent of the influence of natural forces, of course, was R. N. Elliott. Gann and Elliott apparently arrived at their conclusions independently. However, their different approaches are largely complementary.
2. Apparently, Gann spent ten years in research before applying his findings to his trading activities.
3. See, for example, W.D. Gann, *How to Make Profits in Commodities*. Lambert-Gann, Washington, 1976.

4.   Such courses are still available from Lambert-Gann Publishing.
5.   An alternative is to use the *highest* known price – the 'highest high'.
6.   Unity should be used if the lowest price is unknown.
7.   Excluding, that is, the very first number which is also unity.

Appendix 2:

Cycles in the UK Gilt-Edged Market

Using the elementary techniques described in Chapter 18, it is possible to isolate at least 16 cycles in the UK gilt-edged market. These are by no means the only ones. Furthermore, it is quite possible that the periodicities, and the registered timings, of the cycles could be refined using computer-based techniques. The purpose of this exercise, however, is to demonstrate that a reasonable degree of accuracy can be obtained by using techniques which are essentially simple.

The longest of the cycles revealed in Table 19.1 of Chapter 19 is the 54-year cycle. This cycle was originally found by the Russian economist Nikolai Kondratieff, [1] and has attracted a great deal of attention – both critical and favourable – over the years. In the context of the UK gilt market, however, some of his conclusions have been validated by researchers such as Gertrude Shirk of the Foundation for Cycle Studies. [2] Using the price of Consols, it is possible to track a 54-year cycle, dating from the middle of the eighteenth century. The traditional version assumes a 27-year up-phase followed by a 27-year down-phase. (See Table A2.1). There is a consistently good fit between the timing of the theoretical price troughs and the timing of the actual price troughs. There is, however, an apparent divergence between theory and experience at price peaks – possibly reflecting the asymmetry between the slow development of peaks and the rapid arrival of troughs to which we have already referred. The main conclusion from the data is that a very important 54-year price trough (ie peak in yields) was reached in late 1974/early 1975, and that – in principle, anyway – the high level trend for the period to 2005 is basically upward.

Table A2.1. *The 54-year Kondratieff cycle in gilts*

	Troughs			Peaks	
Theoretical	*Actual*	*Difference (years)*	*Theoretical*	*Actual*	*Difference (years)*
1758	1753	–5	1785	1792	–7
1812	1812	–	1839	1844	–5
1866	1866	–	1893	1897	–4
1920	1920	–	1947	1946	+1
1974	1974	–	2005		

The next longest cycle appears to be a 36-year cycle. This cycle was first mentioned by Hugh McDougall in 1958,[3] and still appears to be operating. Table A2.2 shows the theoretical and actual turning points of this cycle. If we assume that both the up-phase and the down-phase last for 18-years, actual peaks and troughs seem to bear a close relationship to the theoretical ones. Reading from the table, it can be seen that the important price peak which was reached in the gilt market in late 1982 coincided with a peak in the 36-year cycle. It occurred exactly 36 years after the price peak in 1946. It follows from this that the down-phase will now last until the year 2000. Such a trend is obviously in conflict with the Kondratieff cycle, and would certainly confirm the *possibility* of the price lows of 1974/5 being re-tested.

Table A2.2. *The 36-year McDougall cycle in gilts*

Troughs			Peaks		
Theoretical	*Actual*	*Difference (years)*	*Theoretical*	*Actual*	*Difference (years)*
1748	1747	−1	1766	1768	−2
1784	1784	−	1802	1802	−
1820	1820	−	1838	1838	−
1856	1858	−2	1874	1876	−2
1892	1889	+3	1910	1908	+2
1928	1929	−1	1946	1946	−
1964	1965	−1	1982	1982	−
2000					

The next cycle for which there is strong evidence is a 16-year cycle. The cycle is symmetrical about the peaks and troughs, with an 8-year up-phase and an 8–year down–phase. The relationship between the theoretical cycle and the actual cycle is shown in Table A2.3 below. The theoretical construct appears to have a very good record of forecasting actual peaks and troughs, although there is often an error of ± 2 years.

In his 1971 book on cycles, Edward Dewey[4] noted the widespread presence of two distinct 9-year cycles, one lasting 9.6 years and the other lasting 9.2 years. *Both* are present in the UK gilt market. The problem is, however, that because of their similar periodicities, the two cycles sometimes stimulate each other and sometimes cancel each other out. Of the two cycles taken separately, however, the 9.2-year cycle appears to be the most widely documented; it was initially reported by Hugh Mcdougall[5] in 1958. The broad details of its influence in recent years are shown in Table A2.4. The cycle appears to have been operating at the price lows in mid-1952, late 1961, late 1970, and early 1980; it also appears to have been associated with the market highs of spring 1966, mid-1975, and late 1984.

(*Note:* in Table A2.4, and subsequent tables, the months are expressed in terms of tenths of years. Hence 1970.9, for example, represents late October 1970.)

The 9.6-year cycle, on the other hand, is not widely recognised. Nevertheless, it was associated with the secular price low in late 1974, and it impacted strongly on the gilt market in mid-1984. The details of this cycle in recent years are shown in Table A2.5.

Table A2.3. *The 16-year cycle in gilts*

	Troughs			Peaks	
Theoretical	*Actual*	*Difference (years)*	*Theoretical*	*Actual*	*Difference (years)*
1746	1747	−1	1754	1753	+1
1762	1762	−	1770	1772	−2
1778	1781	−3	1786	1786	−
1794	1798	−4	1802	1802	−
1810	1812	−2	1818	1818	−
1826	1826	−	1834	1835	−1
1842	1841	+1	1850	1852	−2
1858	1857	+1	1866	1867	−1
1874	1874	−	1882	1884	−2
1890	1889	+1	1898	1897	+1
1906	1907	−1	1914	1914	−
1922	1920	+2	1930	1930	−
1938	1939	−1	1946	1946	−
1954	1955	−1	1962	1963	−1
1970	1970	−	1978	1977	+1
1986	1986	−	1994		

Table A2.4. *The 9.2-year cycle in gilts*

	Troughs			Peaks	
Theoretical	*Actual*	*Difference (years)*	*Theoretical*	*Actual*	*Difference (years)*
1952.5	1952.5	−	1957.1	1957.0	+0.1
1961.7	1961.7	−	1966.3	1966.4	−0.1
1970.9	1970.9	−	1975.5	1975.7	−0.2
1980.1	1980.0	+0.1	1984.7	1984.9	−0.2

Table A2.5. *The 9.6-year cycle in gilts*

	Troughs			Peaks	
Theoretical	*Actual*	*Difference (years)*	*Theoretical*	*Actual*	*Difference (years)*
1955.7	1955.7	−	1960.5	1960.4	+0.1
1965.3	1965.4	−0.1	1970.1	1970.2	−0.1
1974.9	1974.9	−	1979.7	1979.7	−
1984.5	1984.6	−0.1	1989.3		

Following on from the 9-year cycles comes the 7.2-year cycle. This cycle is by no means as conspicuous as some of the others. It has a very good record prior to the turn of the century, after which it seems to have become obscured by the operation of other cycles.[6] Nevertheless, a cycle can still be detected in some of the more recent data (see Table A2.6).

Table A2.6. *The 7.2-year cycle in gilts*

Theoretical	Actual	Difference (years)	Theoretical	Actual	Difference (years)
1953.4	1953.4	–	1957.0	1957.0	–
1960.6	1960.6	–	1964.0	1964.0	–
1967.8	1967.9	−0.1	1971.4	1971.3	+0.1
1975.0	1975.0	–	1978.6	1978.6	–
1982.2	1982.2	–	1985.8	1985.9	−0.1
1989.4					

While the cycles of 7.2 years and longer have a decisive impact on long–term price trends, most investors undoubtedly have far shorter time horizons. In the emotional environment of the market place, where prices are moving rapidly, it is in fact very difficult for an investor to take a genuine 'long-term' view. As we have already discussed, movements in prices themselves tend to shorten investors' time horizons. In addition it becomes increasingly difficult to formulate cohesive investment strategies as time horizons are extended. This is because unexpected shocks (such as political changes, raw material shortages, labour disputes and so forth) become more likely. The long term essentially consists of a series of short terms, and short–term views are justified on the grounds of flexibility.

This partly explains why cycles with a periodicity of less than four years are so influential in markets. The average period of time which elapses between a turning point and the subsequent reversal in such cycles in those cycles is two years or less – and a period of two years appears to be about the maximum that can be incorporated into strategic market views based, for example, on economic fundamentals. Indeed, most investors (better classified as traders!) will take even shorter time horizons than two years: in highly active markets it appears that six months is just about the limit of most people's memory and imagination.

The first cycles to fall within these shorter time horizons are the 4.5- and 4-year cycles. The former cycle has a regular 2.25-year up-phase followed by a 2.25-year down-phase, while the latter travels for 2 years between successive reversal points. The experience of both cycles since the late 1950s is shown in Table A2.7. Interestingly, the turning points of the 4-year cycle always occur during the *winter* months.

The 4.5- and 4-year cycles are not particularly well documented, despite the evidence for their existence. In contrast, most analysts are

Table A2.7. *The 4-year cycles in gilts*

| | **Troughs** | | | **Peaks** | |
Theoretical	*Actual*	*Difference (years)*	*Theoretical*	*Actual*	*Difference (years)*
1958.5	Suppressed		1960.7	Suppressed	
1963.0	1963.2	−0.2	1965.1	1965.2	−0.1
1967.4	1967.4	−	1969.6	1969.6	−
1971.8	1971.9	−0.1	1974.0	Suppressed	
1976.2	1976.2	−	1978.4	1978.5	−0.1
1980.7	1980.7	−	1982.9	1982.9	−
1985.1	1985.1	−	1987.3	1987.3	−
1989.6					

(a) The 4.5-year cycle

| | **Troughs** | | | **Peaks** | |
Theoretical	*Actual*	*Difference (years)*	*Theoretical*	*Actual*	*Difference (years)*
1963.0	1963.2	−0.2	1965.0	1964.9	+0.1
1967.0	1967.3	−0.3	1969.0	1969.0	−
1971.0	1969.9	+0.1	1973.0	1972.9	+0.1
1975.0	1975.0	−	1977.0	1977.0	−
1979.0	1979.0	−	1981.0	1981.1	−0.1
1983.0	1983.0	−	1985.0	1984.9	+0.1
1987.0	1986.9	+0.1			
1991.0					

(b) The 4-year cycle

familiar with the concept of a 3.25-year cycle. This cycle was originally publicised by Professor Joseph Kitchen of Harvard University, [7] and was subsequently broadly validated by Leonard Ayres.[8] Interestingly, the 3.25-year cycle is very pronounced *despite* the influence of longer-term cycles. Both the theoretical and actual turning points during recent years are shown in Table A2.8, and the coincidence of theory and practice is readily apparent. The cycle was last scheduled to bottom out in early 1988.

The precision of the 3.25-year cycle is almost matched by the accuracy of the next cycle on our list, which is the 21.6-month cycle. As with most of the other cycles, the peaks and troughs of this cycle are symmetrical: each phase lasts for 10.8 months.

The record of the cycle since the early 1970s is shown in Table A2.9. Here, we shall change the presentation of the table slightly to highlight the fact that some of the turning points represent only relatively short-term trading opportunities. This is quite important for the shorter cycles, where the cycle is defined in terms of deviations relatively short-term trading opportunities. This is quite important for the shorter cycles, where the cycle is defined in terms of deviations from trends which can be rising or falling quite sharply. The fact that the 21.6-month cycle coincided with the major inflation-induced low of December 1974/January 1975, and then subsequently defined all the most important turning points in the market, provides very strong confirmation of its importance.

Table A2.8. *The 3.25-year cycle in gilts*

Theoretical	Troughs Actual	Difference (years)	Theoretical	Peaks Actual	Difference (years)
1955.5	1955.6	−0.1	1957.1	1957.1	−
1958.8	1958.9	−0.1	1960.4	1960.4	−
1962.0	1961.9	+0.1	1963.6	1963.6	−
1965.3	1965.3	−	1966.9	1967.3	−0.4
1968.5	1968.5	−	1970.1	1970.1	−
1971.8	1971.4	+0.4	1973.4	Suppressed	
1975.0	1975.0	−	1976.6	1976.6	−
1978.2	Suppressed	−	1979.9	1979.7	+0.2
1981.5	1981.8	−0.3	1983.1	1983.5	−0.4
1984.8	1984.6	+0.2	1986.4	1986.4	−
1988.0	1988.1	+0.1	1989.6		

Table A2.9. *The 21.6-month cycle in gilts*

Theoretical	Troughs Comment	Theoretical	Peaks Comment
1969.6	Trough	1970.5	Rally peak 1970.6
1971.4	Trough	1972.3	End of bull 1972.2
1973.2	Trading low	1974.1	Rally peak 1974.3
1975.0	Major trough	1975.9	Peak 1976.1
1976.8	IMF crisis low 1976.9	1977.7	End of bull 1977.9
1978.6	Start of temporary rally	1979.5	End of bull 1979.3
1980.4	Important low 1980.3	1981.3	End of rally 1981.2
1982.2	Falklands crisis low	1983.1	Start of bear 1982.9
1984.0	Trading low	1984.9	End of bull
1985.8	Trading low	1986.7	Trading high
1987.6	Major low 1987.8	1988.5	End of rally 1988.4
1989.4			

The 9.6-month (or 41.5-week) cycle also has a record of exceptional accuracy. The history of the cycle since early 1975 is shown in Table A2.10. Each phase of this cycle lasts for 4.75 months (or 20.8 weeks). The cycle is, of course, a relatively short one and consequently is subject to the influence of higher-level trends. Nevertheless, the cycle can provide some important *short-term* trading opportunities.

The performance of the 7.7-month (or 33.3–week) cycle in recent years is shown in Table A2.11. It has obviously been associated with a

Table A2.10. *The 9.6-month cycle in gilts*

Troughs		Peaks	
Theoretical	*Comment*	*Theoretical*	*Comment*
1975.1	Secular low 1975.0	1975.5	End of rally 1975.3
1975.9	Start of rally	1976.3	Trading high
1976.7	IMF crisis low 1976.9	1977.1	Trading high
1977.5	End of correction 1977.6	1977.9	End of bull
1978.3	Trading low 1978.2	1978.7	End of rally
1979.1	Start of bull	1979.5	End of bull 1979.3
1979.9	End of bear	1980.3	Trading high 1980.1
1980.7	End of correction	1981.1	Start of bear 1980.9
1981.5	Trading low	1981.9	Trading high
1982.3	Trading low	1982.7	Trading high
1983.1	Start of rally	1983.5	Start of bear
1983.9	Trading low	1984.3	End of rally
1984.7	End of bear 1984.6	1985.1	End of bull 1984.9
1985.5	Trading low 1985.4	1985.9	End of rally 1985.8
1986.3	Important low 1986.1	1986.7	Trading high
1987.1	Important low 1986.9	1987.5	End of bull 1987.4
1987.9	Major low 1987.8	1988.3	End of rally
1988.7	Important low	1989.1	

Table A2.11. *The 7.7-month cycle in gilts*

Troughs		Peaks	
Theoretical	*Comment*	*Theoretical*	*Comment*
1975.0	Secular low	1975.3	End of rally
1975.6	Low 1975.5	1975.9	Peak 1976.1
1976.3	Temporary low	1976.6	Trading high
1976.9	IMF crisis low	1977.2	Trading high
1977.6	Correction low	1977.9	End of bull
1978.2	Trading low	1978.5	End of rally
1978.8	Trading low	1979.2	End of bull 1979.3
1979.5	End of correction	1979.8	Suppressed
1980.1	End of bear 1979.9	1980.4	End of rally
1980.8	Trading low	1981.1	Start of bear 1980.9
1981.4	Trading low	1981.7	Trading high
1982.0	Major low	1982.4	Trading high
1982.7	Trading low	1983.0	Start of bear 1982.9
1983.3	Suppressed	1983.6	Start of bear 1983.5
1984.0	Trading low	1984.3	End of rally
1984.6	End of bear	1984.9	End of bull
1985.2	Start of rally 1985.1	1985.6	Trading high
1985.9	Important low 1986.1	1986.2	End of bull
1986.5	Trading low	1986.8	Trading high 1986.7
1987.2	Important low 1986.9	1987.5	End of bull 1987.4
1987.8	Major low	1988.1	Trading high
1988.5	Trading low	1988.7	

The remaining cycles on our list in Table 19.1 of Chapter 19 are far more short-term than anything that has so far been discussed. As such, they are influenced very substantially by the direction of higher–level trends. Nevertheless, it remains true that they have a powerful effect on short-term trading opportunities. They are often associated with the beginning or the end of contra-trend corrections, and indeed seem to have the inherent ability to coincide with higher-level turning points.

They therefore need to be followed very closely. The first of these important short cycles is the 9.2-week cycle which lasts for approximately 65 calendar days or 46 trading days. The cycle is symmetric: both its up-phase and its down phase last for just under 4.75 weeks. Table A2.12 shows the record of the cycle during the period August 1983 to December 1985. In order that its accuracy may be checked, the table lists the actual turning points together with the time periods between successive peaks and successive troughs. It can be seen that the variability of these time periods is actually very small.

Table A2.12. *The 9.2-week cycle in gilts*

Troughs		Peaks	
Actual	*Elapsed weeks*	*Actual*	*Elapsed weeks*
4 Oct 83	9 1/5	14 Nov 83	9
14 Dec 83	10 1/5	17 Jan 84	9 1/5
24 Feb 84	10 3/5	29 Mar 84	10 2/5
24 Apr 84	8 2/5	6 May 84	9 4/5
26 Jun 84	9	14 Aug 84	9 3/5
28 Aug 84	9	8 Oct 84	8 4/5
29 Oct 84	8 4/5	5 Dec 84	8 2/5
3 Jan 85	9 3/5	7 Feb 85	9
6 Mar 85	8 4/5	19 Apr 85	10 1/5
9 May 85	9 1/5	19 Jun 85	8 3/5
5 Jul 85	8 1/5	22 Aug 85	9 1/5
12 Sep 85	9 4/5	21 Oct 85	8 2/5
14 Nov 85	9	30 Dec 85	10
Average	9 1/5	*Average*	9 1/5

Overlaid on the 9.2-week cycle comes the equally important 7-week cycle. This cycle lasts for approximately 49 calendar days or 35 trading days. (Note that the number 35 almost equates to the Fibonacci number 34). The record of this cycle since early 1984 is shown in Table A2.13. This table has the same format as that used for the 9.2-week cycle. It can be seen that, despite some variability (particularly at peaks) the average period of successive lows or highs is indeed 7 weeks.

The penultimate cycle with which we shall deal is the 4-week cycle. The cycle lasts for approximately 28 calendar days or 20 trading days. As in the case of all the other cycles, it is symmetric with respect to turning points, having a two-week up-phase followed by a two-week down-phase. Details of the cycle during 1985 are shown in Table A2.14.

Table A2.13. *The 7-week cycle in gilts*

Troughs		Peaks	
Actual	*Elapsed weeks*	*Actual*	*Elapsed weeks*
24 Feb 84	7 2/5	13 Mar 84	5 2/5
19 Apr 84	7 4/5	26 Apr 84	6 2/5
30 May 84	5 4/5	19 Jun 84	7 3/5
23 Jul 84	7 3/5	14 Aug 84	7
5 Sep 84	6 2/5	3 Oct 84	7 1/5
18 Oct 84	6 1/5	13 Nov 84	6
14 Dec 84	8 1/5	10 Jan 85	8 1/5
28 Jan 85	6 1/5	27 Feb 85	6 4/5
14 Mar 85	6 3/5	19 Apr 85	7 2/5
19 May 85	7 3/5	4 Jun 85	6 2/5
28 Jun 85	7 1/5	29 Jul 85	7 4/5
13 Aug 85	6 2/5	23 Sep 85	8
8 Oct 85	7	4 Nov 85	6
26 Nov 85	7	27 Dec 85	7 4/5
Average	7	*Average*	7

Table A2.14. *The 4-week cycle in gilts*

Troughs		Peaks	
Theoretical	*Comment*	*Theoretical*	*Comment*
15 Jan 85	Trading low	29 Jan 85	Trading high
11 Feb 85	Trading low	25 Feb 85	Suppressed
11 Mar 85	Suppressed	25 Mar 85	Trading high 29th
8 Apr 85	Trading low	22 Apr 85	Trading high
6 May 85	Trading low	20 May 85	Minor high
31 May 85	Trading low 29th	14 Jun 85	Suppressed
27 Jun 85	Trading low	11 Jul 85	Suppressed
25 Jul 85	Trading low	8 Aug 85	Trading high
22 Aug 85	Suppressed	5 Sep 85	Trading high
19 Sep 85	Minor low	3 Oct 85	Trading high
17 Oct 85	Minor low	31 Oct 85	Trading peak
14 Nov 85	Trading low	28 Nov 85	Trading peak
11 Dec 85	Trading low	25 Dec 85	Trading peak 30th

The last cycle to be discussed in the current context is the one-week cycle. This is a seven calendar day, or five trading day, cycle. It is primarily of value only to the *very* short-term trader. Even in today's sophisticated markets, the natural tendency of most traders is to want to *hold* stock: very few individuals have a natural bias towards short positions.[9] Many traders gauge the mood of the market on the Monday, and then on Tuesday morning will either take a contrary view in a falling market or will chase prices in a rising market. Such bull positions are invariably closed either on Thursday or Friday because of the interruption of trading over the week-end. On this analysis, prices should be biased downwards on Mondays and biased upwards on Wednesdays. An analysis of price movements in the gilt market during the 92 weeks prior to 30 September 1988 confirms this to be the case. On 56 Mondays, prices traded lower than the highs the previous Friday; on 72 Wednesdays, prices traded above the previous day's lowest level. This represents a 60 per cent effectiveness for the down-phase of the one-week cycle and an 80 per cent effectiveness for the up-phase, no matter what was the direction of the higher-level trend.

There is therefore strong evidence for the existence of rhythmic fluctuations in the UK gilt market. A similar analysis of other financial markets would result in identical conclusions.[10] Knowledge of these cycles enables an analyst to predict the *timing* of turning points with a great degree of accuracy.

Notes

1. The numbers 55 and 56 are also applicable. Kondratieff himself estimated a variable periodicity of 45-60 years. It is worth noting that the number 54 is related to other numbers in Table 19.1 via the number 360 and its multiples, particularly 1080 and 2160. The number of degrees in a circle is 360 and this and is the classic reference to cycles.
2. See Gertrude Shirk, *Cycle Analysis — A Case Study*. Foundation For The Study Of Cycles, Pittsburgh, 1981.
3. E.H. McDougall, 'Cycles in Consols', *Investors Chronicle and Money Market Review*, 1958.
4. Edward R. Dewey with Og Mandino, *Cycles – The Mysterious Forces that Trigger Events* . Hawthorn, New York, 1971.
5. E.H. McDougall, op. cit.
6. This same phenomenon has also been noted in relation to the 7-11 year Juglar cycle in economic activity. See J.J. van Duijn, *The Long Wave in Economic Life*. George Allen and Unwin, London, 1983.
7. J. Kitchin, 'Cycles and trends in economic factors', *The Review of Economic Statistics*, 1923.
8. L.P. Ayres, *Turning Points in Business Cycles*. Harper, New York, 1939
9. Which is why bear markets develop so suddenly and fall so quickly. They are rarely fully anticipated. If large-scale bear positions were in place, the fall would continuously be resisted by 'bear closing'.
10. Some analysts have argued that the rhythms are either only temporary (in the sense that they will eventually disappear), or a statistical quirk. LaMont C. Cole of Cornell University, for example, has shown that it is possible to obtain evidence of cycles from any set of random numbers. See LaMont C. Cole, 'Biological clocks in the unicorn', *Science*, 1957. Cole's argument was, however, critically flawed because he merely kept on adjusting the data until he 'found' a cycle. There was no possibilty of

finding similar cycles in an alternative set of random numbers, or of finding an harmonic group of cycles in the same set of random numbers. Both possibilities are open to cycle analysis in financial markets.

INDEX

α-wave, 100-102, 107, 109, 120, 125, 126, 128, 207, 220
A-wave, 137, 142, 144
A-B base, 151
A-B-C correction (*see* Corrections)
Advance-decline index, 165
Allen, R.G.D., 194
Armies, 9
Assumptions in economics, 39
Assymetry in investment, 67
Auxiliary price index, 154, 165
Ayres, Leonard, 247, 252

β-wave, 100-102, 107-111, 120-128, 133, 157, 169, 220
B-wave, 137, 142, 144
Base pattern, 91, 99-100, 103, 134, 206, 211
Bateson, Gregory, 10, 12, 15, 19, 26
Bear (*see also* Cycles),
    closing, 60, 63, 156
    investor as, 45
    squeeze, 65
    trend, 48-49, 132
Behaviour,
    instinctive, 11
    linear 33, 39
    mechanistic, 5, 6, 39
    non-rational, 12, 17, 50, 224, 227
    rational, 5-6, 50, 156, 224, 226
Bertolanffy, Ludwig von, 19, 25
Bond markets, 70, 86-94, 99, 165, 202
Bonner, John Tyler, 13
Borissavlietch, M., 83
Botticelli, 81
Box-reversal, 117
Brain, 11-13
Brown, Frank, 193-194
Bull (*see also* Cycles),
    investor as, 45
    trap, 65
    trend, 48-49, 131
Buy signal, 109-112, 126, 152, 165-166, 217, 228-229

C-wave, 137, 142, 144

Call option, 54, 168
Capra, Fritjof, 7, 13
Catastrophe Theory, 55
Charpentier, Louis, 84
Christ, Carl F., 41
Co-evolution, 27-28
Cole, Lamont C., 252
Collective consciousness, 11
Commodities, 150, 234
Commodity Research Bureau, 132, 181
Complex correction (*see* Corrections)
Confirmation of trading signal, 152-168, 207
Contagion, 21
Corrections, 137, 140, 142-150, 167, 177-178, 211-212, 221-222, 237
    A-B-C, 137, 140, 146-148
    complex, 146, 149, 150
    flat, 142, 144-146, 149
    inverted, 142, 144, 145, 148-149
    irregular, 142, 144
    running, 142, 144, 146
    zigzag, 142, 146, 149
Cultural Revolution, 9
Cranshaw, Ralph, 17
Crash,
    September 1929, 54, 226
    October, 1987, 181, 202, 205-226
Crowds, 8-13, 19-25
    altruism and, 10, 16
    behaviour of, 23, 30, 65
    bearish, 46, 49, 50, 52, 53, 56
    belief system of, 10, 12, 14-16, 46
    bullish, 46, 49, 50, 52, 53, 56
    climate and, 36
    conflict and, 16-17, 47, 50
    cycles in 26-37
    emotions of, 39, 48-9, 51
    energy of, 20, 25, 41
    environment and, 20, 23-24
    financial markets and, 41, 45-53
    intelligence of, 12-13
    leadership, 14-16, 20, 23, 26, 27, 49, 51, 52

life cycle of, 26-27
purpose of, 19-20, 26, 49
revolution and, 24
self-organisation of, 19-25
stress and, 16, 19, 24, 25, 47, 50, 52, 56
Cycles,
    bias in, 67, 101
    bull/bear 48-49, 56-72, 99, 101, 137, 149,
        153, 159
    crowd and, 26-37
    earthquakes and, 36
    54-month, 196
    54-year, 196, 197, 215, 243
    4-week, 250-251
    4-year, 213, 214, 216, 246-247
    4.5-year cycle, 196, 197, 246-247
    gilt-edged, 197-202, 243, 252
    harmony of, 32, 186, 196-197, 241
    life, 26-27, 69, 70, 227
    limit, 28-37, 51, 56-64, 68-70, 156-157,
        159-160, 167-168
    metabolic, 30, 41, 68-70
    9.6-month, 196, 197-202, 248, 249
    9.6-year, 196, 197, 244
    9.2-month, 197
    9.2-week, 196, 250
    9.2-year, 196, 197, 244
    1-week, 251-252
    periodicities of, 186, 187, 189, 194, 196,
        246
    planetary, 241
    7-day, 193, 196
    7-week, 196, 250, 251
    7.2-day, 202
    7.2-week, 202
    7.2-year, 246
    7.7-month, 248, 249
    16-year, 244
    stable, 21, 23, 28-29
    34-week, 197
    39-month 190
    36-year, 197, 244
    3.25-year, 191, 197, 213, 214, 216, 247-248
    20-day, 193
    28-day, 197
    21.6-month, 247-248
    22-month, 197
    unstable, 21, 23, 34, 85

δ-wave, 100-102, 107, 108, 109-110, 115,
    116, 119, 120, 125, 127, 128, 131-133,
    160, 163, 207, 220
Darwin, Charles, 24
Da Vinci, 81
Decisions,
    rational, 5-6, 47
    non-rational, 5-6, 47
Descartes, René, 4
Deutschemark, 95, 122-123, 181

Dewey, Edward R., 37, 189, 194, 197, 202,
    244
Diener, Ed, 15,17
Divergences (*see also* non-confirmation),
    162-163, 165
DNA, 83
Dollar, 122, 131, 151, 170
Double bottom, 113, 126, 127, 129, 133, 134
Double Retracement, 142
Double top, 113, 126, 127, 133, 134
Doubling Sequence, 236
Dow, Charles, 166
Dow Jones,
    Home Bonds Index, 93
    Industrial Average, 94, 165, 168, 177,
        205-224
    Transportation Index, 165
Dow Theory, 165-166, 168
Down-trend (or-wave), 100, 102, 131-132,
    133, 168, 170, 220
Duality,
    in nature, 4
    in motivation, 5-6
Dürer, 81
Durkheim, Emile, 16, 17-18

Economics, 38-39
Ehrlich, Paul, 28
Electrons, 3-4, 7
Elliott,
    Ralph Nelson, 134, 151, 174-175, 179,
        181, 184, 186, 207
    Wave Principle, 103, 119, 136-151, 168
Emotions, 11-12, 21, 30, 47, 48, 56
Evolution, 19, 24, 36, 176
Extensions, 140-142, 149-150

Failures, 135, 140-143, 149
Farrell, M.J., 54
Fear, 47, 56, 66-67, 72, 101-102, 156, 164,
    225
Federal Reserve, 202, 220, 226
Feedback loops, 21-23, 27-28, 39, 51
Fibonacci,
    constraints, 210, 212, 213, 214, 216, 220
    Number Sequence, 73-97, 129, 149, 186,
        225, 228, 235-236, 240
    Ratio, 76, 85, 86, 169, 175, 177, 179, 184,
        226
    targets, 170, 174, 175, 177, 223
Fifth wave, 140-144, 150, 163, 207, 237
54-month cycle (*see* Cycles)
54-year cycle (*see* Cycles)
Financial Times Indices,
    FTSE100, 181, 225, 226
    FT30, 181, 208, 224, 225
Five phase (or wave) movement, 131-135,
    137-144
Flat correction (*see* Corrections)
Fluctuations (*see also* Cycles), 25, 28, 69,
    181, 187, 197, 227
Foreign exchange market, 38, 72, 150, 154

4-week cycle (*see* Cycles)
4-year cycle (*see* Cycles)
Fourth wave, 142
Fractal geometry, 103
Freeman, Walter J., 37
French Revolution, 9
Freud, Sigmund, 9, 15, 17, 19
Friedman, Milton, 41
Frisch, Ragnar, 33, 37
Frost, Alfred J., 149, 151
Fundamentals, 38, 40, 42, 60, 65, 70, 111,
   130, 176, 222
Futures markets,
   Eurodollar, 181
   Standard and Poors, 207
   T-bill, 170, 179, 181
   T-bond, 88-94, 124, 154, 177, 181

Gann,
   numbers, 236, 239, 240-241
   ratios, 237, 238
   William D., 174-177, 179, 181, 184, 185,
      186, 196, 233-242
Ghyka, Matilda, 83
Gilt-edged market, 87-90, 95, 98, 117, 171,
   176-178, 195, 197-202, 215
Gold, 95, 165
Golden,
   Ratio (*see also* Fibonacci Ratio), 76-77, 83,
      84, 129
   Rectangle, 77-79
   Spiral, 79-81
Gothic cathedrals, 81
Government Securities Index, 170, 172, 178
Great Pyramid, 81
Greed, 48, 56, 164
Gribben, John, 84
Groups, 8-9, 11, 14

Hambridge, Jay, 84
Harris, Thomas A., 17
Harmony in cycles (*see* Cycles)
Hawking, Stephen W., 7
Head-and-shoulders, 113, 119-125, 128,
   129, 177
Heisenberg, Werner, 4, 7
Herd, 8, 47-48, 152, 222
Hersey, Rex, 30, 37
Highest high, 242
Huntley, H.E., 83

Impulse wave, 100-101, 102, 103, 137, 139,
   140, 142, 148-149, 157-158, 169, 174, 177
Individuals, 6, 8, 9, 10
Information (*see also* Shocks), 12-13, 20-21,
   26-27, 38, 47, 73, 121, 129, 176, 228
Integrative tendency, 8, 14-18, 50, 53, 61,
   64
Inverted corrections (*see* Corrections)
Investment advisers, 52-53

Irregular corrections (*see* Corrections)

Jantsch, Erich 8, 13, 19, 25, 37, 184
Japanese Yen, 181
Jaynes, Julian, 13
Juglar cycle, 252
Jung, Carl, 9

Kaufman. P.J., 129
Koestler, Arthur, 7, 9, 12, 13, 17, 19
Kondratieff, Nikolai, 215, 217, 243, 244
Kitchen, Joseph, 247, 252

Laszlo, Ervin, 19, 25
Law of Vibrations, 233
Leader (*see* Crowd)
Learning, 24, 176, 228
Le Bon, Gustave, 9-10, 13, 19, 20-21, 25
Lefevre, Edwin, 194
Life cycle (*see* Cycles)
Limit cycle (*see* Cycles)
Lowest low, 234, 236, 238

Maclean, Paul D., 11,13
Mandelbrot, Benoit, 103
McDougall, Hugh, 244, 252
Measuring formula (*see* Prices)
Michell, John, 84
Milgram, Stanley, 16
Mind, 10-13
   collective, 11
   crowd, 10-11
   metabolic, 11
Mobs, 9, 17, 23
Momentum (*see also* Prices), 153, 159-164,
   167-168, 192-193, 200, 205, 213, 215, 227
   indicator, 190, 192, 207
   spike, 191, 192, 200
Morris, Desmond, 5, 7,
Motivation, 5-6
Moving averages, 160-162, 187-189, 194
Multiple bottoms, 113, 126, 128
Multiple tops, 113, 125

Natural
   laws, 134-135, 149, 169
   numbers, 179, 181, 186, 236
Neckline, 119-125
New Physics, 4-5, 11
Newton,Isaac, 4
9.6-month cycle (*see* Cycles)
9.6-year cycle (*see* Cycles)
9.2-month cycle (*see* Cycles)
9.2-week cycle (*see* Cycles)
9.2-year cycle (*see* Cycles)
Non-confirmation, 153, 157-167, 192, 193,
   200, 209, 210
Number sets, 239-240, 241
Nuremberg rallies, 9

1-week cycle (*see* Cycles)

One third/two thirds retracement, 174-176, 177
Open interest, 154-168, 207, 218, 227
Options, 54, 154, 167
Overbought, 64-66, 156-159, 161-168, 168, 191, 205-207, 213, 216, 225
Oversold, 64-66, 156, 159-168, 168, 191, 207

Parent-substitute, 17
Parthenon, 81
Penrose, John, 84
Point and figure, 116-117
Postle, Denis, 54
Poussin, 81
Prechter, Robert R., 135, 136, 149, 151, 168, 184
Price pulse, 68, 98-103, 107-112, 120-129, 131-135, 146, 150, 151, 157, 159, 160, 161, 162, 168, 169, 207, 220, 228
Price square, 234-235
Prices,
    acceleration in, 159, 190-191
    change in, 57, 58, 60-66, 70, 73, 156, 160, 161, 190, 197, 207
    leadership and, 49, 51, 57
    patterns in, 107, 112, 117, 132, 134-135, 137, 139, 140, 142, 146, 149, 152, 165-166, 207, 216, 228
    sentiment and, 58, 63-64, 69, 73, 152-153, 156, 157, 159, 160, 167
    targets for, 85-87, 121-124
    velocity of, 190
Probability theory, 4
Profit-taking, 63, 65, 156, 193
Programmed trading, 224
Put option, 54, 168

Random Walk Hypothesis, 41
Raven, Peter, 28
Reductionism, 4, 10, 39
Relative Stength Indicator, 161-164, 202
Resistance, 174-175, 178, 179
Re-test, 63-65, 72, 125, 153, 156-157, 167, 168, 193, 218, 220, 222
Retracement targets, 174-175, 178, 221
Reverse head-and-shoulders, 124-126
Reversal pattern, 65-70, 107, 119-120, 125-126, 131, 165, 166, 167, 169
Revolution, 19, 24, 34
Rhea, Robert, 168
Richards, Steve, 202
Rule of alternation, 149
Rule of three, 186, 236-237, 239-240
Rules (*see also* Trading rules), 134-135, 139-140, 144, 148, 149
Running correction (*see* Corrections)

Santoni, G.J., 41
Schumacher, E.F., 5, 7, 13
Self-assertive tendency, 8, 13

Self-awareness, 5, 7, 11, 15, 38
Self-organisation, 10, 25, 28
Sell signal, 109-112, 120, 122, 130, 152, 166, 202, 208, 216, 217, 222, 228, 229
Sentiment, 39, 57, 58, 62, 63, 64, 65, 70, 71, 72, 133, 152-153, 155, 156, 157, 159, 160, 167, 168
7-day cycle (*see* Cycles)
7-week cycle (*see* Cycles)
7.2-day cycle (*see* Cycles)
7.2-week cycle (*see* Cycles)
7.2-year cycle (*see* Cycles)
7.7-month cycle (*see* Cycles)
Shells, 83
Shirk, Gertrude, 194, 243, 252
Shocks, 27, 33-36, 41-42, 60-66, 68-70, 73, 122, 129, 153, 176, 177, 217, 228, 246
Signal, 109-113, 126, 128, 130, 152, 216, 228
16-year cycle (*see* Cycles)
Smith, Adam, 41
South Sea Bubble, 54
Spiral, 34, 35, 64, 73-86, 91, 94, 122, 152, 169, 175, 211-212, 217, 221, 234, 235
Spiral phyllotaxis, 81-82
Sterling, 95, 131, 170
Stevens, Peter S., 84
Stock market 177, 197
Stop-loss, 220
Suicide, 16-18
Sunflower, 82
Support, 174-175, 178, 179-181, 221, 222
Systems Theory, 19-37

Tajfel, Henri, 15
Talbot, Michael, 17
Target, 169, 170, 175, 177, 211-212, 216, 220, 221, 222, 223
Technical analysis, 40, 103, 113, 128, 129, 152, 205, 222, 228-229
Third wave, 140
34-week cycle (*see* Cycles)
39-month cycle (*see* Cycles)
36-year cycle (*see* Cycles)
Three phase (wave) movement, 131-132, 134-135, 142
3.25-year cycle (*see* Cycles)
Time, 47, 73, 116, 152, 163, 164, 176, 181, 185-202, 212-213, 228, 234, 236, 238-241
Time window, 189, 193, 194
Tobin James, 54
Trading rules, 111, 130, 131-133, 134, 153, 192-3, 220
Treasury bill 170
Treasury bond, 99, 100, 102, 154, 202
Treasury 8.75% 1997, 87, 88, 197, 200
Trebling sequence, 236
Trend line, 113-118, 128, 133, 216, 217
Triangle, 117, 119, 142, 146-148, 150, 151
Triple bottom, 113, 129
Triple top, 113, 126

Turning points, 40, 41, 58, 64, 107, 109, 139, 152, 185, 186, 190, 240
20-day cycle (*see* Cycles)
28-day cycle (*see* Cycles)
21.6-month cycle (*see* Cycles)
22-month cycle (*see* Cycles)

Uncertainty Principle, 4, 10
Up-trend (-wave), 100-102, 131, 132, 133, 168, 207, 218

Venus, 82, 84
Velocity (*see* Prices, Momentum)
Volterra, Vito, 28
Volume, 41, 51, 65-67, 154-158, 167, 168, 207, 218, 226
Vorob'ev, N.N., 83

Wars, 17, 36

Watson, Lyall, 37
Wave Principle (*see* Elliott Wave Principle)
White, Walter E., 84
Wilde, Oscar, 40
Wilson, Louise, 197, 202

x-wave, 101-103, 107, 108, 109, 110, 120, 125, 126, 150, 207, 217, 218, 220
X-wave, 146, 148

y-wave, 101-103, 107, 108, 109, 110, 120, 125, 126, 127, 131, 132, 133, 150, 157, 163, 169, 207, 218, 220

z-wave, 101-103, 107, 108, 109, 116, 119, 120, 125, 129, 132, 133, 159, 163, 207, 220
Zigzag correction (*see* Corrections)
Zukov, Gary, 7